PENGUIN BOOKS
FLASHBACK

Robert John Christo, popularly known as Bob Christo, was born in 1938 in Sydney, Australia. After completing his civil engineering in Sydney, he took on projects which involved supporting the military supply lines of the South Vietnamese army and working as construction supervisor on the film sets of *Apocalypse Now*. Led by his instincts, Christo zealously followed one aspiration after another: chasing after a lost spy ship, running an escort service, modelling for African beer, singing in rock concerts and so on.

Bob Christo landed his first film role at the age of sixteen in a German movie, after working as an extra in the Düsseldorf National Theatre, Germany. Hoping to meet Parveen Babi in India, he chanced upon a part in Sanjay Khan's *Abdullah* (1980) and then went on to act in hundreds of Hindi, Telugu, Tamil, Malayalam and Kannada films. In the year 2000 he became a yoga instructor after shifting base from Mumbai to Bangalore, where he passed away on 20 March 2011.

FLASHBACK
My Life and Times in Bollywood and Beyond

Bob Christo

Foreword by Tom Alter

PENGUIN BOOKS

An imprint of Penguin Random House

PENGUIN BOOKS

USA | Canada | UK | Ireland | Australia
New Zealand | India | South Africa | China | Singapore

Penguin Books is part of the Penguin Random House group of companies
whose addresses can be found at global.penguinrandomhouse.com

Published by Penguin Random House India Pvt. Ltd
4th Floor, Capital Tower 1, MG Road,
Gurugram 122 002, Haryana, India

Penguin
Random House
India

First published by Penguin Books India 2011

ISBN 9780143414629

Typeset in Perpetua by Eleven Arts, New Delhi
Printed at Repro India Limited

www.penguin.co.in

MIX
Paper from
responsible sources
FSC® C047271

Contents

For Roberto, from the heart . . .

The first time I met Bob, he pulled the door handle off an Ambassador . . . He also galloped full speed on a black stallion right past me and disappeared—with the horse—into a nearby bog; and the first thing we saw emerging was Bob's bald head, followed by a stunned stallion. Bob, of course, was grinning from ear to handsome ear—not in the least concerned that he was supposed to have halted in front of me, saluted, dismounted and given me the latest military report—all part of a scene we were shooting for a French TV serial so many, many years ago . . .

Bob then proceeded to borrow my white pants, since his were now a darker shade of pale, and re-did the shot; with me, the commanding officer, waiting for his salute, my lower regions now covered by a towel . . .

This was Bob Christo (for me, Roberto)—largest than life, full of adventure and humour and such strength, of the body and soul and heart . . .

And near the very end of his life, Roberto decided to write his book . . .

As only he could—for no one, absolutely no one, could tell the story of Roberto, except Roberto himself . . .

Marlon Brando, Amitabh Bachchan, Raj Kapoor—these are the level of stars he has shared screen and real time with. For Roberto, nothing could be average . . .

Loves, lusts, longings—they are all there in vivid, even violent detail in this book. And if you thought Roberto was confined only to Hindi films, read on. Australia, Rhodesia, the Philippines, from the Gulf to Goa, Roberto has blazed his trail—fighting, singing, dreaming, loving. He did it all . . .

And the people who star in his story: Bruce Lee's guru—Roberto was so close to him . . . Ian Smith—the man who tried to keep Rhodesia alive . . . Parveen Babi—the siren who lured Bob to Bombay . . . Sanjay Khan—the man who took him under his wing . . . And so many more . . .

Roberto's first forays into learning Hindi, and the strange rules of the Hindi film industry . . . His family life—tragedy in Australia, and fitful happiness in Bombay . . . His children—scattered around the globe, and within Roberto's large heart . . . All this and much, much more . . .

But—and this is what I loved about Roberto and his story—this book also deals with the truths of life: loss and sorrow, and the journey of a tough, tough man to find inner peace in a world he always dealt with on his own terms . . .

Bob Christo's book is as amazing as the man—as complex, as straightforward, as true—and when you read it, you can remember him from one of his wonderful roles, or you can discover him as the mystery he was . . .

Roberto, I tip my hat and my heart to you . . .

You always used to growl, 'Tom, why don't they give me romantic roles?'

The truth is, my friend, your own life was the most romantic role of all.

2011   Tom Alter

Preface

I always liked reading—right from childhood, after I had mastered the English and German alphabets. It opened up a different world for me; a world that I did not know yet. I liked fairy tales as a child but later on I began to enjoy stories that were based on facts. My mind used to delve into the depth of the stories that I read, trying to find an answer to why things happened the way they were described. Why didn't they happen in another way? Sometimes I kept on thinking for hours about a story that I had read and variations of them were born in my imagination. During one period of my youth, I used to tell stories to my brothers and my childhood friends during the day; however, one day they persuaded me to continue narrating the stories to them at night. So my brother and I went to borrow some microphones and speakers from a friend's father who had a repair shop for radios; these, together with some other equipment, we fixed inside our neighbours' children's bedrooms to finish the stories that I had started to tell them during the day. Now they could lie in their beds, happily listening to my fiction till late at night until they drifted off to sleep.

At school, we were sometimes asked to write essays. The topics were varied; it could be about a sports event or a day out, or about a city or village or a volcano that had erupted not very long ago. We would have to write down every detail that we could remember. Occasionally I received top marks and prizes for outstanding essays. Over the years I kept up the practice; whenever I happened to witness strange events or anything interesting or curious or dangerous, I would make notes of it so I could remember it again later on. I was always observing my surroundings. For instance, once when I was in school in Düsseldorf I spotted a squadron of manoeuvring American military aircraft right above me, quite high. Though there was no sound to tip me off, I saw one aircraft hitting the one next to it while the one that got hit bumped into the fighter aircraft right in front of it. All three aircraft burst into flames immediately and within a few minutes hit the ground. Thanks to my observant nature I had noticed what most others would have missed. I jumped on to my racing cycle to the place where the crashed planes had fallen.

When I told people about some of the interesting things that I got involved in or witnessed, they would challenge me in all seriousness to write a book filled with my adventures and anecdotes and the love and affection that I felt for and got from all the different countries to which I have travelled. They said it would definitely be very successful.

Well, I've heard that for years but my reply has usually been, 'If I ever manage to find somebody who would like to do it on my behalf, go ahead, you're welcome. I am not interested, I'm not a writer.' Actually, when I think of my replies now, I feel that I should have tried because deep down I really like writing.

Then, on one Sunday in February 2008 I read an article on the 'Life' page in the *Times of India* by Nona Walia, the columnist from New Delhi. The title of the story was: 'Can one learn how to write a book?' I read the piece, then sat down thinking about it, imagining a situation in which I start talking to an unknown, pretty girl. I let the conversation run through my mind and then wrote it down on a piece of paper. After I read it, I shouted, 'I can write a book! I've got it!' And then I decided that I could and would write my autobiography. I bought paper, a spiral pad and a few pens and visited two good friends of mine, Satya and Aruna, who were friends and also neighbours in a big block of apartments. I surprised them by telling them that I had decided to write my autobiography and I wanted the two girls to be my assistants. Aruna was a good typist, so she would type everything that I hand-wrote in my manuscript. Satya would have to listen to every thirty or fifty pages of my manuscript as soon as I'd turned them out and give me her opinion of the gist and the interest factor of what I had written. At times she made me rephrase or rewrite entire portions of the manuscript. In return I would give both girls yoga lessons every evening.

Most of my life was right there in my mind as though it had just happened recently. Sometimes I had to wait for a few hours or a day to recall something, but most of the time the old memory bank didn't let me down. I was so happy to have made the decision to write the book myself and not depend on a biography writer. Apart from the fact that I would have had to tell all my experiences to the biography writer, which would have been a more expensive and a boring task for me, it would not have given me the joy which successful writing does! Exactly how Nona Walia wrote in her Sunday column: 'I would want to write a book and be alive to read it when my first book is published.'

* * *

After I had an operation in 2006, the post-operative time was a very painful period; however, I was fortunate enough to have had a friend who was helping me during those days. I used to call her Angel. I don't know what I would have done without her; I doubt that I would have survived. So I just say: Thank you again, my Angel. And God bless you.

PART I

Hong Kong—Philippines

One thing that I have learnt over the years is that man changes continuously. I am no exception. When my survival was at stake, I could be so mean, heartless and inconsiderate with other people that I would be shocked or feel utterly ashamed when I later reviewed certain parts of my life.

I often thought about how to successfully control my emotions; how to be fair to everybody without letting anger or other emotions distort my judgments. Eventually this led me to the practice of meditation during the time I lived in India. I started to look inside myself. One day I was meditating with my mind focused on compassion, which reminded me of something I had read by Stephen Levine, who said, 'When your fear touches someone's pain it becomes pity, when your love touches someone's pain it becomes compassion.' During this meditation I was trying how to experience the genuine feeling of compassion. After that I always remembered those lines whenever I felt compassion for something or someone. For me it signified a spiritual beginning. It helped me and I realized how important it is to meditate regularly throughout life. However, it is not an easy task at all.

I have been challenged numerous times by friends and acquaintances to write a book about my life. I usually would say that I'd rather let somebody else write my life story.

With age I changed my mind. Since so much of my life has remained in my memory I decided to sit down and do the writing myself. I do not start at the beginning. I start my story at around the age of thirty-five. The early days will be revealed later on in the narration.

A Girl in Each City

I left Vietnam one day before Saigon became Ho Chi Minh City. I managed to get on a Royal Air Force flight to Singapore with three mates who were with me maintaining the supply routes of the South Vietnamese Army in their struggle against North Vietnam. I had no papers with me, I didn't know where my passport was and I was lucky that the RAF took me up to Singapore, where I had to make an appearance at the Australian High Commission to request them for another passport. That took about three weeks. So I had time to relax and to rejuvenate myself and I spent quite a few days at the beach. We stayed at an Indonesian hotel until I was given my new passport and then we discussed where to go next; the guys who were with me wanted to go to another place with plenty of action—Angola in Africa. I decided to go to Hong Kong and try to get into business.

I had met two Belgian girls in Singapore who had given me their address in an apartment building in Wan Chai, close to Star Ferry. On arriving in Hong Kong, I called them and they helped me get a one-bedroom/kitchen/bathroom apartment in the seventh floor of the same building and invited me for dinner in the evening. When I entered the girls' place, there was a third girl sitting on the sofa smiling at me. She was very pretty, with a Polynesian look and demeanour. Her name was Kisa, and she had come from Apia, Western Samoa, to study dental technology in Hong Kong.

We clicked immediately and left together after dinner. Without hesitation she came with me to my new apartment and we had a housewarming party, talking and chatting in different languages; I knew some Polynesian from an earlier visit to the Marquesas. But it was different from the Samoan tongue of Samoa i Sisifo (Western Samoa). We were both very happy; laughing and enjoying ourselves and crowning the night with a wonderful love session. In the morning she told me in her Polynesian accent, 'Now I have my own "dalling", let's stay together.'

She had a place, but eventually she gave it up because she lived with me from that first day. I helped her change her hairstyle; for some reason she wore a wig. I made her sell it and asked the hairstylist to give her an Afro style that looked very sexy. She invited me to go out with her to celebrate. After that we seemed to be celebrating every night. In those days Hong Kong was cheaper than today, even though the prices had increased because of the soldiers from Vietnam who used to come there on rest and recreation leave. We had a very active sex life and she used to encourage me to do everything with her. 'Please don't forget, I like to do all different positions. As long as you enjoy, I enjoy.' When I told her that I would have to work hard to earn money, she said, 'So long I have money, for you no need to work; if you want to work, you can get job as erotic dancer in nightclub as you have beautiful, strong body.'

I didn't have to work in the nightclub; I met an Indian photographer, Dinshaw Balsara. Most of his clients were models. So I started modelling, mainly for fashion. For the next six months, I went swimming at Repulse Bay beach every morning, and rowing a boat to one of the offshore islands and back in between. Then I did my thing on the catwalk for about half an hour at one of the big five-star hotels and then got changed again and had lunch. I earned well and the food was good, but then I started thinking of a salary enhancement because I had so much free time. I noticed that in Hong Kong there were quite a lot of Jaguar E-type sports cars and some of them were parked in the street but damaged. I made inquiries and learned that these particular cars were involved in accidents where people got injured——and you had to wait till after the court case if you wanted to buy such a car. Many of these cars had not been taken back by the owner, so they eventually were sold at government auctions. I liked that, and finally I bought one——and later another four.

Kisa was very happy that we had a car now and more to come, but she didn't like to drive around in damaged cars and asked me to have them repaired. The labour in Hong Kong was too expensive, so I sent all the cars to Manila by ship. I met Eddy Moses, a Jew who was born in Shanghai. When China started opening up, his family had come to Manila. They used to be in timber logging and were very well off. He had good connections with shipping and freight forwarding and knew the right places to get the repairs done much cheaper than in Hong Kong. Kisa helped me a lot with funding. Once I was short of 20,000 Hong Kong dollars. Kisa didn't have any money left and would have to wait until she received her monthly cheque that her family sent her from Samoa for tuition and expenses. However, an uncle of hers had just arrived from Apia and I told her to go and ask him to give the money in cash, saying it was for something very urgent. In the evening she came and opened her sweaty hand, transferring the money into mine.

Then I was off to Manila. By flight it was only an hour and a half from Hong Kong. My friend Eddy Moses was a member of the Army and Navy Club and he got me a complimentary membership for one year. I was sleeping, eating, drinking and swimming there, which saved me a lot of money. At that time the digital watch had just made its first appearance in the markets of Hong Kong.

It revolutionized the international watch industry. I took a few dozen of those watches with me on commission. I made a lot of profit with the watches and later with the cars after the repairs were over. The cars were all spray-painted in very sexy colours; in those days they called them birdcages. I kept one, painted bright lemon-yellow, for myself.

My poor Kisa never saw the end product of the cars because neither did I re-export them to Hong Kong nor did I take her with me to Manila. She cried each time I left Hong Kong. Often I'd be sitting at the pool of the Army and Navy Club when her call would come. I would hear the attendant announce: 'Phone call for the Count of Monte Christo, please.' Each time somebody called me (it was before mobiles were in fashion), members and others craned their necks to see who this Count of Monte Christo might be (I didn't know myself why that name was given to me).

So my time was spent between Hong Kong and Manila, and later, also in Taiwan. But as faithful and loving as Kisa was, I can't make the same statement about myself. Girls in Manila are also a beautiful race with a slight Spanish influence. Spanish is still the language of high society. I fell for a girl by the name of Maria Antoinette Francisco. That often kept me in Manila longer than I intended until, driven by some kind of guilt, I rushed back into Kisa's arms.

Once when I returned she was laughing and crying all at the same time. She told me that a friend of Eddy Moses, Saha, also a Jew, was making life hell for her. He had told her to become his girlfriend and once had started to take his clothes off while sitting in my apartment opposite her. She had to threaten him that she would call me up immediately; only then did he leave, begging her not to say anything to me. I owed him money, which must have got him worried. Around that time Kisa told me that she had been raped at the age of fifteen. It had not caused her any mental scars, but ever since she had always wanted a man who would love her genuinely, and she hoped that I would turn out to be that man. That reminded me of our first night together when she had told me in the morning with such a happy smile, 'Now I have my own "dalling"!' I took her in my arms and said, 'I hope that I don't disappoint you.'

I was so fond of her and we were having so much fun together, especially when she tried to teach me Samoan. I learned pretty quickly; of course sometimes I made mistakes and she couldn't stop laughing. The strange thing with the Polynesian languages is that they have very few consonants and use mainly the vowels; there are sentences that look like this: 'Ae iolau mea ae tia ou' which means 'what have you made for dinner?' Another thing is that the Polynesians are, or used to be, very kind and sweet people and had no swear words in their vocabulary. The only Samoan swear word is 'ufa', which means backside or ass. It's very bad to say it to someone. But now even this would have changed. The world has become a small place.

I stayed with Kisa over the weekend, and we stayed at Lantao Island, which now accommodates the new Hong Kong International Airport. We had a beautiful weekend; we swam a lot and Kisa introduced me to having sex in the seawater in standing position. We used to go to Lantao Island often. We had to take a ferry across from Star Ferry terminal or Lamma Island for an hour's trip and then a bus to the beach area on Lantao. If you wanted to live on the island, you had to make an application and then wait until a house was free. The island was government property and you also had to make an application for a car. The number of cars allowed was strictly to be adhered to, and you could not bring any more than that to Lantao.

After the holiday, I had to go back to the Philippines. I had been invited by Dr Francisco, my girlfriend Maria Antoinette's father, and her family.

Maria had told her father that she wanted to get married to me even though I had never been to the family's estate or met her father. I had only met her in Manila when we were dating there and driving around in my lemon-coloured E-type Jaguar. Of course all my friends had met her and were also invited to come to the Francisco Estate. So this was the first occasion that my Filipino friends took me to Nueva Ecija, like Manila a province on Luzon Island. My Manila friends were all friends and relatives of the Francisco family as well. I liked the girl very much. She was slim, fairly tall, well educated and had graduated in biochemistry. She didn't smile much but when she did, her whole face would light up like a Christmas tree. When we were going out in Manila and entered any of the restaurants or dancing joints, all heads used to turn; she was beautiful.

Her father was tall and slim and had a dental practice in Nueva Ecija and another one in Manila. They had a hacienda away from the town; there were no big cities nearby and the family owned a lot of land and farm animals. It was obvious that the family was very well-to-do. After taking a tour of the outside of the house and part of the hacienda, we were ushered inside into some grand party room where everybody had assembled. In the presence of her family, Maria was very formal; she smiled shyly and greeted me with two kisses on my cheeks. She looked lovely. Although I felt like taking her in my arms and holding her tight with a lip-lock, Maria was very intelligent and knew quite well how to behave in front of her family in that situation.

All Maria's and my common friends from Manila and Hong Kong were in favour of us getting married. Now only the Francisco family had to be just as convinced. There was a slight hitch—Dr Francisco was so far of the opinion that Maria would be married to Dino Corazon, a kind of childhood sweetheart. He was quite a bit younger than I, which went in my favour because the family liked someone with more maturity. I was absolutely confident that we wouldn't encounter any problems.

We all were requested to take our seats and Maria began to serve me coffee and cakes first, because I was regarded as the chief guest—well, at least by my Manila friends who were mainly women and girls. After coffee-kahlua and other refreshments, Dr Francisco wanted to talk to me in his private office to get to know some more details about me. He liked the fact that I was a civil engineer and that I had a construction company in Sydney. I didn't tell him that I didn't really want to return to Sydney for the time being, but I did reveal that I had lost my first wife, Helga, in an automobile accident that had thrown my family life into chaos just after I had finished the construction of a hotel for an Australian syndicate on Kuta Beach, Bali Island. It caused me to accept an offer by Vinell Construction's liaison agents, to work for the South Vietnamese Army, in charge of an engineering unit to support their military supply lines. My three children, one boy and two girls, stayed with my friends who had taken them to California until I could sort out whatever problems had arisen because of the demise of my dear wife. After our talk it was decided that I may continue to rendezvous with Maria and an engagement date would be fixed after about three months if everything turned out satisfactory. After that we shook hands and I was told to address my future father-in-law henceforth as 'Santo', short for Santozo. I would be Bob to everybody; but some people in the Philippines liked to address me as Christo, which stands for Christ both in Spanish and in Italian. With persons who liked me or respected me a lot, I often was requested to bless them which I didn't mind, if I thought they deserved it.

I remained as the Francisco family's guest for two and a half days and then left in a happy mood to go back to Manila. Maria and I made a date to meet after three days in Manila or Quezon City.

A Typhoon, and Apocalypse

If I got married to Maria I'd have to break off with Kisa, but when I arrived at my place in Hong Kong I was looking forward to seeing Kisa. However, when I entered the apartment I was surprised to see Kisa together with three other Polynesian girls; wow, good-looking too. Kisa embraced and kissed me and introduced the girls as Maeva, Liana and Aemia, friends from Western Samoa who had just returned from a four-week show tour singing and dancing Polynesian songs in Tokyo. Forgotten were my thoughts about how to work out my separation from Kisa.

We decided to go out that night to the Peninsula Hotel dance club. What a hit; the girls all danced so well, and I was the only guy; except later on Jimmy Shaw, an old friend from Sydney, turned up and joined us. This we did for the next four days, dancing every night. Then the Samoan friends of Kisa had to leave. On the last day, however, I persuaded the girls to bring for the dancing their lava lavas, which is a Samoan national outfit similar to a sarong to wear at beaches and at home. It was very sexy-looking and they did a few Samoan/Polynesian song and dance numbers.

After they finished, a gentleman introduced himself to me as Angelo Graham, the art director for a Hollywood film called *Apocalypse Now* which was under production in the Philippines. The film was based on the Vietnam War. At the time the crew was on a hiatus because of heavy rains in the Philippines, but they were supposed to continue their shooting after about a week. The film was being directed by Francis Ford Coppola with Marlon Brando as the leading man. When Angelo heard about my history in films and modelling he said he was sure that he could get me a role, but I had to go to Pagsanjan, about a two-hour drive from Manila. He gave me his card and asked me to ring him before going there. I was excited but Kisa made a long face. 'If you get a Hollywood film role, God knows when we'll see each other again!' she complained.

The next day Maeva, Liana and Aemia departed for Samoa i Sisifo (Western Samoa). The other part of Samoa is American Samoa, known as Pago Pago locally and pronounced Pango Pango. Western Samoa used to belong to New Zealand. Lucky for the girls to have left that day, because on that day a typhoon started. By evening the storm signal was already a No. 3 and two days later it was 10; the highest. It was right on top of Hong Kong. At that strength nobody is allowed outside; no public transport or any other vehicle is allowed to ply on the roads. This lasted for three days. We didn't have much food in the house. I had only rice and plenty of onions and some oil. That's all we ate for three days; no milk, no beer, only water.

So, as the saying goes, we lived on rice and love. Starting in the morning we made wild love under our sheets. I was usually the first to wake, and I would squeeze some cold cream (during the night I put it in the fridge) into Kisa's pussy, which made her wake up immediately, giggling; it turned her on. If her friends would have been there still, we would have requested them to stay with us instead of remaining in the hotel. I think it would have been much more fun! Kisa and I were alone, and we made love only in the morning and then again after lunch; imagine what a difference three more beautiful girls aboard could have made.

The nights we reserved for sleeping and joking. Sometimes it was also interesting to observe the neighbours. There were illegal squatters who had set up home on the roofs of neighbouring buildings and it was fascinating to watch them go about their daily lives. Since we were staying on the seventh floor, we could see the buildings that were three floors below us from our bedroom window. Everything was flying away; the roofs, TV aerials, the broken windows. From our window it looked like a disturbed anthill. From the kitchen window we could observe the harbour. Ships were anchored, since there was not enough time to shift them into the storm shelters. The water from the waves that roared into the harbour and hit some of the ships and the quays shot up to unbelievable heights. We could even get glimpses of some of the streets; people who had ventured out were getting hit fiercely by flying debris; they probably hadn't listened to the warnings on radio and TV. It certainly was an experience, and it brought Kisa and me a little closer yet, especially since we were cooped up inside the apartment for several days.

By then, I was wondering if *Apocalypse Now* had given me the excuse to separate from Kisa to marry Maria—or hadn't it? Of course, I couldn't be sure yet if Angelo Graham had been straightforward with me. He had said that he lived in West Hollywood, and that was where most gays lived. Anyway, I'd find out soon enough, and one thing was for sure, if he was after my ass, he'd be disappointed.

After the typhoon, I had a few days. Kisa and I spent the evenings and nights together. I described the nightlife in Manila to her. 'One thing that is great in the Philippines generally is the music. The Filipinos are great musicians and singers. Filipino bands are always in demand for entertainment, that's why there are so many dance bars, nightclubs and even day clubs in the big cities.' At that time the country was ruled by the military with nightly curfews in Manila from midnight till morning, and in the provinces from 11 p.m. till 6 or 7 a.m. The bars and clubs had to close by midnight and after that some of the girls came accosting guys, asking if they could come with them to their place for the night because they lived too far to get home before curfew hours. That way you could always pick up a girl every night; most of those girls were prostitutes. Another thing in the Philippines was that because of the good-quality bands you could always get permission to take the microphone and sing with one of the bands; they knew all the songs and were happy when persons like The Count of Monte Christo would sing a few Nat King Cole songs or even some Filipino songs like *Kapantai ay langit*. Kisa pleaded, 'Please let me come with you to Manila. I want to see you sing on the stage.' I told her that she shouldn't miss her classes. 'I can take you for two or three days, or we can go to the Jockey Club on Hong Kong side right now, because there they normally have some good bands. Anywhere they have a Filipino band, I don't mind singing.'

So we went straight to the Hong Kong Jockey Club and as we walked in, who was on the stage? 'Willy', a Maori entertainer (he had a Sri Lankan manager, a lovely lady named Roma). I'd known him from Australia; that's where entertainers went first after they graduated in New Zealand, then Hong Kong, Japan and London. He said immediately, 'Bob, you've got to sing, I've got a sore throat,' and Kisa sat down with a tomato juice, while I took the microphone and sang *When I fall in love* and *Unforgettable* by Nat King Cole, *Somewhere over the rainbow* and *We can make it happen again* by the Stylistics. I was in a happy mood and the band was good and people applauded and got up to dance, and Kisa was thrilled. I was glad Willy was here. I often say that it is important to meet the right people at the right time. And don't drink alcohol for inspiration! Drink coffee or kahlua and have a beautiful, cool companion by your side! After that we went back to our apartment, not far from the Jockey Club. We needed some rest after the three stormy days which we'd survived on rice and love. Now maybe we would try without rice.

After two days I received a phone call from Angelo Graham. He was in Pagsanjan and requested me to come within the next two or three days to meet the casting director of *Apocalypse*. Angelo wanted me to inform him on what flight I'd be arriving so he could meet me at the airport and take me to the production office. I rang up Maria again and told her that I'd come to Manila in the next two or three days, as soon as I had my plane ticket. The flights between Hong Kong and Manila were full most of the time, so I went to the airline office right away.

I also got some mail from a friend who promised to find out where my karate guru Oshiro was staying those days. I had met Oshiro around 1963–64 in Sydney. He had come to train army recruits and he had trained me also. He was also the guru of Bruce Lee. I hadn't seen him for about two years. Even though he was Japanese, he trained in Hong Kong. Although I'd made inquiries, there had been no results. Now Jimmy Shaw sent me a message that he was in Zamboanga, right down in the south of the Philippines. Well, I couldn't go there now, I had to go to the *Apocalypse* office first. I wondered what Oshiro was doing in Zamboanga. Was he training down there? He had taught me the soft Japanese martial art of Goju-Kai in Sydney and I wouldn't have minded catching up with some good sparring to stay in shape.

Two days later I arrived at Manila airport around lunchtime. I had had lunch already in the flight. I was looking for Angelo; instead someone much prettier put her arms around my neck from behind. Maria! Soon Angelo found us. He said that since they didn't require me at the production office that day, I should be prepared to stay overnight. Maria had to go back to work, so I told her I'd phone later on, we'd have to meet.

Angelo and I were soon driving towards the famous Pagsanjan Falls. He said to me, 'Man, every time I see you, you're with some beautiful babes. But to be honest, I think you have a great body for your age. You're in top shape. By the way, I'm gay. I hope you don't mind.'

15

'As long as you leave me alone I don't mind talking to you,' I said.

He said that he was of Greek origin; there were quite a few Greek-Americans with *Apocalypse* and also Italians, like Coppola. I said that I was also of Greek origin on my father's side. But I was born in Sydney, and professionally I was a civil engineer. 'Oh, that's interesting,' he said. Angelo was driving, and we took less than two hours from the airport to the Pagsanjan Hotel, where there was the production office as well. That's where we went straight away.

The casting people asked me a lot of questions about my education, my acting experience and what I was doing in the Philippines; then one of the assistant directors, Fred Roos, came and said they could give me a relatively small role in the beginning of the film with Martin Sheen who was playing Captain Willard, the lead. I was to play a CIA officer who had to brief Captain Willard about his task, which entailed eliminating a rogue US colonel called Colonel Kurtz (played by Marlon Brando) who stayed with the Montagnard natives in Cambodia and killed US soldiers. I had to fill in a form and sign it and was told the fee I would earn per day. They were not sure when the shooting of that part would take place, maybe in two weeks' time; I would be informed a few days earlier.

I was looking for Angelo to tell him that I was leaving when I saw him talking to an Italian-looking man. He introduced us; John La Sandra, the construction boss. 'When he heard that you're a civil engineer, he said he needs you,' Angelo said. Angelo also told me that the role I had been given was pretty small. Probably it would be over in four days and the money would also be less than what I was expecting. 'See, we need someone who we can put in charge of Kurtz's compound.' Kurtz's compound was where Colonel Kurtz (Brando) lived. 'The set builders couldn't do that complex because it needs proper foundations; we're in the middle of the rainy season and the set has already been washed away twice. We don't have the right man in charge; you will be the right man. You'll be busy for about four months. You can see the drawings, they are based on The Angkor Wat temple structure with two big towers; you and the sculptor, James Casey, can do it together. You'll be the construction supervisor and you will earn much more than they were going to give you for that crummy little role of a CIA officer. How about it?' OK, I was happy with that. I could start the next day.

That was how I came to refuse the role they wanted to give me and start building Kurtz's compound together with Jim Casey, the sculptor and artist. My role was given to an actor called Harrison Ford who was a carpenter but had tried to become an actor for a long time. After this little role he hit the big time with *Star Wars* and *Raiders of the Lost Ark*. He became one of the highest-paid Hollywood actors of the eighties and nineties.

I called Maria to tell her about my new role as construction supervisor. 'I'm going to be working with *Apocalypse* for at least four months, how do you like that? $2,500 a month!' We made plans to meet at the Army and Navy Club the next day, a Sunday, before I started work on Monday.

'I have to go to Manila but I've left my car there because Angelo picked me up from the airport,' I told John La Sandra. He asked me how I was going to go back to Manila.

'Oh Bob,' Angelo intervened, 'you can stay here overnight. I can get you back to Manila in the morning.'

'That's fine,' I replied. 'You can arrange a room for me in the hotel.'

'Oh, if there is no room free you can always double up with me.'

'I don't think you would like it, I'm a terrible snorer,' I said hastily.

'That's no problem Bob, I've got some anti-snore tablets with me.'

'Never heard of anti-snore tablets before! I think you're kidding; just get me a room, please, and I'll start my job the day after and bring my own car with me.'

Once that was settled, John shook my hand and said, 'Welcome to *Apocalypse Now*.' He asked me if I'd join him for dinner in about two hours, we'd have a couple of drinks first.

Angelo also joined us for drinks. After a few drinks, he asked, 'Would you like some Thai Stick—it's unbelievable, hits you like dynamite. A friend of mine brought it with him only yesterday.'

'Maybe I'll try it, just for the heck of it, although I'm not into all that stuff,' I said. 'I smoke enough as it is. Every time I think of Vietnam, I feel like giving it up.'

'Why, what happened?' asked Angelo.

'Oh, when we were working on the supply lines near Talat one of our guys got hit in the chest by shrapnel from grenades. The doctor had to perform emergency surgery to find the stuff and remove it. I went inside the tent with them to watch, hoping the guy would survive. It was Jerry the Pommie. I wasn't allowed to go too close, but I wore a mask and saw that every time Jerry exhaled, there was a bubbling noise and black slime came to the surface. It was disgusting. I said to the doctor, "He's finished, Doc, isn't he?" He replied, "No, no, he'll be all right. These are the signs that he's a smoker." So I asked him, "If I smoke cigarettes and cigars, mainly panatellas, but I inhale, how long would it take to get rid of all the nicotine and tar?" "It'll take at least two years if you stop totally, and if you live in a reasonably unpolluted environment." That shows you what a dirty and unhealthy habit smoking is, as if there are not enough other pollutants in the air.'

I looked at Angelo, who took a deep draft from his Thai Stick or whatever it was called. John La Sandra had only just lit a cigarette but he extinguished it and took a hearty sip from his beer. I joined him, feeling very thirsty suddenly. I didn't feel like smoking that Thai hash that Angelo was puffing on, but I had a few more beers.

Then I met Jim Casey, the sculptor, who had just walked through the door. He was about sixty. We shook hands. He'd heard already about us starting to work together. So he explained everything about Kurtz's compound and how much work was pending. I told him to make sure that we had enough material so we didn't have to wait for that, especially if it had to be sent all the way from Manila. We also needed a crane for the towers, but first we had to do the foundations properly.

'OK,' I said finally. 'Let's eat and then I'm gonna hit the sack. What time are we leaving, Angelo?'

'Seven o'clock. Your key is with the reception.'

Next morning I called Maria at home from the Army and Navy Club in Manila. I told her to come for breakfast and bring her bikini along. 'But come in my car, because I get good parking here.'

The Army and Navy Club was very nice, with a beautiful pool, tennis court, barbecue area and drinks; whatever you ordered was brought to your deckchair. While I waited for Maria, I called Jimmy Shaw in Hong Kong and asked him where he had got the information about Oshiro. 'I've been searching for him ever since I've come back from Vietnam, but still haven't found him. What the hell is he doing in Zamboanga? Do you have a phone number?'

'He doesn't have a phone number but there's an address where he is training.' In retrospect, without mobiles or e-mail things used to be quite difficult, though we didn't realize it at the time.

By the time I got off the phone, Maria had arrived.

'Hello, my darling,' I said. 'Oh, today I get a kiss, better than in Nueva Ecija! You're looking absolutely beautiful. Now tell me the news.'

She smiled. 'My parents both liked you very much. My mom said she likes your sense of humour; by the way, you got kisses in Ecija too, only more formal than today's.'

'Hey, once I'm working in Pagsanjan for a few days you must come and visit me. You can stay with me. How has Dino taken the changed marriage plans? He is quite a nice boy, but I think you need a man like me. Come, sit down; let's order a nice breakfast for four.'

'Why, who else is coming?'

'I am hungry for two, and I don't think a little more weight would do you any harm either! See, I plan to look after your health properly from now on!' Maria laughed.

'Later on,' I continued, 'we'll swim for an hour and if Eddy Moses brings the boat, we can go to that waterskiing place. Have you ever been to the Pagsanjan River? You go uphill till you come to a big waterfall. When you get there, you have to turn the boat around and go downhill. The boatmen who row it up have to push and even sometimes carry it over the rapids. It's amazing. These boatmen are guys with huge muscles, and tourists are so in awe of them that they pay them big tips.'

Our food arrived. 'Oh, have a look at the size of those omelettes!' I marvelled. 'And what is this on the other plate? Yes it's some very appetizing fish and kalamansi juice with pan de sal, your famous Filipino bread! Actually it's like Spanish bread, isn't it? OK my dear, bon appetit! We'll have some fruit after this, and maybe some more omelettes.'

After breakfast we relaxed in the sun and chatted about the past and the future, until the announcer's voice called out that there was a phone call for the Count of Monte Christo. It was Eddy Moses.

Whenever he went to someone's office or past a hotel he went in and made all his phone calls. He'd have been a big success for the cellphone revolution in the eighties! But then it was only 1976. Eddy said he'd come around 3 p.m. because we had to do some digesting before we start waterskiing. Actually we should have gone in the morning. Before lunch we had had a pitcher of cold sangria and after the sumptuous lunch we slept for a little while, half snoozing and half chatting. Then we drove down to the waterskiing place at Manila Bay. Eddy was already on his ski. Maria was still on two skis, but that day she kicked one of them off and managed on mono for some time; she enjoyed it tremendously.

After that, I went to Maria's place to discuss our programme for the next two to three weeks and then I was on my way back to the set. This time I met Jim Kelly, the chef, and his huge catering van. The food of the *Apocalypse* cast and working crew was excellent. But Jim Kelly was a man of other talents; he had a ham radio that he used to pick up information——I used to call him intelligence snooper and I feel that was his greatest talent.

After that Jim Casey and I sat down and made a flowchart of all the work we had to finish during the next month with the details of materials to be ordered. That would take care of the foundations and then we'd start on the structure.

Earthquakes and Body Bags

I'd been working on the set's footings and foundations, and everything looked solid; it was all near the Pagsanjan River and it was definitely not being washed away. Most of the actors had not been there when I had first touched base with everybody else. Even Francis Ford Coppola had arrived from the USA only a few days earlier. The film shooting was only going to start now.

There was a long weekend, two holidays and a Sunday. I decided to use this to fly down south to Zamboanga to try my luck in finding Oshiro again. It wouldn't be a problem to be back in three days, with or without Oshiro. Actually my secret plan was to bring the karate guru to Pagsanjan and offer the shooting cast and the working crew evening classes in Goju-Kai Japanese karate. He was an excellent teacher, and could do with some extra money. I was a black belt myself and I had been taught by Oshiro.

Maria wanted to come with me. She'd never been to Zamboanga and neither had I, but I had to travel by air to be back fast. If I had enough time, I would've been happy to take her by car or better still to take the boat ride. But then either way it could have been risky, because Zamboanga is the Islamic rebels' stronghold in the south. It was not yet too bad, but it was getting worse by the day, and I didn't want my Maria getting kidnapped. I told Francis (Coppola) where I was going and that I'd be back in three days. I met Maria at her place, had a cup of coffee and she drove me to the airport. I checked in and then we had time for another cuppa. I said, 'Be careful my love, and if I find Oshiro, I'll bring him here. Then you will have to take a course in Goju-Kai, and we will be a two-man army.'

She embraced and kissed me, and I saw that tears were running down her face. 'What's the matter, my darling?' I asked.

'Just take care, Bob. Please don't stay any longer. I love you, you know!'

'I love you too, Maria; bye my honeysuckle-rose!'

In the plane, I relaxed in my seat, reading the morning paper. It was a sunny day and very impressive to fly across the whole island nation, all the way from north Luzon down to the southern point of Zamboanga in Mindanao. You could get a notion of the great depths between the Philippine islands. One could tell by the dark blue, occasionally black-blue patches; that's where you have the greatest depth in all the oceans of the world.

As soon as we touched terra firma, I found a taxi driver, gave him the address I had and sat back hoping he was good enough to find the man. We did eventually, after over two hours of driving around and asking other people. Nobody seemed to know him. Finally, a few hours after noon, somebody took me to an overcrowded, colourless hovel that was supposed to be a hotel and pointed us to a person who he said was the manager. This manager said, 'Oshiro told me that he'll return tonight, and then he'll be leaving for Taiwan tomorrow.' I asked if he had a room for me in this kind of questionable place. He said, 'Yes, one place next to Japan-man room.' I told him to show me the room. He pointed to a room and said, 'This room, Japan-man room and that room, your room. You give me money now. 200 piso.'

I gave him 250 piso and told him, 'You put new bed sheet and new pillow and pillowcases, OK?'

'Yes sir, new.'

'And when Japan-man come, you wake me, you call me! OK?'

'Yes sir.'

I thought I'd find a good hotel where I could eat, have a drink and maybe take a shower, before coming back to this hovel with a thousand people in it. I wondered what happened to Oshiro—he used to be such a clean, fastidious person. I hoped to God he was not on drugs.

I found a five-star hotel, and had some nice sangrias and then a first-class dinner. Then I went to the band and asked them if they could play *Autumn leaves* for me. 'OK,' they said. So I asked, 'May I sing it?'

There was a lady singer, so I asked her, 'What's your name?'

'Lila.'

'You don't mind if I sing a song?'

'No sir, you sing.'

When I have a few songs to sing with a decent band, I always get in a good mood. After a few songs, the band was going to sit down for a break and they invited me to join them. I had another cool sangria. When Lila asked me how long I was going to stay, I said, 'I have to leave again tomorrow.'

'Oh, sir, don't stay long time in Zamboanga, bad city for ground moving all the time.'

'What, you mean earthquakes?'

'Yes, sir, all the time making noise.'

That was enough for me. I left quickly hoping that Oshiro had already come. There was nobody in his room, so I just took my shoes off and rested on the bed.

I must have fallen asleep and started dreaming something weird; I remember the face of that singer Lila as she shouted at me: 'Don't wait for earthquake, get up, get up, get up!' And then I was awake and heard a thunderous noise—de-de-de-de-de-de-de—faster and faster, and then rrrrrrrrrrrrrrrrrrrrrrrrrrrrrrr and everything was shaking terribly. I got out of bed and ran to the door of the room and waited for a while under the door frame until I heard something collapse above me and people shouting and a lot of noise from outside. I checked Oshiro's room but it was empty. So I ran down the stairs. Something fell on my shoulder and then I was in the street.

I stopped and looked at the other side of the street. Several buildings were collapsing and people were running out. Some people were falling down from wobbling houses. There were no lights, only moonlight. Some sirens started blaring and a fire engine passed by. Now a lot of people were in the street; some of them were bleeding and others had towels over their heads. I saw a lot of people with helmets on their heads; they all must have been motorbike riders. The problem was the darkness. In some places where vehicles were parked, people had turned on the car lights and the fire trucks were also trying to create some light. Some flares were also shot up in the air to illuminate the city.

I thought it was pointless to walk around aimlessly unless I could help somebody who was in trouble. So I walked back to the hotel where Oshiro was supposed to be living, but how was he going to come back when the city had been hit by an earthquake? The hotel looked pretty bad. The top half had broken down. I went back to my room and retrieved my overnight bag.

I went down again, and walked around as I waited for daylight. Now there were two helicopters with searchlights flying over the city. There was a lot of damage. I could hear cries coming from some of the collapsed houses. I passed one street which had a long wide crack disappearing into a big heap of rubble. I had to be careful not to fall into cracks like this one. I asked some military personnel how I could get to the airport. They told me that Zamboanga airport was closed. I would have to go by ferry to Davao and try to get a flight from there. They told me where to go to find a ferry.

The streets were in bad condition, because they were full of rubble, stones and cracks in the road surface and every time there was another tremor, more houses were collapsing. Some people had transistor radios on and I could understand from the announcements that the strength of the earthquake had been 7.6 on the Richter scale. A few thousand people were dead and trains and flights were out of order, so I rushed to find the ferry station to make it to Davao fast. My God, in daylight it looked totally devastated. Groups of workers and army personnel were digging to free trapped persons from beneath the rubble. To get to the ferry station took me about three hours. I walked partly and got a lift in a car for the rest of the way. The scenes of destruction that awaited me en route were absolutely horrendous. There must have been a tsunami, because I saw quite a few overturned boats scattered on the shore far away from the water, as well as big puddles of seawater above the high-tide mark.

I was lucky because a ferry was ready to leave. But there were too many people trying to get on board, and nobody was stopping them. I had to tell the captain that if he didn't stop the inflow of more passengers the ferry might capsize, like it had happened so many times before. I used to read about so many capsizes in the headlines of the Philippine newspapers. I also told the other passengers that we had to stop more people from getting on the ferry as it would definitely sink and most of the people on board would drown. That galvanized everybody on the ferry to stop more people from boarding. This led to scuffles with those who wanted to board. I told the captain to take off—and off we went.

Despite the overcrowded ferry, we managed to go fast enough to get to Davao in a reasonable time. Once we were there, I took a taxi to the airport and bought a ticket to Manila. It was a waitlisted ticket. Then I finally found a phone to call Maria. Of course, she was waiting for my call because the newspapers were full of news about the catastrophic quake. Papers estimated 6000 dead. I told Maria that I was still not sure whether I could get on that flight, and that I might be a day late.

I also called Jimmy Shaw in Hong Kong to find out where Oshiro was headed after he'd left his room in Zamboanga. He had told the manager at the boarding house that he wanted to travel to Taiwan. Had he known that there was going to be an earthquake? I felt frustrated at having been thwarted by the earthquake. I hadn't come over here to waste my time, and my shoulder hurt like hell. The last call was to Kisa. I apologized that I hadn't called her earlier, and I told her what happened and that I had to get back to the *Apocalypse* set. I promised to go and see her as soon as I could.

Love Breeds Worries

I arrived in Manila on Tuesday morning and by the grace of God, Maria was waiting for me at the airport. She looked worried. But when she saw my smile, she cheered up. I asked her if she had any visitors at her apartment, but the answer was negative.

At her house, I said, 'Maria, I haven't had any sleep, I must sleep for a few hours and then I'll start work tomorrow morning.' As I took my clothes off, she came over and looked at my shoulder which was bruised and swollen. I had difficulty moving my left arm.

'What happened to your shoulder, Bob?'

'Something fell on it when I got out of the house during the earthquake. Actually, I hardly noticed it when it occurred. Now it's suddenly very sore.'

Before lying down I got John La Sandra on the phone and told him I'd be late by one day for work. He just said, 'Have a good sleep.'

Then Maria lay next to me, holding me very tight and kissing me softly. That's all I remember. When I woke up again, she was still there next to me. I said, 'Don't you have to go to work?'

'Bobsi, I've just come back from work, you must have slept all day long. You didn't touch any of the food I prepared for you.'

'Oh, mon dieu, quel malheur!'

'Don't you wanna see a doctor about your shoulder?'

'There is a doctor for the whole team at *Apocalypse*. I'll be OK. For me there is no physical work, I'm the supervisor.'

I really slept well, but in the end I was dreaming again. The next day, I was at Pagsanjan bright and early. I had my breakfast in Jim Kelly's fabulous catering van. Afterwards, as I was going on a round with Jim Casey to check the work on the Kurtz's compound set, I noticed that the sculptor had a very conscientious assistant. She was his timekeeper, making sure that each of his workers signed in and out at the right time. Her name was Flores, and she was not more than twenty. Jimmy had also used her portrait as the head on the four-faced towers. She seemed to be in love with him—and vice versa. There was at least a forty-year age difference between them. I was sure that when he returned to the US, Jim would take her with him.

Jim had finished the formwork for the Angkor Wat towers and was ready to pour the mix with lightweight aggregate and cement. They were being poured in small segments, lifted up to the base by cranes after drying and put together again. So work was continuing on several fronts. We couldn't go wrong, we'd be on time. I asked Jim Casey how much work he had done in the film industry. He said he had done all the sculpture work on Disney World, Florida, and set work for a lot of movies. He lived in Venice, Los Angeles, where he had a huge backlot full of material and cut-outs. He invited me to visit after we'd finished *Apocalypse*.

Then Jim asked me to meet Sandy, the property (props) master, who wanted to talk to me.

I strolled over. 'Hi, Sandy.'

'Yes, Bob. Francis asked me to find out where to get real dead bodies from. You know, to be used for shooting war scenes—burnt by napalm, hanging down from trees, all kinds of gruesome spectacles.'

'Well, I know a funeral parlour in the old part of Manila. It's called Funeraria Popular, which means popular funeral parlour. They use it for a great deal of unclaimed bodies. I don't know how much we have to pay for them, but we'll have to return them after use, and we mustn't damage them. They should look as good as new. Well, put it this way, how much will Francis pay for them?'

'Maybe he wants a hundred bodies at the rate of $100 per body.'

'I'll get them. I'll check it out tomorrow morning and let you know. Do you have Vietnam body bags?' There were a lot of surplus body bags remaining from the Vietnam War and they would come in handy for the film.

'Yes, plenty.'

'Why don't you come with me tomorrow, OK? After breakfast.'

I immediately ordered half a dozen workers to get some wooden beams and erect a hut 12' X 6' with plenty of ventilation and two doors fitted with padlocks. Then I had a look to see if Francis was around. I found him and told him about the funeral parlour and that he'd probably get the first ten bodies the next day and that a hut for the corpses was already under construction. Then I informed him that the staff working as costumers to dress and undress the bodies would probably not touch the corpses. So we needed to get a mortuary assistant. 'If I can get one from the funeral parlour, I'll bring him with me, OK?' Francis gave me the thumbs up.

Next morning I drove with Sandy, the props master, to the Funeraria Popular in a small van. They had ten corpses and we were given to understand that they were unclaimed bodies—just in case some people came to claim them. Although there was a time limit for that, we still had to turn them over to relatives if they intended to bury or cremate them. All the corpses were put into the body bags which we had brought with us from the property department. The undertaker told us that they had performed post-mortems, after which they had all been embalmed. Then he took us to the embalming room where the embalmer would cut the heads open to check for the cause of death, after which he would cut open the front of the bodies to check there as well. Then he applied formalin, the embalming liquid, after removing the intestines and part of the brain; after that everything was stitched up again. The embalmer's assistant asked me if we could give him a job. I told him he could work in the costume department, where the corpses had to be dressed and made up. He wanted to come with us right away. I said OK, we'd find him a place to stay with some of the costume guys.

The embalmer told us to wash our hands before leaving. The mortuary assistant took us to the tap, which was outside in the yard at the end of the corridor. Suddenly I heard an 'oink', and when I looked across I saw the biggest pig I have ever laid my eyes on. I thought to myself, *That must be the animal that's eaten all the intestines and whatever else is removed during the post-mortems!*

I didn't feel too good after that, neither did Sandy. Before we washed our hands the embalmer asked us if we wanted some old corpses. He opened the doors of an old hearse, filled with dried-up corpses which could be picked up with one hand. They must have been several years old. I was surprised that they would keep them for such a long time at the back of their funeral parlour for no apparent reason. For us they would be of no use. Anyway, we said goodbye and told them that I would ring up next week regarding some more corpses. Before leaving, we washed our hands thoroughly.

When we arrived at the set, we placed the ten bodies alternately staggered on their backs, covered them lightly and locked the doors. I told them not to install any lights so nobody could see what it really was. I mentioned that they were artificial bodies but a faint smell was noticeable. Someone must have talked, maybe the mortuary assistant, because the next day one of the costumers booked a ticket for himself back to the US, saying he didn't want to work with dead bodies. So far we had only acquired ten, which meant another ninety were still needed.

Soon Marlon Brando started his shooting. He only had nineteen days with us and he lived in a houseboat which was anchored in a lake near Pagsanjan River. He socialized quite a lot with the other actors, make-up people and Chinese and Vietnamese coordinators. In fact there were quite a number of good-looking Asian girls with various departments. That's why I wondered why he had selected as a regular companion who would have meals with him, a Vietnamese coordinator whom I would have classified as neither pretty nor ugly but pretty ugly! In fact the ugliest of the Asians; she had no chin. I had nothing against her; it was just an observation. Tastes vary from person to person, which goes to prove that for every individual in the world there is a suitable partner, and love has no limits, be it from the physical point of view or from the point of intelligence. Marlon even invited that particular girl to his island paradise near Tahiti after his shooting was over. Whether she joined him, I am not aware of, but he was a good companion. I had a few conversations with him, but mainly in the morning because that was the time of the day when he was generally in a good mood. Most people are governed by moods. For instance, I would never phone my Indian wife any time before lunch. I would preferably wait till evening, then she would be civil and not without humour. I told her one day just after her menopause, 'From now on we shouldn't make love any more; it may be construed as incest.' She didn't think it was funny at all; I had made that remark in the morning. But from then on she stuck to my recommendation!

I enjoyed the few days with Marlon Brando. He had put on a lot of weight; that's why the film took so long to finish. Coppola waited for him to lose his excess weight, but instead he kept putting on more. Then we couldn't wait any longer.

One morning Brando was shooting in the area around Kurtz's compound when he stopped at a heap of little artificial arms which were supposed to be the arms of North Vietnamese children who had been vaccinated by the Americans against malaria. In the film, Colonel Kurtz declares, 'The Vietcong cut them all off, a heap of little arms. See the genius of it. If I had soldiers like that, our troubles here would have long been over. The horror, you have to try and make horror your friend. If you don't make horror your friend, horror may be an enemy to be feared.' Brando looked at the arms suspiciously, sniffed and then caught sight of a fence in front of him on which hung a carabao hide which emanated a stench of decay. 'Take this shit away. Why do you subject me to that stench in the morning. I am going to relax for some time.' His mood was spoiled. Later on Coppola mentioned to the property master, 'If Marlon's reaction to a smelly carabao hide is that fierce, he won't stay a minute longer if he comes to know that we're working with genuine cadavers. I think we've got to abandon the idea.' We didn't see Marlon for the rest of the day; he asked for his favourite coordinator to give him company.

His fifty-second birthday was a few days later, and he requested the production to give an afternoon birthday party for the whole unit. The party was fun, but about halfway through some people fell ill, vomiting and running to the toilet. It turned out that over a hundred people had become violently sick after eating a lovely squid salad; the supplier admitted afterwards that the squid had been deep-frozen twice, which can be deadly. I thought for some time that I was going to die. Luckily Maria, who had come for that party, didn't try the squid salad. She stayed overnight to look after me.

In the morning a group of military personnel was moving around making inquiries about a person by the name of Bob Christo. They asked me if those dead bodies were mine. I replied, 'No, they belong to the film company. I only brought them here from a Manila funeral parlour.' They further inquired whether I had a certificate for corpses in transit. I told them to see me in the

32

afternoon because I was not well, I had food poisoning. The military police returned towards evening and told me that those bodies could not be used for the Vietnam War shooting unless I produced the necessary certificates.

'What if I don't give you any certificates?' I asked.

'Then the corpses have to be taken back to the funeral parlour,' they said.

'OK, take them back.'

'No, you have to take them back personally and you have to pay us a fine of 25,000 pisos because you didn't have any certificates.'

I said, 'Fine, we'll take the bodies back tomorrow morning. We'll see about the money later. I have to get it from the company.' So we returned the ten bodies. In any case, Coppola had decided not to use them because of Marlon Brando. Only this one Filipino military police asked me every day for the money, which obviously was going into that low-ranked policeman's pocket. So I told one of my army friends, a colonel who often shared drinks with me at the bar in the evenings. I explained the story to him and after three days I heard that the policeman was beaten up and transferred to an unpleasant outpost. So that was the beginning and end of using genuine bodies in war scenes in an American movie.

Unfortunately I didn't get to see Maria more than once a week, but whenever she stayed with me for a night or a weekend I was in a happy mood and usually sang in the hotel with the band. By now I had learned two or three Filipino songs which I sometimes used to show off with. Maria was surprised when I sang *Kapantai ai langit* (*The sky is the limit*), the favourite song of the First Lady, Imelda Marcos, owner of thousands of shoes.

It took a few days before I was able to eat properly again; it was the worst food poisoning I had ever suffered from. Finally, I got up and walked around Kurtz's compound. It was just about ready. It looked real, very much like an old temple ruin. Filming had already been done in the areas that had been completed earlier. Now we could finish the rest of Marlon Brando's scenes. The Montagnard natives with whom Colonel Kurtz was staying lived in Cambodia, which was at the time of the *Apocalypse* shooting involved in a horrible war and genocide (because of this the area had come to be known as The Killing Fields). So we were using the people of another tribe whose home is in the mountain areas of Central Luzon near Baguio in the Philippines. They are the Ifugao tribes. They were found by our research team to be very similar with regard to looks and lifestyle of the Montagnards. We supplied them with wool of different colours and the right tools which they used to weave a lot of things. An old woman of about eighty made me a charming blanket of blue, red and green wool. I've kept it with me since that day in 1976 and still use it while sleeping whenever it's cold. At the moment, as I am writing this book, thirty-odd years later, I am using the blanket every night in Bangalore, India. I can still remember the face of that beautiful old woman with her snow-white hair and her lovely features.

Another morning, as I took my habitual round along Kurtz's compound, I took a deep breath and detected a spicy fragrance in the air. Everywhere around me were coconuts, thousands of coconut trees, but I couldn't figure out where that spicy aroma originated from. I felt something in my pocket. Putting my hands in it, I came up with a big cigar someone had given me a couple of days earlier. I put it in my mouth, lit it and took a deep draft. I didn't like the taste; it destroyed that spicy aroma which I had been enjoying a minute ago. Then I remembered Vietnam, the operation in the tent, and the black slime in the lungs of the soldier. *I must be crazy*, I thought. *Why do I still smoke cigarettes, cigars? I should have stopped long ago. Smoking is bad for your health, it is a dirty habit. I only lit that cigar because of a habit. I've become a slave to my habits. No, not any more, never again.* I threw the cigar away, never to smoke again. Then I took another deep breath and held the air in my lungs for about thirty seconds, and there it was, the spicy fragrance, I could smell it again. It was worth it to give up smoking for that pleasure. My lungs have been clean for thirty-five years now. Later I also started to practise yoga—I have been doing so for almost thirty years now.

In Search of Oshiro

I received a message from Jimmy Shaw asking me to call him soon for news about my Japanese martial arts friend. I called Jimmy in Hong Kong and he said, 'Oshiro is in Kaohsiung (Taiwan). His wife is staying in Taipei, but if you go to meet her, she will take you to her husband. Go as soon as possible.' I decided that I'd go the following weekend. I had earned well on this job, but I wouldn't be able to do any business with Oshiro through *Apocalypse*.

My main work was done, but I had agreed to do a few stunts for the film and those remained to be filmed. How I got into stunt work is an interesting story and dates back to my days in Sydney. On Sundays, my wife Helga and I used to go to a beach very close to home on the north shore of Bondi Beach—I think it was called Whale Beach. One day, around lunchtime, Helga said she was hungry, so we decided to go and get some burgers and fish and chips and some drinking water. After buying lunch, we decided to take the forest route back to Bondi. As we were driving through the bush, we noticed a lot of smoke in the distance. Bushfires! Sydney used to get plagued by bushfires and lost a lot of property and trees every year. Helga was scared and wanted to take the roads along the beaches, but that would have been too long a route. I found a place safely away from the fires and we had our lunch, but the wind was blowing the fire towards us. After lunch I continued driving through the bush, trying to bypass the fires. It worked up to a certain point, but then there was no option but to drive through a fire to get safely out of the area. Helga was terrified. 'I'm not coming!' she said.

'Fine,' I said. 'Tell me how to go and I will come with you.'

She shouted, 'I don't know! I don't know!'

'OK,' I replied. 'I know how to get through. If you trust me, do as I tell you.' As we neared the fire I wrapped the petrol tank in a beach towel soaked in water; we had plenty because we had prepared for a hot day. Then I soaked Helga with more water and told her to lie down on the back seat and close all the windows. I gave her a thick cloth and told her to keep it against her face and nose and asked her to breathe slowly. Then I drove like a maniac through the fire, trying to avoid the hot spots on the ground. We drove for nearly a kilometre through the fire, and then another kilometre till the fire was well and truly behind us. We stopped the car, checked the tyres and our stock of drinking water. Our car was still drivable, and not far away we found some burnt outhouses with working water taps. Helga smiled and we hugged each other.

A short time after the bushfire incident, a Hollywood film was produced near Sydney and I heard that stuntmen were required for some dangerous shots. After having successfully negotiated a real-life bushfire, I felt capable of tackling any dangerous shot! I asked Helga if we should apply for a job; she declined but I went ahead and was accepted. I didn't have to drive through any more fires but I was paid for jumping from several high cliffs and about sixty metres from a helicopter into the water. That was the first of a number of stunts that I did for movies; I did some more in Hollywood later, and a few in Bollywood. I also did a stunt for *Wild Geese* in Cape Town.

So when I learnt that there was some stunt work to be done for *Apocalypse* I had asked to do it and had been accepted. That scene would be shot only after I returned from Taipei.

I called Kisa. I told her that I'd come to Hong Kong on the weekend. I'd take the Hong Kong flight to Taipei instead of taking the Manila flight.

When I arrived at Kai Tak Airport, Hong Kong, I was pleasantly surprised to see Kisa running across to me. I hadn't realized how much I had missed her. I took her in my arms and kissed her on her mouth. 'Is everything OK, Kisa? You told me on the phone that you'll be leaving for Samoa soon.'

'Yes, Bopsi, and I want you to come with me.'

'Darling, I have to finish a few things first in the Philippines and I'm on my way to Taiwan, because Oshiro's wife is taking me to him in Kaohsiung. If you want, I can take you to the filming location in the Philippines for two days when I return from Taiwan. Let's go out to the Jockey Club tonight and celebrate.'

'Oh Bopsi, let's make love first.'

'Sure, my turtle dove, let's go and do it on the runway. Can you imagine the headlines in the paper tomorrow?'

'Let's go home fast,' she laughed.

'Yes, you have to teach me some more Polynesian words.' The moment we were in our place, she removed her clothes and attacked me, trying to remove mine too. We fell on the floor and started a wrestling match that turned out to be the best foreplay we had ever had. After the act, we showered, got dressed and I called Jimmy Shaw to request him to join us at the Jockey Club. Then I told her to lie face down on the bed, and keep herself totally loose. After she was in the right position, I started to trail my nails and fingertips of both hands ever so lightly from her shoulder blades down her back, veering to the waist and then continuing slowly to her bottom, in between the buttocks, to the top of her thighs. She had goose pimples all over her skin and she shouted, 'Let's do it again, Bopsi, please!!!'

After that we both were very happy and we got ready to go. Outside our apartment block everything was dug up, because the government had started work on the Hong Kong mass transit railway (MTR), which would run on both sides of the harbour and also underneath. About a year before I had received an invitation for the position of a government building inspector for the MTR. After I started on *Apocalypse* I could not accept the position, but there were some positive write-ups in the newspapers about my educational background and my occupations of modelling and film work in various countries.

We arrived at the Jockey Club, just as Jimmy made his entry with his Chinese girlfriend. As we walked in, we found Willy, the Maori entertainer, tickling the patrons with his latest joke: 'A Catholic priest was taking a ferry across a wide stream. The ferry was heavily loaded with people and capsized. The priest fell down on his knees and prayed to God, "Oh holy father, please have mercy and save all of us from certain death." Right after the prayer another ferry came very fast and the captain of that ferry shouted, "Get in quickly!" But the priest assured him, "No, no, don't worry, God will help us." But things became worse, and a few moments later a big boat came roaring along to help the people, but again the priest sent the boat off shouting, "We'll be fine, thank you, God will help us!" Right after that big boat came a third boat, a powerful tug, and the crew threw a rope across to the sinking ferry; now the priest threw the rope back and said, "Everything will be all right. God will help us," and the tug left. That was the end. Everybody drowned, including the priest. When the priest arrived at heaven's door, he asked God, "Why didn't you save us?" The Lord shouted back, "What nonsense are you talking? I sent you three different boats and you sent all of them away telling their captains, 'We're OK. God will help us.' You made me look a fool, off to hell with you!'"

At that time it was the latest, but after a few years it died down and I never heard the joke again, until one of my friends heard a priest recite it during the Sunday morning service, saying, 'See, these are the ways of the Lord.'

We had a few bottles of wine and ate a Chinese dinner for a change; I usually stuck to Filipino food or global cuisine. Jimmy had worked in quite a few movies. I kept running into him, here and there in different parts of the world. Now Jimmy told me that he had a movie with George Brown about the Japanese Silver Dollar, which was a fortune that had been sunk into the Bay of Manila by the Americans who were stationed in the Philippines until the end of the Second World War. Now the Japanese wanted that money. They were trying to find some of the soldiers who knew where it was dropped in the sea. Somewhere near the rock of Corregidor.

Anyway, Kisa kept urging me to sing; at least three songs, she said. So I sang *Didn't we* by Engelbert Humperdinck, *My cherie amour* (Stevie Wonder) and the *Godfather* theme by Al Martino. After that we went back to get some sleep. I had to catch an early flight to Taipei.

After arriving in Taipei, the Taiwanese capital, I rang up Oshiro's wife. I'd met her before and she remembered me. We arranged a meeting place where we had *chin cha* (Chinese tea) and something to eat. Mrs Oshiro trusted me, because she knew that I was her husband's friend. I asked her if he was all right. She didn't reply.

I asked again, 'Is he sick?'

She made a gesture like injecting something intravenously in the arm.

I asked, 'Heroin?' She nodded.

'Who gives him the drug?'

'Triad people. When they heard that Oshiro knows who killed Bruce Lee, they wanted to murder him.' Oshiro's wife was Chinese and she knew about the Chinese Triad secret societies.

'You must stop him from taking the drug,' I said. 'Don't let anybody come to visit him. I will help him. I will stay with him for seven days and work with him to give up the drug, but then you have to take him to Tokyo. Nobody is allowed to give him drugs. I will work out with him to give him his life energy back.' I had studied all this as part of my martial arts training and was confident I could help him with his withdrawal. 'He will remember Goju-Kai. If we work together, his power will return. Do you have enough money to go to Tokyo with him?'

'His family will pay for the fare.'

'Don't give him cash until he is totally cured. Take me to Kaohsiung. I'll pay for the flight. Let's go to the airport.'

We got on to a flight a little later in the day. I wanted to reach Oshiro's place during daylight, because I would have to stay with him and nobody else was allowed to come into his hideout. Mrs Oshiro and I entered the airplane separately and stayed away from each other. I thought it was better to be careful in case someone from the Triads was watching. They surely would know Oshiro's wife. If I went with her I would draw their attention to myself also. Even when we arrived in Kaohsiung, I stayed a few steps behind her. As we were walking down a main road, she suddenly turned left into an alleyway, then after 100 metres she walked through an opening into the compound of a three-storey structure. She opened a door and we climbed the stairs to the third floor. Oshiro's wife took a key out of her bag and opened a door. I went in and Oshiro was lying in bed, but his eyes were open. When he saw me he jumped up, but fell down again. He must have become very weak from all those drugs. I pulled him up, and when I saw that he recognized me, I embraced him and told him that I had come to help him and make him strong again.

We sat down, but first I wanted to see how big that place was. There was his bedroom, another bedroom adjacent, a kitchen and a big bathroom. There was a terrace above the third floor. I told Oshiro, who looked very weak and had lost a lot of weight, that he had to stop taking drugs immediately. 'We have to work fast on the withdrawal. We have no time to waste with slow, step-by-step withdrawals.' Turning to Oshiro's wife, I continued, 'Once he is in Japan they can put him into a hospital for junkies.' Oshiro's wife would stay with us and do the daily shopping. I would not leave the house, because I didn't want to be seen. Oshiro's wife would make us breakfast and other meals she could buy at a restaurant.

I checked Oshiro physically, asked him to bend forward and backwards, stretch his arms up, sideways, place his fingertips on his shoulders and rotate his elbows, try to do squats, which were difficult for him. I remember that he could do at least 1000 squats non-stop and 100 with a six-foot guy across his shoulders. We used to do it together. I said, 'You have to do it all again. Bit by bit. For seven days, then you go to Japan. Your family will look after you. Your wife will come with you. Just be fully aware that you must never again take any form of drugs. Now let's see if you still know how to do your katas?' Katas are karate movements, to be done in a particular sequence with grace, speed, power and technique. When I started the katas in front of him he joined me and did it properly, though he was a little rusty.

I wrote down for Oshiro's wife what she was to buy at the pharmacy. 'We have to give Oshiro high-protein food and add protein substances to his meals. Because of the withdrawal symptoms he'll become very weak and won't be able to keep the food in his stomach. He will vomit a lot.'

41

I worked out with him a little more to get him tired so that he could sleep during the night. Oshiro's wife went to get medicine and food. I told Oshiro that he had to be tough and do whatever I told him to do. If he did his workouts with me and ate his food, he would regain his energy soon. His craving for the drug had already started. He was moaning and calling out, and at night he was restless and sometimes screaming, then sobbing to arouse my pity to give him a fix. I expected that it would go on like this all through the seven days. Normally at that stage it takes at least fourteen days but I didn't have that much time.

I was very surprised when his withdrawal symptoms simmered down after four days. I knew that it was because of our workouts and the Goju-Kai exercises which made him forget the pain in his system. The first three days he vomited after meals, but now that had also stopped. He slept right through the night, took his medicine and drank a lot of purified water. He started smiling. He remembered a lot of things from the time of our earlier workouts and our sparring in Sydney.

On the fifth day I took him up to the terrace. We worked on some martial arts breathing exercises which involved screaming, from the core of the body, using the abdominal muscles. It was good because the air was beneficial in spite of the pollution, but as we continued, someone came upstairs to find out what that ruckus was about. It was a policeman. I told Oshiro to stop, and called his wife to translate. In Taiwan they speak Mandarin, not Cantonese like they speak in Hong Kong. I don't speak Mandarin. The Chinese don't speak all the languages, but they can understand if it's written down. The script is the same in all the different Chinese tongues. If you want to find an address somewhere in Taiwan and you don't speak Mandarin, you can ask somebody to write it in Chinese characters and a Chinese person will understand it. I told Mrs Oshiro, 'Tell the policeman that that man has epileptic seizures and I do special exercises to help him. Tell him I'm a doctor.' The policeman seemed to be sympathetic to us, and he was smiling. I asked him if he could stay with us for two more days. I didn't want to mention the Chinese Triad secret societies, because often the police are partial to them because of the money they get from the societies. He seemed to be willing to stay for two days if his commanding officer would give him permission.

So I told Mrs Oshiro to go with him to the police station, but not to mention drugs. I knew that I would have to pay something but that was better than possibly having to fight it out with some Triad guys. So I decided to play it cool, at least I had one policeman. The Triads are always very well armed. In China you always are best off if you don't carry any weapons or drugs but always carry a smile. The policeman came back with a second guard for the night and the blessings of the police station. When they heard that I was Australian, they wanted to shake my hand. They like Aussies better than the British.

Oshiro improved at an impressive rate. His energy started coming back and his voice didn't sound like the voice of a sick man any more. I kept hammering it into his brain that he was the famous Oshiro and he had to be the same again for the rest of his life. He shouted, 'I am Warrior Oshiro!' We had to take it easy on the last day because his muscles had become very sore, but then we continued for the last few hours, because it would help him. In any case, once he was in Tokyo he could relax. I think I was just as worn out as Oshiro was that last day. I gave Mrs Oshiro some more money, and the two policemen said they were also coming to the airport to see Oshiro and his wife off and perform their guard duty to the end. I ordered a limousine for the airport trip. I gave Oshiro a bear hug and kissed his wife and stayed with the policemen for a couple of hours before I took the next flight to Taipei. Now I felt free and happy. No more danger to Oshiro or his wife.

Bunnies, a Helicopter and a Spy Ship

When I reached Taipei, I booked my ticket directly to Manila, because I couldn't go to Hong Kong again after spending so much time away from *Apocalypse*. I rang Maria and told her to bring the car. Then I rang Kisa and told her that I couldn't keep my promise to take her for two days to the *Apocalypse* shooting location. I described for her the details of my meeting with Oshiro and what it took to get him back on his feet again to send him to Japan. 'Now I have to go back to the location right away. Some other changes have developed. I will inform you about them after some days,' I promised.

In the aircraft to Manila, I read an interesting article in one of the flight's newspapers. I think it was a private news agency. It just mentioned that an important American spy ship of the CIA had disappeared in the Mediterranean Sea not far from the African coast. There were no further details published, but it sounded quite ominous that a spy ship could not control its own safety. I would keep my eyes open for further news in this matter. First I had to apologize to Francis and the production designer about my delayed return from Taiwan. They said it was OK; the accountant would probably cut it from my salary.

Then it was time to prepare for my stunt. The scene was of a USO entertainment programme for the American soldiers in Cambodia on the Mekong River, with six sexily dressed Playboy Bunnies and loud American music. In the scene, the Bunnies arrive to entertain the troops. After the chopper lands and everybody gets out, the GIs push their way towards the Bunnies to get their

Playboy copies autographed by the respective Bunnies. The military police keep everybody away from the stage. It goes on for a while, the music gets louder and the girls are in a teasing mood; finally the GI soldiers break through the police, and some of them fall off the stage into the water. Someone starts to fire flares up in the air and commands are given to the girls to reboard the chopper. The blades start whirring; the choppers slowly rise into the air. Some GI soldiers jump up and hang on to the landing skid and undercarriage of the helicopter. As part of the scene I would have to jump into the river from one of the choppers—my pants were rigged to come off just before I fell; I'd be wearing boxer shots underneath. 'I'll be ready any time,' I told them.

Then I went to see James Casey, and on my way I saw Jim Kelly's van parked at Kurtz's compound. I went up to check what was for lunch. Kelly said, 'Today you'll have the best pasta you've ever had in your life.'

'Well, that's great, I've had so much good food from this van that I don't have the smallest doubt. Now tell me the truth, Kelly, have you heard anything about a CIA spy ship disappearing in the Mediterranean yesterday?'

'As a matter of fact I have, Christo, I was listening on my ham radio.'

'Aha, I read it in a paper on the flight from Taipei to Manila.'

'Oh, what were you doing there?'

'Again the same thing I went to Zamboanga for, only this time no earthquake! I found the karate master Oshiro. He was hooked on heroin and it took me seven days to sober him up slightly. He was relatively strong but I had to train him with Goju-Kai and katas which gave him back his energy and willpower. He had been on the run from the Triad society because they found out that Oshiro knew who killed Bruce Lee. It was one of the Triad guys, a revenge

45

killing—chop to the Adam's apple. So after Oshiro's health had improved, I sent him to Tokyo with his wife. They can get him back into top shape there. I felt I owed him, because he was the guy who trained me ten years ago and that helped me at a time when I really needed it. Now Kelly, tell me what else you heard in your radio about the spy ship. They must have had more details than in the newspaper?' I told him that I was thinking of finding that spy ship—these spy ships were very valuable because of their expensive parts. Of course, it would not be easy to wrest the valuables away from whoever was in control of it.

'Christo, if you want, go for it, I'll help you. I can find out all the info, but you have to have manpower and weapons to get what you want,' Kelly said. 'I might come with you. The only thing is, I'm scouting for another movie in the making, here in the Peenes (Philippines). It's a war film called *The Boys In Company C*.'

'OK, Kelly, I tell you what I'm gonna do. The manpower and weapons I'll get from Rhodesia. I'll write to Ian Smith's government and tell 'em that I want to join up with their Special Air Service (SAS). Once I'm in, I'll just take whatever I need. But I need your info, Kelly. Please don't let me down.'

'Don't worry, Christo, you know that you can trust me.'

Wow, I thought, *it looks like after all the work and preparations, I'm not destined to get married again. Kisa I can handle, but Maria, that's really a pity. I'll have to work out how to go about it.*

When I called Maria to tell her the news, she sounded excited. 'Hi Maria, what is it, you sound so excited.'

'Actually I was just about to call you too,' she said.

'OK, you first. Is it news?'

'Yes, but I don't want to tell you over the phone.'

'Well, is it good news or bad news?'

46

'Good 'n' bad. Good because it's ours and bad because it's too early!'

'Ohhh, darling, you better come over here tomorrow!'

'Yes, let's meet tomorrow,'

'Mekong River delta, OK? Bye!'

Next morning I walked around Kurtz's compound again, and from there to the lake on the Pagsanjan River where we would be taking the helicopter up and shooting the scenes that were supposed to be shot on the Mekong River in Cambodia. At night it would look like the Mekong River. *But the lake is deep*, I thought, *I must do a trial jump first or at least check the depth for rocks. What's that music? Oh, must be Larry Fishburn, one of the new actors.* He was only sixteen or seventeen. He was with Martin Sheen and another two guys on the river patrol boat. He always carried a huge transistor radio with the volume as high as it comes. 'Are you trying to wake everybody up for the call sheet?' I shouted.

'I can't hear you,' he bellowed. Larry has also made it as a big actor now, like Harrison Ford.

I arrived at the lake. The water was calm, and a couple of guys were swimming near the bank. One was the stunt master and the second a stuntman. Jerry, the stunt coordinator, explained, 'See that kind of corner between the trees on that stretch of shore and the ninety-degree angle just here. We'll jump into the centre of that. The pilot will get the chopper in position and give you a beep and Jack pulls the wire connected to Bob's pants. Bob's pants will come off as Jack falls. Ten seconds later Bob falls. Now, let's swim across into the triangle and take a few dives.' We jumped and dived into the water from the trees on the banks and from the elevated ground near the river for about half an hour and didn't see any dangerous obstructions in the water. So as long as the chopper was in the correct position we had nothing to worry about. The stunt scene would be shot either that night or the following night.

I walked back to have some breakfast and see if I could find Maria. I couldn't see anybody, but the sun was just visible above a grove of coconut trees and the air felt fresh and clean. There were some boys who asked me if I wanted *buco*, which means coconut in Tagalog, the national language. In those days I never would say no to a tender coconut. One of the boys opened the nut and I drank the water in one long swig; it was so sweet and slightly effervescent. Then I slurped up the tasty white flesh and followed it with one more of these delicious gifts of nature.

I saw somebody coming. Oh, yes, a couple, he very old and she very young and attractive. Who else? James Casey (sixty) and his model and timekeeper Flores (twenty).

'Hi, James, when are you two getting married?' I asked.

'It's already done, you weren't here Bob. An all-Catholic wedding.'

'Did you invite the Pope?' I joked.

'He was busy, but he's gonna come for the first baby.'

'Oh congrats, you two. I'll definitely see you in Venice, LA right?'

'Absolutely, you may sleep in our mobile van.' When I visited them about five years later in LA they gave me the bedroom and the two of them slept in the mobile van. They were both so happy. Flores was working in a bank; there were quite a few of the Filipino workers from *Apocalypse* living in the area who had made their way to the USA.

Well, I also wanted to get married to my beautiful Maria. But it was not to be. I wanted to get to that CIA spy ship. We would be able to make a fortune, with all the data and the unbelievable technology in there. I was quite sure it was in Libya. How much would the US government pay for getting it back undisturbed?

Oh, there was Maria! 'Hi, my love. How are you feeling? Is it kicking already? Do you feel like getting something to eat? I haven't had breakfast either. Kelly makes great omelettes. Better than the Army and Navy Club!'

While we were eating and having coffee, I told Maria the story about the spy ship and that I wanted to find it and save it, and what I had to do to get the weapons and manpower. If anything went wrong, the wedding may even have to be cancelled. 'Before I go to Africa, I want to spend a couple of days with you on Lubang Island. Dino will have to arrange it. He knows the owner of that house where we can stay. Please tell Dino to call that owner so he can tell someone to be there when we are coming. It's a nice island. Where that Japanese soldier lived until 1972 and didn't know that World War II had been over since 1945! Every morning we'll swim across the lagoon and walk on the other side. Go and call Dino. We'll probably go the day after. Tonight I have to work, jumping about eighty feet from a chopper into the water. Maria, have a coconut, they're so fresh and tender around here.'

I impressed Maria ordering the coconuts in Tagalog language. She said my Tagalog had improved since I'd been working on the set. 'Well,' I said, 'if I don't know the language, it'll be pretty difficult to communicate properly. I like learning languages.' The Americans couldn't talk in foreign languages decently. The natives never understood when the American staff were trying out their Tagalog. That's why the Americans spoke to the locals in English. Most of the Filipinos spoke English with an American accent because the Yanks had been in the islands for years. During the War I'd also started learning the second most important lingo in the Peenes, Visaya. It's in the south and all around Cebu.

'Maria, I'll just go and make a phone call while you drink your coconut water.' I went and called Kisa to find out when she would have to leave for Samoa. Kisa had told me that she'd have to return to Samoa i Sisifo when her studies were over. When she came on the line, she told me that Eddy Moses, his father and Saha, who had behaved so badly with Kisa a few months ago, were on their way to Pagsanjan, to have a look at the shooting and the impressive sets. They had said they'd try to meet me too. That was no problem; I had been meaning to talk to Saha for a long time anyway. Kisa told me that she'd leave for Samoa by the end of the year.

I said, 'It looks like I might have to go to Africa for some urgent work. If it works out OK I can come back to Hong Kong. I'm telling you now, just in case, so that it doesn't come as a surprise! When I am leaving, I will go directly from Hong Kong airport via Colombo and the Seychelles. I'll try to come to Hong Kong soon my darling. Aloha!'

I put down the receiver, turned around and found myself staring directly into the face of Eddy Moses. 'Hi Bob, haven't seen much of you lately.'

'Yes, you're right. What took you so long to get to this place?'

'Oh I thought you might invite me and show me around. I've never been to a film shooting before. Here's my dad, and Saha has also come along. How's everything going?'

'Pretty good, Eddy, I've done a lot of work over here.'

'Bob, you were pretty lucky to find these old temple ruins,' said Eddy's father, surveying the set. 'You can use them for the film work.'

'Well, I'll tell you something; these old ruins were all built by me, along with one of the biggest sculptors in Hollywood—James Casey, who has worked on a lot of Walt Disney Casey. I'll introduce him to you, he is around somewhere. We didn't get it that easy. We had to build islands in the river and ruins and temples all over the place and by the side of Pagsanjan River. That's supposed to be the Mekong River in Cambodia. They paid me well,' I remarked, looking in the direction of Saha, who picked up the taunt and said, 'Then it shouldn't be too difficult to pay me back the money that you owe me!'

'Why, is the court case over already, for indecent exposure in front of my girlfriend in my apartment and for threatening to rape her in my apartment?'

'But you owe me money, blood money!'

'One more word from you and I'll teach you a bitter lesson, and have you removed from this place by our security personnel,' I shouted. I stood inches away from him, glaring. He started to scratch his head, turned around and slowly walked away without another sound.

To Eddy and his father I said, 'You can have a look around the set, and if you have any questions, you can come and ask me.'

'Hi Bob, one moment please,' called Eddy. 'My father said that we gave you a membership with the Army and Navy Club for a few weeks or months, not a lifetime.'

'Oh, I see. I appreciated your gesture to give me that membership on your account, but I was never aware of any details like time limitations.' My voice was heavy with sarcasm. Because of the Saha episode, I was miffed with Eddy as well. 'Maybe the staff thought I am royalty, because whenever they called me to the pool office or front office, they made announcements like: "The Count of Monte Christo is requested to please answer a telephone call, thank you." You please sort that out with the management, Mr Moses, and let me know. By the way, during the last few months I've hardly taken full advantage of the benefits that you so kindly put at my disposal. I shall be happy to meet you at the synagogue. Good day, gentlemen.' That last remark was another taunt. They used to invite me to their synagogue earlier, when they talked business and afterwards we'd have breakfast right inside the temple.

Maria had enjoyed her coconut water and flesh and was back from a round of the sets. She told me that there was a private and confidential letter at the *Apocalypse* counter for me. We went to get it. It was from the deputy minister from the Department of the Prime Minister in Rhodesia.

I still have the letter in my possession with the Rhodesia letter stamp, over thirty years after it became Zimbabwe under that blackguard Robert Mugabe, who by the look of it has now reached the end of his misrule. They thanked me for the letter I had sent to them and said they were obliged at the response from those who were prepared to identify themselves with the cause that they defended. My letter had been passed to the appropriate personnel officer within their security forces who would reply to me directly.

Now I had to have another talk with Jim Kelly, caterer and intelligence snooper. Maria asked me why I was getting that letter from the Prime Minister's office in Rhodesia. I told her, 'I'm just trying to make them believe that I'm interested in their struggle for freedom and the unilateral Declaration of Independence in order to take manpower and weapons to the place where Kelly will tell us to go and liberate that CIA spy ship. That's where my bread and butter for the next few years is supposed to come from.'

At lunchtime I spoke to Kelly about the ship. The only news he had was that there was an underwater bunker somewhere off the coast of Libya where a ship could have access and disappear from view. We'd have to wait for Kelly's magic radio to spill out more news. Meanwhile Maria said, 'If you want, we can go to Lubang Island tomorrow or the day after. The domestic help and caretaker are there for the next four days. It's a twenty-minute flight from Manila airport.'

'Tonight I'm possibly doing the stunt work for the USO entertainment show with the Playboy Bunnies and Billy Graham and his band. That means we can go to Lubang Island tomorrow. After that, I'll be off to Seychelles and then Joburg.'

There were so many other things to see here in the Philippines, I thought. It would have been nice to take a ferry ride from Manila to Cebu, or only halfway to Legaspi with its ever-smoking volcano right on the beach, or to the mountains around Baguio with the Ifugaos and lovely strawberries in springtime. If you are looking for a female companion, go anywhere in the Philippines, best in the cities like Manila, Quezon City and Cebu. There are so many attractive girls wherever you go and they like to please you and give you a great time. There is only one affliction that is visible with a lot of girls the moment they open their mouth—they have a denture clamped in between their teeth with a wire that holds it in place. Maybe by now dental technology has improved the cosmetic aspect of it, and you don't notice the dentures any more. Possibly I should have sent Kisa back to the Philippines to cause a dental revolution. A lot of females from the Philippines are employed in places like Abu Dhabi and Dubai as domestics and nurses. In general their employers are very pleased with them.

I was lost in my random thoughts until I saw Maria looking at me quizzically with her big eyes. 'Oh, I'm sorry Maria. I was just thinking about the Philippines. Would you like to travel? What do you think we're going to have, a boy or a girl? I think it's going to be a girl, maybe even twins; imagine?'

Maria thought it'll be a boy. 'Let's call him Bobby?'

I laughed. 'Come on, let's go to the stage; the helicopter is arriving with the girls and the band. The GIs are all in their seats already.'

The cameras started rolling for my shot. I was hanging on to the outside of the helicopter with Jack Cooper hanging down from my feet. The helicopter went up fast and we were given the signal. Jack let go and fell, while pulling my trousers off. At about 80 feet height I was given a signal to let go, and I had a nice fall into the cool water of the lake. Bingo!!!

I was not required any more, so I went to get changed and gave Maria a signal to follow me.

'Hey Bob, after you jumped from the chopper, I was waiting for you to resurface, but you took such a long time to come up again, I was afraid you got stuck at the bottom of the lake in the mud!'

'Hey darling, I'm right here, can't you see me? Have you eaten the snacks they passed around or do you want to eat something more substantial? Not hungry? OK, let's go to sleep, get up early and do some exercises. Come on.'

'OK, Bob, let's go to our room.'

Bingo!

The moment we were in our bed, Maria started to cry, holding me tight and asking me not to go to Africa. 'Our baby is on the way, we will be very happy together. Please don't leave me!'

'I don't want to leave you,' I said, 'but there is no other way. I will try to be back before the baby is born. Anyway, that's why I want to go to Lubang with you, so we can discuss everything thoroughly. If you want, you can ask Dino to come with us also. He can come and stay in another room. Come baby, let's sleep if you can.'

We held each other till we both fell asleep. I really felt terrible because it looked possible that I would have to abandon my sweet Maria; it was difficult to find such a well-spoken, tender, affectionate, loving girl. Should I forget about the spy ship? But it was my opportunity to make a lot of money just before our marriage. Santo would be proud of his son-in-law.

Anyway, we took off early from Pagsanjan and called Dino before we left, asking him to come with us to Lubang Island. I paid for his ticket and told him it would be nice to have him with us, because he knew all of Hiro Onoda's hangouts and the places from where he used to steal his food and where his caves and hideouts used to be. Hiro Onoda was the Japanese soldier who didn't believe that the war was over. His understanding was that no Japanese would be alive if Japan had lost the war, because the emperor's troops would all have committed *seppuku* (suicide) because of their great shame. When it became known that one Japanese soldier was still on Lubang Island, the Japanese were informed about it by the Philippines government. They sent a group of Japanese together with Onoda's brother, attracting the soldier's attention by announcing through loudspeakers that the war was over and Japan had lost the war, but everybody was living in peace. It took a long time before Hiro Onoda believed the whole story and surrendered to President Ferdinand Marcos by handing over his samurai sword, which was returned to him later.

The island was quite small but now there were a number of villages scattered around, and a mayor was the head of a population that earned its living mainly by farming, fishing, salt panning and drying coconuts. Our quarters were in one of two houses that belonged to the friends of Dino, and there were two bedrooms in our house. After arrival and meeting with the housekeeper and her two little children, we changed our clothes, put on our swimwear and walked down to the lagoon. We enjoyed the warm salt water and swam happily for an hour. When we returned to the house, we were served some nice Filipino food. Most of the Filipinos are non-vegetarian. They eat chicken, a lot of pork (except in the south), beef and buffalo.

In the late afternoon the three of us sat down to discuss our problem. The problem was that Maria and I were to be married and we were not even officially engaged yet. Now Maria had become pregnant even before the engagement ceremony. My adventure to find and salvage the CIA spy ship could take up to three months' time, depending on how fast I got the information from Kelly. So in other words, the situation was slightly vague.

'What to do?' Maria said, 'I'll wait for Bob.'

Dino kept quiet. I said, 'Dino, please excuse us. I want to discuss my thoughts with Maria first. Just give us twenty minutes.'

'No problem.'

After Dino left the room, I turned to Maria. 'OK darling, I suggest that if I am not back within a month, you get married to Dino. Waiting any longer would be unfair to the Francisco family, and since there is a pregnancy already, it would be unfair to you also. The month will start the day I leave Hong Kong on the flight to Rhodesia.' After all, Maria had been as good as engaged to Dino before. Her father had been surprised that the bridegroom has been changed. I loved Maria with all my heart and I was sorry that my adventurous spirit had caused us this complication. But I was quite sure I'd make it back before the one month was over. 'One more question has to be answered. Dino will have no problem with getting married to you, he'll be happy, I dare say. But what about the baby? Is Dino happy to marry you and be father to a baby that has been sired by me? What do you say Maria?'

'I have no problem with any of that, we'll have to ask Dino and let him answer himself.' At that moment Maria broke down. Her face twisted into a grimace, tears were streaming from her eyes. I had to hold her to prevent her from falling down on the floor. Her arms were around my neck and she was sobbing bitterly. I sat down with her for about fifteen minutes until she managed to control herself again. I kissed her tears away, and wiped her face with a cloth. She was snivelling and moaning and said, 'I can't help that I love you so much Bob.'

When Dino came back inside, he looked at us and I asked the question. Dino said instantly that he would be proud to raise my child together with Maria and he would look after it as though it were his own biological child. After this the three of us embraced each other. It was a very emotional moment. I heaved a sigh of relief and hoped that everything would end well; if I could make it back in time, that would be wonderful.

It had started to get dark. I asked the housekeeper if the kids had gone to pick the cashew nut bulbs we had asked for. 'Oh, yes they're already back,' she said.

We made a fire, roasted the cashew nut bulbs (they popped open—bang, bang, bang) and ate them accompanied by a bottle of red wine. It was good that red wine doesn't have to be chilled too much because there was no electrical power. We had a couple of kerosene lamps only. But we had a nice evening. We took one lamp to the bedroom to check that the feet of the bed had been put into small tins of water so that the ants couldn't climb into the bed and bite us. The bed had a mosquito net but without the water tins under the bed you'd think there were holes in the mosquito net! Then we extinguished the kerosene lamp because of the smell. After that Maria and I made love very slowly, softly and tenderly with lots of kisses.

The next morning we went for our lovely swim again, crossing the lagoon. After breakfast, consisting of pan de sal with coconut syrup and papaya, we had a look around and saw some of Hiro Onoda's hideouts and some of his weapons that were behind a glass case. In the afternoon we took the flight to return to Manila. The three of us were in quite a good mood. I think that we were pretty sure that the wedding was going to take place as planned. I was going to Pagsanjan to get my luggage and say my goodbyes and collect whatever money they still owed me. Maria would stay with me until I left for Hong Kong. Tonight, I decided, we're gonna sing a few songs in the Pagsanjan Hotel. I also had to see if there was any message from Kelly. He'd be in Hong Kong for a couple of days, because he had to meet some people there. The message for me read: 'Christo, please meet me at the Imperial Hotel tomorrow by evening or the next morning. Kelly.'

I hope he's got good news, I thought. Kisa must be angry with me, because I hadn't taken her to the film shooting. Maybe she'd already gone. I called her, hoping she'd answer the phone. She did.

'Hello, Kisa.'

'Yes, Bopsi, are you coming?'

'I'll be there tomorrow after lunch.'

'Oh please come, I'm also leaving around lunch. I've paid the bill for the rent. It's all cleared.'

'OK thanks, Kisa. I'll give it to you tomorrow. Bye my darling!'

'See you tomorrow, Bopsi, aloha!'

As I put down the phone, I found Maria right behind me. 'Who was that Bob?'

'That? Oh, on the phone?' I played for time as I thought of an excuse. 'Well, that was the landlady of my Hong Kong apartment. I'm checking out tomorrow and moving to the Imperial Hotel, because that's where I have to meet Jim Kelly. You know what they've got written on the back of their business cards?' I asked, trying to change the subject.

'No, what?'

'The Imperial Hotel is like sex, if it's good, it's very very good, if it's bad, it's still good!'

Maria laughed.

'There is someone who wants to buy my E-Type, did he call you up?'

'Yes, Bob, he said he'll come today and he'll pay US dollars in cash; he took the car for a drive and he's very happy with it.'

'OK that's great, my love. You know, Jim Casey and his young, young wife have already left for the States.'

'Oh, have they? That's right. I saw them on that morning when we had breakfast made by Kelly.'

'We are invited to see them in LA at a suburb called Venice.'

'I'm so thirsty, come let's have some coconut water. It's supposed to be good for your daughter!'

'Is she moving much?'

'Only occasionally. Is that why you made such tender sweet love to me last night?'

'It was the mood we were in, remember, my Bong Bong Baby?'

At my farewell party at the Hotel Pagsanjan lounge that night I said my goodbyes in my customary way, with a few songs—*Memories* by Barbara Streisand, *If* by Nat King Cole, and finishing off with *My pretty little girl* by Stylistics.

I signed off with a small speech. 'Dear friends, let me wish you all a safe return to your homes or wherever you may travel after you leave this beautiful place. Some of you who worked with us on *Apocalypse Now* will surely have started a career with great promise. My best wishes are with Francis Ford Coppola and his production. Meet you for the premiere at Ziegfeld theatre in New York, 1979.'

The next day Maria called me and said, 'That young man who wants to buy the car is here.'

'Oh, good evening,' I greeted him. 'I am very sorry. I've changed my mind; I'm going to keep it for a little longer.' His face fell. 'Whenever it is for sale again Madam will call you,' I assured him. 'Thank you. Goodbye.'

Maria was mystified. 'But Bob, are you going to take it with you?'

'No, my darling. Where is the key?'

'Here,' she handed it over to me, still perplexed.

'OK. Tomorrow you can take me to Manila Airport in your new lemon-coloured E-Type Jag. It is your wedding present in advance. Take your key and this kiss from me.'

And that's the way it happened. Maria came with me up to the departure lounge. The flight was late—I hoped I would not miss Kisa. Maria and I sat down outside the lounge and kissed a very sad goodbye and farewell. I never saw Maria again except in photographs with our children and with Dino and the Francisco family.

Eventually the Philippine Airlines flight to Hong Kong took off. I was always happy flying on this route because on either side there was always somebody nice waiting for me! After arriving in Hong Kong I took a taxi and told the driver to go fast. Maybe Kisa was still there. As the taxi pulled up opposite my front door, Kisa was already standing on the footpath. She came running up to me. I told her my flight had left late.

'I have to go up again,' she said, 'I forgot something. You also come up.' I told the caretaker to watch the luggage and we took the elevator to the seventh floor. The moment we went inside the apartment, Kisa slammed the door shut, fell around my neck and meowed, 'Let's make love, Bopsi, please. When will we see each other again?'

Kisa was wearing the sexiest jeans I have ever seen this side of the equator, but they were lying on the floor already, below her underwear. 'Oh Kisa, I tell you, I'm gonna miss you.' She was sitting on me, working hard, and then she turned around and she called and cried and put her tongue inside my mouth and we rode towards a wonderful climax. She wanted to continue but I stopped her. 'Don't miss your flight, baby, we'll continue when I come to Samoa.' It was such a rush, that Kisa had barely finished her climax before she was boarding. That was the last time I ever saw her.

I went straight to the Imperial Hotel. The atmosphere was pleasant, the AC was cool. I went to the bar, that's always where I met my friends. I left word that in case Mr Jim Kelly arrived, he could find me in the bar. I asked for a sangria and wondered where that spy ship could have disappeared without a trace. Didn't they have any drones around in the area to keep track of an important valuable gadget like that? Could it possibly have found shelter in the belly of a especially designed vessel? If there were no eyewitnesses, how were we ever going to know more about it?

Kelly's appearance cut into my thoughts. 'Hallo, there you are Kelly, good evening my friend. Do you have other visitors?'

'Yes, all about that film they want to shoot at the same location as *Apocalypse*.'

'But you can't shoot right there at Mekong River. You have to go far away from there.'

'I know, we're using choppers for the scouting, I know where to go; I just have to get their bloody approval.'

'OK, Kelly, I have to know where to go for the spy ship. I'm leaving Hong Kong tomorrow for Africa. Are you gonna be in it with me, or are you gonna take time? I can stop off in the Seychelles for a few days, but you have to be in touch with me every day!'

'I'll send faxes to the British High Commission in the Seychelles daily addressed to Bob Christo, SAS regiment.'

'OK, let's have another drink!' We drank and had dinner together and the film people of *The Boys in Company C* narrated to us the script of their movie. There was music, but it wasn't a Filipino band and not the right girls that get me into a good mood. Actually I was not in a good mood at all. I felt like Marlon Brando when he smelled that carabao hide, and I excused myself and had an early night, dreaming of Maria, Kisa and the spy ship.

In the morning I tried to call Jimmy Shaw, but then I remembered that he had gone for shooting that American diving film about the Japanese Silver Dollar. I'd have to try to find the number of his film production in Manila at the location of Corregidor rock. I also had to go back to my apartment in Wan Chai to see if there was anything of mine or Kisa's belongings left, or any mail. When I arrived there I asked the caretaker to open my apartment and let me check for mail. There was one letter from Karin, my friend Bob's wife, and a piece of paper from Kisa, where she had noted down her full name and family particulars. Her father was the chief of their tribe in Western Samoa and Kisa's full name was Temukisa Penaia. She wrote also that she loved me and would like to get married to me, and that she was sure that her four brothers would all like me and be happy if I stayed with their family in Samoa.

Karin's long letter mentioned that she and Bob and my kids had left Sydney now and moved to California. They lived not far from Napa Valley, the California wine area. I didn't feel like going through the whole letter right then. There would be plenty of time later, or after a few more years. Now I had to get ready to make my way to Africa. I had heard nothing new from Kelly.

PART II

From Africa to India
via the Middle East

Seychelles: Plotting a Coup

I was back at Kai Tak Airport, this time for the trip to the Seychelles islands. I'd stay there for a few days until I got news from Kelly.

This flight was also delayed. A fellow sat down next to me asking, 'You Australian, mate?'

'Yeah, Bob Christo's the name. I'm on my way to the Seychelles.'

'Oh, are you? I'm Jack Onslow. I'm a farmer from Mullindullingong, but now I'm selling aircraft.' After that he tried to convince me that by selling aircraft you could make a lot more money than by selling cows.

'But,' I said, with a wry smile, 'cows give you milk and meat which you can't get from an aircraft.'

Soon it was time to board. There were a lot of Japanese on the flight; I think they were all alighting at Colombo, where there was a stopover. A lot of Japanese are Buddhists and there are many Buddhist temples there. I'd been to Ceylon (later Sri Lanka) several times. In my younger days, I used to travel a lot by passenger liners like P&O Liners, Sitmar Line, Messageries Maritimes, Flotta Lauro, etcetera. From Australia to Europe and back, sometimes via the Suez Canal and sometimes via the Panama Canal or round the

Cape of Good Hope. I found travelling by sea very relaxing and interesting. You'd always wait for special food menus to give you surprises; you know, like chicken surprise—when I was a child I used to have this image of the cook opening the pot and a chicken flying out! Sometimes there'd be fights breaking out in bars, or some wild storms that caused everybody to rush to hang their heads over the railings to throw up, although I must say by the grace of God I never had that problem, else I wouldn't have liked sailing so much! A heavy sea didn't affect me in the least.

I usually didn't drink too much alcohol on long-haul flights because it prolongs jet lag and it's no good to keep drinking water or juice. In those days, there were no in-flight movies either. So I had a nice sleep till we touched down smoothly on the Seychelles runway. As we landed, I could see this huge green overgrown mountain. As usual I had no trouble getting through immigration or customs; with an Australian passport you normally encounter no difficulty, everybody smiles at you.

A taxi delivered me and my luggage to a kind of pensione or guesthouse. It felt quite cosy and comfortable. I liked it, so I checked in there. After a short chat with the management and another guest from Zaire, I withdrew to my room and hit the sack. In the morning I got ready and had a nice breakfast of fruit, juice and bread. In those days, getting ready in the morning meant brushing my teeth and having a quick shower. For the last twenty-nine years, yoga and meditation have been added to my morning routine.

I took the address and the phone numbers of the British High Commission from the management and left to have a look around outside. Wherever I turned, I saw water; on one side, the open sea, on the other a lagoon where people were swimming and sailing. In that instant I fell in love with the place.

As I walked on, a girl got up from where she was sitting and approached me with a 'Bonjour'. She was a dark, pretty local girl. Very soft features, big black eyes, straight black hair and a slim but well-rounded body. She asked me if I was looking for something. I said, 'I want to hire a car, self-drive.' She said to come with her. Just around the corner was an Avis rent-a-car. I asked for the prices and selected a nice Citroën; just the right vehicle for a few days.

In front of us was a hotel by the beach. The girl said, 'The Beau Valon, good hotel. The President comes here every day.'

'The President?'

'Yes, Jimmy Mancham.'

'Oh, I've heard the name, but I've never met him.'

'I'll introduce him to you,' she offered. 'He comes here in about one hour.'

'OK. *C'est bon*. What is your name?'

'Vila.'

'My name is Bob Christo. Now you say it!'

'Bob Christo.' She took my hand as a gesture of greeting; then she escorted me to the guest lounge of the Beau Valon. We selected some drinks and chatted until a chauffeur-driven limousine pulled up outside and two men exited.

Vila said, 'The man with the beard is Jimmy Mancham.'

When they entered the lounge, the President looked at Vila and greeted her. She rose from the chair and shook hands with him; then she looked at me and said something. I arose, introduced myself and uttered some pleasantries. The President requested both of us to join him and his friend at a table.

Three men were sitting chatting at a table nearby and kept looking in our direction. One of them had a drooping moustache, which he was stroking habitually with his fingers. We had coffee and after we finished, Vila and I excused ourselves. Mancham invited us for lunch on the following day. He said he had some foreign visitors as guests and I should come with Vila, who knew the venue.

'OK,' I said, 'until then.'

Vila and I drove off in the Citroën. I told her to guide me along the coastal road so I could get to know the area. It was called Victoria and it was the capital of Mahe, which is the largest of the Seychelles islands. For lunch we went to a seafood restaurant which was excellent. Later Vila said, 'If you like, we can meet every day and in the evening I can sleep with you in your room.' At night, she said, she'd go home. If I could drop her there, then I would know where to pick her up in the morning. Everything was very simple and without complications.

The next morning I decided to go on my own excursion. I reached the middle of the village, which had a clock tower at the corner of a cluster of buildings. These buildings all housed coffee lounges and restaurants. A lot of men were sitting around, sipping their drinks and talking seriously. I had a coffee at one of the lounges and then went to meet Vila at her house. She came running down quickly, got into the car and kissed me on the cheeks, French style.

I asked her, 'What kind of party is Jimmy Mancham having over for lunch?'

'There will be foreigners and lots of attractive girls,' she said. 'Mancham uses them to make business deals and sell land to the tourists.'

'Aha, I see!' I exclaimed. 'I've heard about his reputation.' Jimmy Mancham was known as the playboy President——he travelled around the world with glamorous girls by his side, promoting the Seychelles as a tourism destination. In the Seychelles he hosted huge parties graced by beautiful ladies for wealthy foreigners, and invited the rich and famous to buy land in the islands. Many in the country were disenchanted with Mancham; the poor benefited little from his policies.

'Before we go to the party, let's go swimming,' Vila suggested. 'Near the Beau Valon there are some rocks on one side, and on the other side the water is beautiful and full of waves. Let's go there!'

'That's lovely.'

But as we approached the Beau Valon, a thought struck me. 'If we get our clothes wet now, what will we wear at the party?'

Vila laughed as she took her clothes off. 'There are no people here. We'll put our clothes behind that rock until we've finished swimming, OK?' So I also removed my clothes, island style. Wow! It was great and the water was so warm. We swam, played around, dived and grabbed hold of each other. Vila's body was so smooth, it really turned me on. She embraced me and kissed me on my mouth. Her lips tasted salty. We swam ashore and made love on the sand, then washed the sand off in the water and went in between the rocks. She leaned with both hands on a rock, turned around to look at me, touched her bum and called me, 'Come!' We had a great time in and out of the water. Nobody was there except us; I didn't even care if somebody was watching us or not. Then we lay on the sand and rolled over until our bodies were covered in sand. I said, 'Let's go to the lunch party like this, in our "casual clothes",' and Vila laughed. After our bodies were dry enough, we got dressed and went for lunch.

It looked like everybody was there already. I could identify one American, two South Africans, one or two Australians and another three or four nationalities, but only men, no wives. However, there were about twenty attractive island girls, ready to do anything. Vila had joined the other girls by now. She must have taken part in a lot of these parties, I realized; she was one of the girls in Mancham's circle who were used to attract foreigners to buy or lease land in the Seychelles.

Mancham shook hands with me and ushered me to two big boards showing plots of Seychelles land on them, which were supposed to be for sale. I didn't think that the land would be sold outright; most likely it would be hired out for whatever production the foreign buyers had in mind. They probably get promises for deals which they would not be able to implement anyway under Mancham's rule. I was not really interested in Mancham's business, so I just helped myself to a few glasses of delicious sangria. The lunch spread was also very good and I was hungry. Later I asked Vila if she had to do any work, or if we could go. She said, 'We came together, so we can also go together.' We said adieu to the President, thanked him, and wished him best of luck for the future of the Seychelles.

We went for another drive across the island. There were some other beautiful spots which I hadn't seen yet, and I probably wouldn't have time to see all of them on this trip; I would have loved to see the famous Bird Island. Towards evening we went and had a few drinks. After that I took Vila to her place and promised her that tomorrow she could stay with me in my room. I had to check for mail again at the British High Commission to see if there was any word from Kelly.

The next morning, I went for breakfast by the clock tower again. As soon as I arrived, I saw a man beckon and call my name. He was part of a group sitting around a table, and they invited me to join them for breakfast. The man pointed at someone seated next to him and said, 'This is Henri. He remembers you from Beau Valon.'

Now I also remembered him; it was the man with the drooping moustache. 'Bonjour,' I said. Now everybody was shaking hands with me.

After a few pleasantries, we got down to what I suspected they actually wanted to talk about. 'Mr Bob, do you like Jimmy Mancham, our President?' asked Henri. 'Yesterday I saw you talking to him.'

'I don't know yet, I only just met him. I've heard things about him.'

'Oh, yes, what things?' asked the moustached man, Henri.

'Well, I heard he is a playboy, squandering the money of the citizens. Maybe he is too young, that's why they made him grow a French beard before they took the official photos for letter stamps and political posters.'

'You are right, Mr Bob, a lot of people in the Seychelles don't want Mancham, they want Albert René, the prime minister. He is a more serious and reliable politician. He has been in Great Britain for over ten years and is a member of the communist party. But he is not a hardliner. Do you have military experience, Mr Bob?'

'Yes, Henri. I was in Vietnam until the end of the War and I've been trained in the SAS regiment in Australia.'

'Mr Bob, will you help us to depose the President of the Seychelles? We would like your advice.'

'Well gentlemen, I'm only here for a few days. Then I'm on my way to Rhodesia. But my advice is: if you wanna get rid of Mancham, do it without bloodshed. Wait till he goes abroad. When he's out of the country, you inform him through a decree of the opposition that he cannot return to the Seychelles; Albert René is now the President. Very simple. Don't start a war.' All the men at the table looked thoughtful. 'He is bound to go abroad sooner or later. That's the time you should make use of! But discuss all the details beforehand. You should know exactly what's to be done. Before the coup, send your emissaries to Albert René and make certain that he is willing to cooperate with you.'

'Mr Bob, thank you. Before leaving please have our special coffee, only reserved for special guests—coffee-kahlua.'

'OK, gentlemen.'

After the coffee, I wished them good luck. I went to the British High Commission to check for messages (there were none) and proceeded to the beach near the Beau Valon. Vila was sitting on the beach but I was distracted by two windsurfers. It was a new sport at the time; before I left Australia, I had not heard of it even. Now, this looked great, a mixture of board surfing and sailing! I wanted to learn it.

Vila came running over and hit me with her morning kisses. 'I was waiting for you,' she said.

'I had to go to the British High Commission. Now I'm free. I wanna learn that sport, windsurfing. Have you tried it, Vila?'

'Yes, a few times. It's not easy. You keep falling down all the time.'

'Do the rigs belong to the Beau Valon, or are they privately owned?'

'They are privately owned. I know the boy who owns them— Pierre. You've seen his father at the Beau Valon, when you met the President the first time. The father has a very big moustache.'

'Ah, that's Henri. I had breakfast with him this morning. Do you know where they live?'

'Yes, sir,' she said.

'Come let's go there. That boy Pierre *has to* teach me and let me use his windsurfer! We'll talk to Henri, he can't refuse. I want the rig tomorrow, after that I'm leaving for Rhodesia.'

Everything was arranged after Henri spoke to his son. Pierre was very happy to help me out with the windsurfer. He said he'd bought it in Durban, South Africa. 'If the wind is good, we'll start in the morning, otherwise later in the day,' Pierre promised.

I was at the beach early in the morning. There was a slight wind. In another hour the wind would pick up enough for a beginner like me, I guessed. They would be surprised if they were expecting me to fall. It wouldn't happen; I used to be a good board surfer and that was a big advantage. And so it happened, I hardly fell at all. It only took some time to learn how to change directions and go downwind. I was going pretty fast. Pierre took the other board and we went out together. I told him to teach Vila also after I'd left the island. It was a wonderful day. I must find a place somewhere by the seashore to live, I thought, then I can go windsurfing whenever there are good, windy conditions. A few years later, I became one of the windsurfing champions in India.

What was worrying me now was that I'd heard nothing at all from Kelly. I had to leave on the next day's flight to Johannesburg. Maybe he had sent the message to Salisbury and it was waiting for me there?

I booked my flight to Salisbury via Johannesburg for the next morning. I let Vila sleep with me in my room during my last night, like I had promised her. We both slept naked and held each other right through the night, enjoying each other thoroughly and waking up fresh and relaxed. In the morning we kissed goodbye tearfully. Even Henri and his son came over, and I wished them and their island population best of luck.

Rhodesia: Armed Combat

A military delegation met me at the Salisbury airport and booked me into a hotel for two or three days until I was given quarters at the military barracks in Salisbury, the capital of Rhodesia. The hotel was an old colonial hotel, well-kept and with an old-world charm. All the waiters were local, wearing white uniforms with white gloves, well trained and very polite. The hotel and its guests reminded me very much of some of William Somerset Maugham's stories.

As soon as I received my military kit and my quarters in the barracks, my training started immediately with the SAS regiment. In those days, there were only three countries that still had regular Special Air Service (SAS) regiments: Australia, Great Britain and Rhodesia. Rhodesia was divided into Northern Rhodesia and Southern Rhodesia. Northern Rhodesia became Zambia in 1963 when it became independent from the British. Southern Rhodesia was then renamed Rhodesia; they did not agree to independence at the time, because the power would then be back in the hands of the local population who were governed by the terrorists (or terrs as they were often called) who were fighting with the white farmers, the majority of whom were born in Rhodesia. In 1965 the prime minister, Ian Smith, made the Unilateral Declaration of Independence and Rhodesia was on its own, without the support of Great Britain. In 1980 Joshua Nkomo and Mugabe came into power and Rhodesia was then named Zimbabwe, with Harare as the capital.

But this was 1977 and my training was to continue for a minimum of two weeks, maybe longer. It started off with a daily run of five kilometres and after ten days it went up to ten kilometres daily. I was glad I had given up smoking in the Philippines, although the sergeant major, who was in charge of physical training and always ran in front of the recruits, smoked while he ran; he was a chain smoker! It was totally against my personal fitness and health rules.

On my second day in Rhodesia, I received a letter from the Philippines regarding the demise of Jim Kelly, caterer and intelligence snooper. He had been conducting the last of a number of scouting flights by helicopter to identify suitable locations for *The Boys in Company C* when the helicopter had crashed with eight aboard. Jim Kelly had been among the seven who had lost their lives. God rest his soul. The reason for the crash was given as engine failure.

After I got over the shock of his demise, I started thinking about the spy ship. Should I ask the Rhodesian government for help? Probably the kind of help I would get from the Rhodesians would involve being court-martialled for personal gain or for attempting to use the manpower and weapons of Rhodesia to help the USA find one of their lost spy ships in the Mediterranean! I just had to forget about the whole thing. I had to continue to work with the Rhodesian SAS for the time being. What a drama!

After two weeks of training and sweating we did some trial parachute drops from an aircraft for a few days, and finally ten of us were selected for an important operation in Mozambique. Rhodesia was a land-locked country which was predominantly attacked from its borders by terrs who got their military hardware from communist supporters, often from Russia, who sent ships close to the Mozambique coast where they were unloaded inconspicuously on two small islands. Everything was later transferred bit by bit to the mainland quietly and sent by rail towards Rhodesia and divided among the terrs. In 1976–77 this was not possible because the railway lines were all under water due to heavy rains. The ground had become muddy. To accelerate the urgent deliveries, the two Russian ships had been taken directly into the harbour at Beira to be unloaded on to special amphibian vehicles. In order to prevent the military hardware and other goods from getting into the hands of the terrs, the Rhodesian intelligence had ordered destruction of the Russian ships before they could be unloaded. The order had been passed on to the SAS regiment with immediate effect.

We were air-dropped twenty kilometres off Beira harbour after sunset, along with two self-inflatable rubber boats, explosives in waterproof magnetic housings, electronic detonators and underwater diving gear with aqualungs. When we were ready to start the operation, eight of us started moving towards the ship; all our gear was transported in a noiseless underwater buggy. The other two members of our team would move to our meeting point along the beach in the early morning after anchoring and deflating the boats. Four of our team swam to one ship, the other four to the second ship, to attach the bombs to the ships. It was a slow and tedious job since everything had to be done in the dark so that we wouldn't get spotted by the night watch. Once everything was in place we had to check again to see that the timings of the explosions were synchronized so that all bombs would detonate within two minutes of each other. By then we would all be inside the aircraft that would be collecting us from a predetermined spot ten kilometres away along the coast.

The operation took the whole night. We had to swim with flippers under water for several miles, using special phosphorescent lights so as to avoid the risk of discovery. When everything was over, we ran like crazy to get to the meeting place on time and to get the rigged ships behind us. There were no taxis but we had trained well for a few weeks, ten kilometres every morning. The detonations shook the area even before the plane made its appearance. It was 5 a.m. and all hell broke loose; first the noise of the detonations, then the sirens of the harbour and the ambulances, and then the landing of the aircraft. Because of all the other noise, I don't think anybody heard the aircraft landing or suspected us, though some cars stopped and the military was there in the distance.

When we arrived at Salisbury we were asked to go to our cots and sleep and write our reports later or the next day. The Rhodesian intelligence agency monitored all the papers, local and international, for the next few days, but there was nothing at all regarding the destruction of those two Russian ships and the harbour; even the Russians didn't complain. They must have all had guilty consciences and decided to keep mum. So far, so good.

After my first military operation for Rhodesia my monthly payments were increased. The thing I didn't know at the time though was that my pay was in Rhodesian dollars and not in US dollars. When I found out and complained, they said they'd see what could be done, but I knew that it was not going to happen. Anyway it was a good reason to go away when I had had enough. Another thing I came to know through TV while I was in Salisbury was that one of the boys who had been working with me in Vietnam and had left with me to Singapore had got executed by the Angolan terrorists because he had been a mercenary for the Angolan government troops. He was a young German fellow who had wanted to see some more action after Vietnam. They had hanged him.

Soon I was back to exercising, like running and walking with a backpack and weapons, which could be very tough. Afterwards a Rhodesian who I had met in the pub in Salisbury one day would come and take me to his house for coffee and cake after which he wanted to play jigsaw puzzles; he was a jigsaw puzzle collector with a whole cupboard full of puzzles. It was really boring for me, but occasionally I played with him just to keep him happy. He felt proud whenever I went to his house, because I was an Australian who had come to Rhodesia to fight for his country.

Then came another call for the SAS boys. The Selous Scouts, a regiment of the Rhodesian army, had discovered a huge weapons cache which was guarded by terrs about 200 kilometres from Salisbury. Six of us were flown there early one morning and air-dropped about twenty kilometres away from the cache, right in the bush. We coordinated on the radio with the two Selous Scouts who had discovered the weapons, and continued together. They said there could be about ten heavily armed troops in the area; we had to go in and eliminate as many as possible without making any noise. 'Use your automatic rifles only after they're already dead.'

We advanced stealthily. We found two black terrs asleep—they were dispatched with the bayonet. For two hours we could not locate any more. So we just waited in hiding. Then the two Selous Scouts returned from their search and took us to a very bushy area, then stopped us and pointed straight ahead. Nine people with automatic rifles by their sides were sitting on the ground eating and drinking. One of us shouted in the local language, 'Don't move; put your hands slowly up in the air.' It was understood that the moment any of those nine picked up a rifle or put his hand in a pocket, we would shoot; our automatics were in our hands. Then one shot was fired. We couldn't see where it came from, but at that moment some of the nine men picked up their rifles. Immediately we all fired, except the Scouts. Five of the terrs dropped. After another round, the rest also fell. Where that first shot came from I still couldn't see. So we had to be careful. There could be some more terrorists in the area.

We retreated into the bush, then lay flat on the ground scrutinizing the terrain around the nine fallen men. Some of them could have been alive, but we didn't want to take a risk and walk into a trap. So we just stayed in hiding. I signalled to the Scouts to search and see if they could find anything. After another hour one of the Scouts came back and told us to follow him slowly; there were three more enemies. At that moment the Scout pointed and we saw the three terrs right in front of us, checking on their fallen comrades. We decided to shoot. That was the end as far as we could make out. Fourteen enemies dead and we hadn't lost a single man.

We radioed for the aircraft and asked the pilot if he could make a safe landing before sunset. He said he would try to land about two kilometres from where we were. Meanwhile we checked the cache to see if there was anything valuable. We put the brand-new automatic rifles on the side to take them with us and the rest we decided to blow up with all the hand grenades and explosives that were at our disposal. We radioed the aircraft, asking if we should send some men to clear the terrain for the landing. The pilot replied in the positive, so some of our party went ahead, taking some of the Kalashnikovs from the cache with them to put in the plane. Then we checked the cache for some good explosives and rigged it. We'd fire it just before take-off. The aircraft managed to land successfully. We threw the remaining rifles aboard, took the dead bodies to the 'crematorium', blew it all up, then flew back to Salisbury.

That night we were back in our barracks. The High Command was impressed with the execution of the one-day operation without any loss of Rhodesian manpower. Of course, there were not only Rhodesians in the Rhodesian army. Look at me, an Australian. There also were Americans, Canadians, British and other Europeans. But everybody had some reason to fight for Rhodesia.

After a day's rest, I started my training again. Now I was only running ten kilometres in the morning on one day and on the next day I was doing 500 push-ups. Then we were supposed to spar. Actually they asked us to box. I said, 'I'm gonna fight my own way. I've got a big nose, which may cause me some damage.' One of the sergeant majors didn't like what I said, so he told me, 'Don't talk shit, if you wanna fight your own way, then come on, fight me. I don't care, you come and hit me. I'll knock you out in a minute!' This was ridiculous. In martial arts as well as in military situations, you don't fight to show off technique or win points. I said in front of everybody, 'I want a CO (commanding officer) to be here and witness the fight, because if something happens to you, I don't wanna take the blame and get court-martialled.' My SAS team was showing their support for me with thumbs-up signs.

A CO was called for and we got ready in shorts and T-shirts, our hands and feet bare. After the referee blew the whistle to start, the sergeant major moved forward on his left leg quick as a flash, his right arm swinging at me so fast at the same time that I could hardly see it; but I knew that he was trying to hit me on the nose after what I'd said. I was prepared for it and blocked his right arm with my left forearm, which lifted him on to his toes; at the same time I drove my right fist with all my Goju-Kai speed and power into his chest. One or two ribs must have cracked. The sergeant major buckled, almost went down on his knees, but I continued with a round-house kick, spinning my body to the left and crashing my right foot into his face, again with full force. The sergeant major fell on his back and blood spurted out of his nose.

The referee stopped the fight and said, 'You can't do that.' I replied, 'You heard his answer when I announced that I'm gonna fight my way. When I'm involved in close combat with the enemy, I fight to kill, to knock the enemy out as quick as possible. That's the way I have been trained by a Japanese karate master. I am sorry that I hurt him, but he challenged me in front of witnesses. I came here to fight against terrorists and not against Rhodesians. Please forgive me.' The SAS guys who were there all shook hands with me approvingly.

The next Sunday morning my Rhodesian jigsaw-puzzle friend looked me up at the barracks and requested me to visit him after 4 p.m. for a few of our favoured games. I said, 'Let's have a bottle of Lion lager with it, because today's gonna be a hot day. I've also got a story to tell about a fight between me and one of our sergeant majors.'

'OK, Bob, see you in the evening then!'

During the day I took a walk through Salisbury and watched the people. On Sundays there were lots of white folks of the farming community in town, perhaps to enjoy lunch in the city. That's what I wanted to do as well. The native population usually stuck to their own hangouts, where they could make more noise. There were also a lot of black females who tried to attract my attention inside the restaurants; however, I was not interested in this type of companionship, because firstly my mind was acutely aware of the reasons that had brought me to Rhodesia. Secondly these girls didn't give the impression of being my type. This has nothing to do with racism; it was because they looked unhygienic and illiterate. I like my women clean and educated, no matter what her race.

So I went and had a nice lunch of local vegetables and some mutton. Afterwards, I strolled along some quiet streets and admired the colourful jacaranda trees with their lovely blue flowers and their sweet-smelling wood. I thought of Maria Antoinette and our soon-to-be-born baby. I couldn't go back now, although I missed her awfully. I kicked myself for letting her go because of that stupid spy ship. Perhaps it was my destiny or my karma. Was I destined to marry somebody else? Did I have to go through my life and accomplish something first? I felt that so far I had not achieved anything worthwhile, nothing to talk about or sing about. Maybe I should start singing again to alleviate the pain in my heart, I thought.

I trudged along slowly until I stood in front of the door of my jigsaw-puzzle friend; I can't remember his name after all these years. He, along with a friend, was waiting for me with cake and a few bottles of Lion lager beer from South Africa. When I told him and his friend about the fight with the sergeant major who wanted to beat me up as though his life depended on it, they had a hearty laugh and agreed that I had done the right thing.

When I got back to the barracks at night, I wrote a long letter to Maria, then decided to cut it down in size and wrote another shorter one so as not to upset her too much.

In the morning the military High Command briefed us about an urgent matter. 'Our intelligence has revealed that there is an increasing number of attacks on farms, particularly farms that have less security than they should have. Repeatedly, farmers' families and their staff have been brutalized and killed. To thwart these menaces, we have decided to keep some SAS troops on the ground in areas that are highly vulnerable. They'll be in contact with Selous Scout units. Even though we only have about a hundred SAS elite troops, we have to spread out forty of them in these vulnerable areas while the rest of them will be ready to fly any moment they are required. Please have a look at those two maps on the wall for the indications of the vulnerable farms and note down the numbers in the circle to identify their locations correctly. SAS soldiers on foot will wear the full dark-blue uniform with black berets. On the blackboard you can read the names of the troops who will be dropped in their respective areas tomorrow, early morning. Get all your gear ready and prepare yourselves fully so we won't have any delays. Thank you, and good luck.'

I found my name among the many scribbled on the blackboard. We were told to be prepared to be on call for ten days. Every three days we'd get food and water supply by air. We should carry plenty of biltong, a salt-dried smoked meat of either kudu or ostrich, as special ration. I had the whole day to clean my shoes, take an extra uniform, clean my rifle and other weapons. Next day we were on time. I was glad that members of the Mozambique operation made up the six men of our team. We were all first-class shots; we were all fit, and all deadly in close combat. These are the prerequisites of SAS soldiers, apart from parachuting and other survival techniques.

We had a look at the map to orientate ourselves. There were only two farms in the immediate area of fifty acres. We would move from farm to farm and talk to their families and workers. A lot of farms had black staff and maids, which could make it quite tricky, because you never really knew who they were siding with. Some of them could be very loyal to their long-time employers, but they were still scared of the hard-line terrorists who would have no mercy and put a knife in their back before they could say Jack Robinson.

When we got to the first farm, the farmer greeted us and we introduced ourselves as SAS troops. He offered us breakfast and we gratefully accepted. The farmer's name was Howard Smith, his wife's was Shelly. Howard said they only had one security guard. They had been attacked before, but only machinery and cars had been damaged. 'They can always come back,' he said ominously.

'Do all the farms have phones and stay in touch with their neighbours?' we asked.

'Yes, of course.'

'Well, we'll be in this vicinity for the next ten days and nights.'

I said to Mel, a Canadian in our team, 'Listen mate, this is ridiculous. How can they keep us here on foot in an area of fifty acres with only two farms? We have to be motorized; otherwise we'll just have to stay on one farm with six men. That's crazy! We're not Selous Scouts that we should be expected to patrol on foot. Let's make a call to Salisbury barracks.' They apologized and sent us a troop carrier by evening. OK, now we were cooking with gas!

We decided to take a drive to the other farm. We were there in about one and a half hours. We met the farmer's wife, Mrs Gillian, and a security guard. Her husband was still out in the field. So we radioed the Selous Scouts and asked them if everything was all right.

83

After we told them where we were, they informed us that they had noticed some movements near that farm earlier that day. 'It may be better if we keep somebody there during the night.'

We called Howard Smith and told him that we'd stay at the Gillians' place during the night, and to call us back if they had any problems. We put the troop carrier into a barn so it couldn't be seen from outside. We got plenty of drinking water from the truck. I'd been chewing that smoked salty dry meat (biltong) all day, which made me very thirsty.

We sat inside the living quarters of the family on the second floor, keeping watch in turns; two people kept watch while the rest slept. Occasionally we spoke to the Selous Scouts because they were scouting around all night and if there was anything moving towards the farm they would let us know right away. We heard nothing from the Scouts, but at about 1 a.m. Mel and Jan (a Dutchman) noticed some shadows in the moonlight downstairs near the entrance to the farmhouse. Mel imitated the call of an owl which was meant to warn us.

We were awake instantly and fell to the ground in a crouch. We heard somebody in front of us and turned on our high-powered torch lights, weapons at the ready. We saw two black men shooting into the lights, but at the same moment we fired two of our automatics and dropped the two guys. We lit another torch, shining it on the faces of the terrs; their eyes were open, but they weren't moving much. We took their weapons and secured them. We shook them and somebody from our team asked them in their local lingo where the others were. They were bleeding from the stomach area, but they said nothing. We put the point of the bayonet against one fellow's throat and he pointed outside. Someone asked how many and the guy showed two fingers.

We left two men with the wounded terrs and four of us moved

out on our bellies, carefully scanning the area. Suddenly somebody started firing with an automatic rifle into the windows of the farmhouse. The shots were fired from behind a cluster of bushes and two of our men ran around to get them from behind. These fellows kept firing until their magazines were empty and then we got them. Yes, another two.

Meanwhile, Gillian and her husband had come out of the house. We showed them the wounded terrs. Gillian's husband said he'd tie them up and keep them outside and have them taken away in the morning. The other two were dead.

We spoke to the Scouts on the radio. They reported some terrorist activity but no attacks. There had been no incident on Howard Smith's farm.

On the second day we drove along slowly towards another area with more farmland. That day there was no incident in our area. On the third day we changed our area of patrol again. The Selous Scouts had noticed the presence of quite a large number of armed terrorists. We followed the trail given to us by the Scouts and searched and checked the whole morning. After that we received a call from the Scouts. They had been called from a farm about thirty kilometres from where we were. The farmer was on the line and said that they had been attacked by an armed rabble of about ten blacks. The farmer had escaped with his wife and their two children in the car, but they didn't know what had happened to the security man.

'OK, boys, let's go quick. They must still be there.' But it took us about two hours to get to the farm; we couldn't drive fast because of the rough terrain. It was the Houser farm. We jumped out of the truck and checked behind the farmhouse and the other buildings. There was a group of blacks behind the farmhouse who was holding down another black man. In front of that guy was one black man

85

with a knife which he had inserted into the abdomen of the fellow the others were holding down. I could see from afar that he was trying to cut the liver out of the abdomen. Some of these blacks believed that if they ate a strong man's liver raw, they would become more powerful. We immediately shot the man with the knife, and then the black whose liver was already hanging out was half cut off. We came to know that the guy whose liver was being removed was the loyal servant of Mr Houser, the farmer.

'Where are the other hoodlums? Come on boys, let's go have a look, they must be here; and I can smell booze. I think those bastards have raided Mr Houser's liquor cabinet,' I said. We found another five black Rhodesians scattered around, full of booze and sleeping. We tied them up, took their weapons and put them inside the barn. They'd be picked up later on and jailed.

We were still at the farm searching if we could find anything else, when Jan found a body in a bushy area near a field about two kilometres away from the farmhouse. It was a white man, probably the security guard who stayed at the farm. He had been shot in the back. We called Salisbury and gave them our report and told them to let the farmer know that he had to come back to the farm and identify the bodies of the security man and the servant. We'd wait for him and his wife.

The terrorists and the dead bodies were removed in the evening. We stayed for the night. In the morning Mr Houser returned with another man and had a look at the damage done to the house. Then we left on a drive to check on two farms within the next sixty kilometres.

The Selous Scouts had no other emergency for the following two days. It was raining during those two days. We met four Selous Scouts on the second day just as it was getting dark. They saw the troop carrier and stopped us. We got out of the truck greeting each other. I noticed the wet grass around my feet and realized that I had taken off my military boots in the truck. At the same moment I felt a sharp pain above my ankle. I bent down and tried to feel around with my fingers; and whatever it was jumped on to my wrist. One of the scouts said, 'It's a bullfrog; they're nasty things. You can't take them off so easily.' He took out his knife and gave it a jab, and it was gone. It left bloody tooth marks on my ankle and on my wrist.

It reminded me of an incident in Papua, New Guinea, about ten years before. Papua, New Guinea, was still an Australian colony then, and my friend Jack Cooper and I were on a voluntary mission for something like a peace corps for a month. We were clearing some land which was reserved for the construction of a hospital for New Guinea natives. Papua, New Guinea, was full of snakes and some of them were deadly venomous. Now, Jack recognized all the venomous snakes when he saw them. I was chopping down a tree when I heard Jack shouting. I looked across. He was about a hundred feet away. He had an axe in his right hand. He put his left forearm against a tree and cut his left hand off with a powerful blow of his axe. I rushed over to see what was going on and saw a green viper, a fairly small snake, lying on the grass with its head off. Jack had dropped his cigarette on the ground, and hadn't seen the snake when he'd reached down to pick it up. That's when it had bit him, and Jack knew immediately that a bite from the viper kills in sixty seconds. Cutting off his own hand was the only way to save his life, before the venom got into his bloodstream. He'd been living in the USA for many years now. And he'd got an artificial hand with some kind of black glove. Well, compared to the green viper the bullfrog wasn't that bad.

The next day we were called back to Salisbury barracks. It was a little earlier than expected, but I was happy. I didn't feel like staying any longer. I wanted to go to South Africa. I decided to take

87

two days' leave to prepare myself for the journey, and then desert. What I didn't like was that I was being paid in Rhodesian dollars. I had expected American currency, since they had recruited me from abroad. The Rhodesian dollar was hardly worth anything. So I collected all my luggage from my quarters and as an afterthought also took a *Time* magazine which someone had put on my bed. Then I left my luggage with my jigsaw-puzzle friend and told him, 'I'll pick it up after two days and go on an indefinite holiday. Don't tell anybody about it.' The next day I withdrew all my Rhodesian money from the bank. I noticed that the government had also reimbursed me for the money I paid to travel from Hong Kong to Salisbury, but in Rhodesian dollars. The bank advised me to get the Rhodesian dollars exchanged into South African rands because the latter was a more stable currency.

South Africa: 'Downing a Lion'

Now I was a civilian again. I bought a ticket from Salisbury to Cape Town, changing trains at Bulawayo, the second-biggest Rhodesian city after Salisbury. From there the train took me to Cape Town through Botswana and the Kalahari Desert, a journey of almost four days. I had a comfortable compartment all to myself; all meals were served there and at night the compartment would be turned into a bedroom. It was very interesting to chug through bushman's country and see lots of animals. I even saw two lions run through the desert and many ostriches and gnus or wildebeest. Along the railway line I noticed kraal after kraal, the African village huts. I had taken a lot of biltong with me. Even if I got thirsty, there was enough beer available on the train. South Africa's most popular beers were Lion Lager and Castle Lager; even Australians liked to guzzle them, and we Aussies sure know how to differentiate a good beer from an ordinary one.

Once we were in Pretoria, the capital of South Africa; it was just another three and a half hours to Cape Town, which you could also reach by the super-luxurious Blue Train. After the train made its final stop at Cape Town railway station, I stood on the platform with my luggage and accosted people who were about to enter the coaches marked 'Bulawayo–Rhodesia'. 'Excuse me, madam, I have just arrived from Salisbury. I was doing military service with the SAS regiment. You'll require Rhodesian dollars; please buy some from me! I'll give you a relatively good rate; here I need rands. God will bless you.' I sold about 30 per cent of my Rhodesian money, and the rest I'd sell over the next few days when the trains from Bulawayo pulled in every day. I found that people were much quicker to help with the currency exchanges when they saw my SAS beret; I'd wear it again next time, I decided.

After that I took a taxi to the Sea View Hotel. I checked in, put my luggage in the room, changed into my swimming costume and ran down into the water. I was feeling so hot, but when I hit the sea, I almost had a heart attack. The water was ice-cold! I had to come out again. Then I realized that I was at the southernmost point of Africa—where the Indian Ocean meets the Atlantic, which is cold because of the cold stream from Antarctica, while the Indian Ocean is warm because of the warm stream from the north. The beach at Muizenberg, just outside Cape Town, would have been nice and warm as it was on the Indian Ocean. So next time I'd have to make sure to enter the right ocean for a swim. The thing was that it looked so inviting from outside.

When I came out of the cold ocean, I turned around and stood facing the sea. I could see Robben Island in the distance. That's where the South African government was giving free lodging to all their political prisoners like Nelson Mandela, who after almost thirty years in prison became the prime minister of South Africa in 1994.

I went back to the hotel and took a bath. As I took some fresh clothes out of my luggage I found the *Time* magazine which had been on my bed in the SAS quarters in Rhodesia. The publishing date was 1 March 1977. On the cover was the photograph of a very attractive girl, apparently an actress, and the cover story read: 'The Indian Film Industry and Parveen Babi'. I leafed through that magazine and discovered some more photos of the actress. I read with interest that India is the biggest film production country in the world. According to *Time* the industry released over a thousand films every year, that is, about three films every day. I put the mag in my briefcase and hoped that I'd meet that lady soon.

The next day I had a look around Cape Town and I found the Heerengracht Hotel, a five-star hotel in a good location, not far from the railway station and the sea, and close to the city. I went there often, to have a drink at the bar, and to chat with the staff to find out what were the interesting things happening around town. Then one day at a party, I met two gentlemen called Bob Harman and Wesley who told me that the Sybil Sands modelling agency was the best one in town. I went there the following day and was registered right away. From then on, I kept getting regular work for advertisements for tea, coffee powders, shoes, brandy and whisky, and also some fashion shows.

Then I met Luke Van Führen, an African who offered to move me into his and his wife's flat, so that we could share the rent. It was a nice place in Tamboerskloof, a small suburb of Cape Town. I could use his car as well, he said.

I also registered an office for travellers or business people who travelled alone and were in need of a companion—an escort service. I started by providing escort girls and when I found that there was a demand for escort men, I started hiring them too. That was doing fine after I received permission from the police department who gave me a No Objection Certificate. I had an office in Tamboerskloof and two secretaries; later I had three young secretaries and one old, fat one who was very honest and looked after collecting the fees from guests. We called her 'Auntie'. During that period I didn't have much time to spend in the escort business, because I was so busy with a lot of modelling assignments.

One day Bob Harman took me out for dinner and told me part of his life story. He was a jolly fellow, full of the latest jokes. He suggested that we have a shellfish dinner, because those days you could hardly get any lobsters or giant prawns due to a ban on catching shellfish; it had something to do with the mating season and the fact that shellfish were fast becoming extinct in South Africa because people ate so many. So they put a ban, particularly on the large lobsters and large prawns, for about eight months of the year. The restaurant where we were to have dinner that night had a permit for that weekend only. Bob Harman said that there was a big black market for shellfish. Some people took big risks, fishing stealthily on quiet islands and then selling their catch for high profits. He said that he had been roped in by a friend a couple of months ago and his job was to sell the shellfish. It was a lot of trouble for Bob Harman to sell the goods, because if he went to the restaurants during business hours, there often would be cops or special check commandos who would look into guests' plates to see what they were eating. If they caught the restaurant selling forbidden fruit (like fruits de mer!), the fines and punishments could be very severe.

After Bob Harman had gone to all the trouble of getting rid of his black goods, he had not been paid one single rand by his so-called friend. I felt sorry for Bob Harman and promised him that I'd do something to set things straight as soon as I had a bit of spare time. Bob's face lit up and he promptly told me one of his latest jokes: 'Little Johnny came to school one hour late. The teacher asked him, "Why are you late by one hour, Johnny?" Johnny replied, "Oh, my daddy got burnt, sir." "What a shame," said the teacher. "Did he get burnt badly, Johnny?" Johnny replied, "Why sir, they don't fuck around in the crematorium!"'

Then our plates arrived, stacked with the most delicious giant prawns barbecued in butter. 'I haven't tasted anything like this since I left Australia,' I exclaimed.

'People have to wait for eight months until they're allowed to put this kind of food on the table again,' Bob said. 'Just fly over to Mauritius. There prawns, lobsters and anything else from the sea is just as good.'

At about that time I got a big modelling contract for Lion Lager beer, along with three other male models. The ad was about a big brai in the mountains (a brai is a South African barbecue). The theme was that no barbecue is complete without beer and in South Africa it had to be Lion Lager; the catchphrase was 'Down a Lion'. The four of us were flown from Cape Town to Durban on the east coast of South Africa. From there we were taken up the highest mountain range in South Africa, the Drakensberg, by Land Rover.

During the trip from Durban airport to Pietermaritzburg we were listening to the radio when we heard an interesting news flash from the Seychelles: 'The latest about the coup d'état in the Seychelles islands: while Jimmy Mancham, the former president of the Seychelles, was in London for the Commonwealth conference, a coup d'état took place in the islands and Albert René was declared the new President of the Seychelles. Jimmy Mancham was informed that he could not return to the Seychelles until further notice. He will remain in the UK after applying for asylum. It was a quiet takeover by Albert René and his supporters without a single shot fired. Only an elderly man succumbed to a heart attack.' Wow, they had done it exactly like I'd advised them to just three months ago. Fantastic, well done, Henri!

Now the mountains were in front of us. It was quite pretty, but for me the most beautiful trip is definitely by car from Port Elizabeth to Cape Town—it's called the garden route and it's so picturesque and captivating you'll never forget it. Our Land Rover was climbing the road that also led to Lesotho (capital: Maseru). Lesotho had approximately two and a half million inhabitants and a gate that could be locked from inside the country and from outside the country. Our shooting location was very close to Lesotho. I could see people working as we ascended the mountain. It was a camp with production and direction personnel, and costumes and make-up people. Everybody was there, waiting for the four of us. If we couldn't finish the whole shoot that day, we would stay in a hotel in Pietermaritzburg and finish the next day.

It was simple: four guys eating barbecued steak and drinking mugs of beer, that's all; plus close-ups showing laughter and contentment. The actual shoot was nice, a picnic. We only went back to Cape Town the next day. In the morning, after the sun had risen, they wanted to take some alternative shots to make absolutely sure that we had done a good job—and it paid off. This was shot in 1977; in 1978, it won the Best Commercial Worldwide in Cannes—and that without a female face or body! Later on when I was living in India, Zia Mohammed, one of the secretaries of my escort service in South Africa, used to write to me and insist that even if she wanted to forget me she was not able to, because every day and night she'd see my face on TV in 'Down a Lion', with beer running down my chin and the smoke of the barbecued steaks providing a pretty haze.

When we were ready to drive back to the airport in Durban, the road from Lesotho was blocked with trucks full of Lesotho beans that were being sent to some other country. As we willed the truck to hurry up so that we could reach the airport without missing our flight, another convoy, also laden with beans, was waiting to drive into Lesotho with United Nations Organization assistance. I was wondering what kind of trading that was supposed to be.

Soon we were flying back again.

South Africa II: Fishy Business

One day I was walking down a street in Cape Town when my eyes were captured by a sign advertising a martial arts school. Taekwondo and kung fu. I thought of Oshiro immediately, but I was sure that South Africa would be the last place for Oshiro to start a martial arts dojo. Nevertheless I went inside the place. On the ground floor was a young man of about thirty who welcomed me and introduced himself as Berooz Nejad from Iran. 'Would you like to join my school?'

'I wouldn't mind doing some sparring, but I am trained in Goju-Kai, the Japanese soft art of karate. I am a black belt third dan.' Berooz said that he was a taekwondo fifth dan and kung fu seventh dan. I asked him, only half jokingly, if we should start a two-man army. He just laughed. He told me that he had been the Shah of Iran's personal bodyguard, but he had left because the Shah would not last long now and Ayatollah Khomeini would come back to Iran. So he had decided to open a martial arts school in Cape Town. Then he proceeded to show me two floors, one for taekwondo and one for kung fu; and in the basement he had an underground shooting range. That was interesting for me, because I'd been trained to be an expert marksman. We could do some shooting practice together.

From that day on we met often; mostly in his dojo or his basement shooting range. Sometimes we went for a cup of coffee or a glass of beer. One hot afternoon, we went into a pub to have a beer. We both didn't drink much, about two large glasses each was normally enough. Berooz told me that he eventually wanted to settle down in the US. 'Maybe I'll set up a martial arts school in California, but I'm not certain yet. You know what you should do? You should go to Muscat—you know, in Oman. There is so much construction happening, you'll be able to mint money as a civil engineer.'

I agreed in a way, but I wanted to stay in South Africa for some more time, particularly in Cape Town, my favourite city.

As we were talking the door burst open and ten or eleven guys stormed inside the pub shouting for beer. They looked like they were part of some sports team and it turned out that they were the South African football team. They must have just won a match to judge from the way they behaved. Anyway, we kept our conversation going. But it seemed as though the footballers were not happy with us. We were minding our own business, yet these guys were jostling us. Even the publican behind the bar told them to leave us alone.

The moment the publican said that, one of the footballers poured his beer over Berooz's head. Berooz looked at me, we nodded to each other almost imperceptibly and Berooz hit the footballer with a straight and powerful right in his upper stomach. The guy fell down and as one of the others advanced to attack Berooz, he found my knee in his crotch and also sank to the floor. Berooz was a very fast fighter and his blows were spot-on, but we were fighting slowly enough to know exactly what we were doing, ducking and blocking the footballers' blows. When one guy wanted to hit me on the head with a bar stool, I gave him a karate kick against his knee and got hold of the bar stool and hit two fellows with it at the same time. When they were on the floor I kicked one of them under the chin; I used my legs a lot, so did Berooz. Two guys were thrown through a window and remained outside on the footpath. One bloke who wanted to hit Berooz on his head with a bottle was thrown against the bottle rack behind the bar and broke his jaw. Then one footballer was about to punch me I don't know where, but I got hold of his arm, turned, got his arm into a lock and broke his bone. These footballers were huge guys; Berooz looked like a dwarf next to some of the big oafs. But they had no coordination; they were brute strength without speed or power.

Suddenly the police came in two vans and told us to stop. The football team was in a shambles. They were lying on the footpath, behind the bar, under a table. They were bleeding and couldn't move their arms or legs. Berooz and I had a few minor bruises and we were laughing. I offered to pay the publican for the damage, but he said right away in front of the police, 'No, no, you don't have to pay anything. I am a witness. The football team started the whole thing. You did a wonderful job; I never expected that.'

The police inspector asked the barkeeper incredulously, 'Those two guys took care of the whole football team?'

The publican nodded and said, 'You better believe it, it was a great fight!' So the cops took all of them away in the vans and we gave the inspector a handful of Berooz's martial arts school visiting cards for future business. We shook hands with the publican, gave him a visiting card too and left.

Outside the pub, a crowd of people had gathered. We walked towards Berooz's dojo as fast as possible. As we were walking, a Bentley pulled up right next us. 'Excuse me please,' said a well-dressed gentleman, and handed us two business cards. I looked at the card in my hand. It had the name of a company on it under the name Paul Getty II. I looked at the man again and stated with certainty, 'You're not Paul Getty II.'

'You're quite right, but he was there at the bar and saw your fight—or most of it rather. He would like to meet you, as soon as possible. It's about some work. Would you mind to come and see him at the address on the business card?'

I looked at Berooz and asked, 'Tomorrow morning, 11 a.m. OK?'

'Fine. 11 a.m.,' Berooz confirmed.

'Thank you gentlemen, good evening.'

On the next day at 11 a.m. Berooz and I entered an office complex and took the elevator to the ninth floor. We gave the lady at the reception our card and waited. Within five minutes the person we had talked to the evening before called us inside. He pressed a button on the office intercom and a voice said, 'Come in, the door is open.' We entered. A person sat behind a large desk, wearing a blackish-grey suit. He said, 'I would have liked to see the whole fight yesterday; I would have given anything for a ringside seat.' He smiled slightly. 'I am Paul Getty II.'

'I am Bob Christo,' I said, 'and this is my friend Berooz Nejad. I am pleased to meet you, sir. Now how can we be of service to you?'

'I'm about to ask you to do a job for me. The two of you together. It is something which should remain highly confidential, even after the work is done. Somehow I have the feeling that I can have trust in both of you. I have been informed about your martial arts school also, although I have a few questions about your personal backgrounds before we go ahead.'

I was interviewed first and then Berooz. My interview took about an hour and Berooz's, thirty minutes. Then Paul Getty's associate joined us and mentioned that his name was Sorensen. He showed us the menu of their private cafeteria and requested us to select our lunch. 'You'll have about one hour before Mr Getty will meet you again. Your lunch will be served in the room next door.' I had French onion soup, a pepper steak with mashed potatoes, and for dessert, crêpe Suzette. What Sorensen called cafeteria food was five-star cuisine.

Fifteen minutes after Berooz and I finished lunch Paul Getty returned and coffee was served. Getty said, 'I have decided to let you do the job.'

We looked at him quizzically.

'I want you to accompany a luxury Range Rover van transporting $20 million in cash to a place in Cape Town,' he continued, by way of explanation. 'I don't want any professional bodyguards or special vehicles for the transport. That sort of thing attracts attention, which I want to avoid. It will be done tomorrow morning, leaving at 7 a.m. from here. The money will be packed in large suitcases. Sorensen will come with you. He knows the place. Bob, you will drive the van, Sorensen will give instructions. Both of you will behave totally normal. No whispering as though you're hiding something. Wear some smart but casual clothes—and no weapons. You don't need any; you two can take care of yourselves. Is that clear?'

'Crystal clear sir,' we said.

'If everything goes according to our plan, each of you will be paid $20,000. Just remember that no word about this should be leaked to any soul. If you have girlfriends, remember: ninety-nine out of hundred girlfriends are not able to keep any secrets. Any questions? Berooz?'

'No, sir.'

'Bob?'

'Where do we meet after the job is done?'

'You will not meet me again, unless I call you for another job.'

'Sir, you said each of us will be paid $20,000 in cash *if everything goes according to plan*. In your opinion, what can go wrong?'

'For example, if the next day's headlines in the newspapers say "Paul Getty hoards $20 million in such and such a place", then you'll have to return the money.'

'Fair enough. OK.'

'Right, warriors, that's all for today. Be on time. Tomorrow morning 7 a.m. No weapons. And keep your mouths shut. Good day.'

Berooz and I got into the lift and walked out of the building in silence, each of us occupied with our different thoughts—why he wanted us to do that job, why no weapons. Well, I could see quite a few reasons why it had to be kept quiet. The Gettys are a very strange family. Over the last ten years they'd had three kidnappings. The last one had been when Paul Getty III was kidnapped at the age of twelve. When the ransom wasn't paid, the kidnappers cut one of the boy's ears off and mailed it to his father and his grandfather, with the threat that if the ransom was not paid quickly, they'd send the second ear also, and then the fingers, toes, etcetera, etcetera. Well, they had sent the ransom pretty fast after that! Maybe the cash we would be transporting was for some ransom again; or perhaps it was a stash for a rainy day. Black money? Let's see where the money would go tomorrow.

A thought struck me. 'Paul Getty is an American, isn't he?' I asked Berooz. 'And yet he lives in South Africa. Why?'

'Because he is in gold mining and in the South African wine business. His money comes from South Africa.'

'All right, Berooz, let's get some sleep. Oh, I meant to ask you, I wanna get myself a pistol. Since we have started shooting in your range together, I feel like I should have my own weapon. At least I'll get used to it. Can you get me one? There are so many weapon dealers in Cape Town and Johannesburg; tell me who you recommend and I'll buy it there. OK? Goodnight.'

Next morning we were at Getty's company on time. The van was in the parking bay, and suitcase after suitcase was being loaded on to it. All the suitcases had posters all around with the name of some vintage company situated in Stellenbosch on it. I assumed there'd be wine bottles inside.

I said to Berooz, 'I have to drive carefully, so that the bottles don't break. There could be anything inside; for all we know, drugs. It's too late to speculate now. I can't ask Getty to open the cases to check if everything is there, can I? We're not gonna meet him again.' Sorensen strolled up, interrupting our conversation. 'Everything ready to go, Sorensen?' I asked.

'Yes, guys, let's go! Bob, we're going to Stellenbosch. Know the way?'

'On the highway, isn't it?'

'That's it; I'll tell you when we come to the turn-off.' Sorensen directed me to a very large wine godown like a mammoth wine cellar, stocked with products of different wineries. You could drive right in. Sorensen opened the doors with his keys, then the door to a strongroom. We wheeled the cases in, then locked the strongroom again. Then we drove out, locked the main gates behind us and returned to Cape Town.

Sorensen let us off at the dojo and handed each of us a packet. We shook hands and he left. Berooz and I went into the martial arts school. Then we counted our money; 20,000 dollar notes in each packet. That was the best part. Whatever I didn't spend, I could always change back into dollars. Looking back, the whole incident seems so surreal; this is but one of many examples in my life that shows how fact can be stranger than fiction.

After the Paul Getty episode I bought myself a Czechoslovakian pistol which I started to use in the underground shooting range. I intended to take it with me whenever I was travelling abroad. I would first wrap it in some aluminium foil and place it into one of my shapeless bags in which I stuffed a lot of clothes. Whatever is wrapped in aluminium foil will show up as just a black spot when it's being X-rayed, and in a big shapeless bag it would not attract any extra attention. Today I would not risk it, of course; but thirty-odd years ago I took it with me to so many countries and never got caught. I always planned to give it to someone as a present, but it took a few more years until that day came.

Sybil Sands, my modelling agency, called me and said there was an offer for a film role in an English movie called *Wild Geese* with Richard Burton, Roger Moore and others. I can't remember the rest of the cast. I didn't have enough dates to do the film role, so I just agreed to do a stunt scene. It involved riding in a cable car up to Table Mountain. I had to do a stand-in for one of the main characters who had to jump from the cable car going up into the one going down while they passed each other. It was a big jump and very high, so we had a moving platform fixed under the cable cars to make it safer. It turned out all right, but it took almost a whole day because it took time to get the camera placings right, with some of the shooting being done with the cameraman partly suspended in the air!

After that I had to spend some time sorting out matters in my escort company. Zia told me that two of the secretaries had made some money on the side; they hadn't checked it in with accounts. So I threw out those two secretaries and kept only Zia and Auntie.

They were both honest as far as I could make out. After a few days I'd go and recheck again.

Now I was thinking seriously about going to Muscat, in the Sultanate of Oman, to return to civil engineering. Meanwhile, I had enough money for some time, so I could take it easy and go to the beach, surfing and swimming in the sea. One of the hang-glider guys who I regularly met on the top of Table Mountain or down by the beach had promised to teach me how to do it on his rig. On the sunny days with the right kind of wind you always had somebody, sometimes many hang-gliders, overhead, particularly above the area which was reserved for nude swimming and nude sunbathing activities! Some of these hang-gliders stayed up for eight hours sometimes without landing.

The most difficult part in the beginning is to take off properly. Then you have to learn how to make use of the wind in the right way in order to change direction. To go up and down you use your legs and operate the rear of the hang-glider. Once you're flying it's absolutely thrilling. On the beaches it's lovely; hang-gliding is also very popular on the Hawaiian beaches. The most difficult hang-gliding is in the mountains, because of irregular winds and sudden updraughts and cold streams. If you hang-glide in the mountains you must wear gloves and ear protection. When I was trying to land in the beginning, I sometimes scraped and cut myself on trees and thorn bushes and lost a few litres of blood here and there. But now I am glad that I learned it.

One other thing I still had to do——I had promised Bob Harman that I would help him take revenge on his so-called friend Kepler Wessels (not the famous cricketer but a namesake) for cheating him with the shellfish. I called Bob Harman and told him to introduce me to the guy. He called both of us and made it a party. I had insinuated myself with Wessels by the end of the party. He instructed me to give him a call after three days and he would let me know as soon as he had enough shellfish for me to start selling it for him.

I went to the restaurants where I knew the owners and told them that I'd be getting a fresh catch of shellfish in two or three days. I also mentioned the rate of the moment for fresh, first-class lobsters and giant prawns. Then I also talked to the Heerengracht kitchen, whose chef was familiar to me, and the chef of another five-star hotel as well. They all instructed me that as soon as I had the merchandise, I should come before lunch, and they'd buy on the spot.

I called Kepler after two days, and they had received a large delivery already. Next morning, I went to the Wessels' house and Kepler's wife gave me three iceboxes filled with lovely big lobsters and huge prawns. She asked me to let her know as soon as I had sold all; there was another delivery the next day. I put everything into Luke's station wagon, turned on the AC and started my rounds. I had to work very fast, because I could not afford any mishaps. I needn't have worried; the two five-star hotels bought everything I had in the car. They were going to have a party in the evening. I managed to convince them to give me cash cheques, which was very lucky. That saved me at least two days' wait for the cheques to be cleared. I didn't want them to start searching for me for another four days. The delivery which I'd get the next day was as good as sold; they agreed on the rate and that they'd pay me cash—I just had to give them an invoice. They wanted to sell their food as much as I wanted to sell my shellfish.

They all probably thought that I was going to come back for another delivery, which I wouldn't. At the end of the day I netted a tidy sum. I never expected that much. Even though I did it for Bob Harman, my 50 per cent of it was a great inspiration. I called Bob Harman and asked him to meet me. When I showed him how much shellfish I had sold, he was surprised and a little scared, because he felt that Kepler would put the blame for his loss on him when he realized that he was not getting any money from me. I gave Bob exactly half the proceeds and advised him not to reveal that this was his revenge on Kepler. 'Keep the revenge silent, because it's your right. After all, Kepler cheated you first. Put the money in your bank account, and if you can't keep your big mouth shut, then just don't see Kepler and his wife any more.' I told him that I was going to Johannesburg for a few days. He suggested a few suitable hotels in Highbrow. I thanked him, wished him well and said goodbye.

Then I continued to Berooz's dojo. I told Berooz that I was ready to go to Muscat soon to get back to civil engineering. Berooz gave me the names and addresses of his builder friends in Muscat and mentioned that he had already spoken to them on the phone. 'Before you leave for Muscat, just telephone them and someone will come to receive you at the airport.'

'Come, Berooz, let's have one last round of target shooting with our pistols.' One round became two hours, and then I had to stop over at my office in the escort agency to check for mail. When I got there, I called Zia inside and explained to her that I had to go to Johannesburg for some time. 'Once I'm there, I'll let you know how long I'll be. You and Auntie can continue with the agency and take your salary out of the cash flow.'

Zia said, 'Auntie hasn't come today, she'll probably be here tomorrow.'

'OK then, I shall phone you from Joburg, Zia.' Before I could say any more she put her arms around my neck and kissed me on my cheeks. I looked into her pretty face and gave her a long kiss on the mouth with my tongue, holding her tight and feeling her body against mine.

At that moment the office bell rang. Zia quickly sprang away from me. It was the postman delivering the mail. Zia took the mail and put it on my table. It was a letter from the Philippines from Maria. She'd given birth to a pair of female twins. I was relieved to read that everybody was happy about the twins; only Maria had been depressed for a few days because I couldn't be there. I consoled myself with the thought that if I had been there with the view to leave again, it would have been much worse. Well, I'd read the letter again later on.

As I walked down the stairs to the ground floor, I saw two girls standing there chatting and laughing. They seemed to be what they call Cape Coloureds, with not black but brownish skin. They live in the area around the Cape. Often they have a disfigurement which you see when they open their mouths. The four front teeth of their upper and lower jaws are missing. It reminded me in a way of the girls in the Philippines with the wires in their mouths. Of course, the teeth right out missing looks much worse; looks like they've been purposely knocked out. Some of those girls could be very pretty, but without the front teeth they look unsightly and unpleasant. It seems that they have them removed at puberty—I never managed to figure out why. An example of beauty being in the eye of the beholder?

The last night in Cape Town I decided to go dancing in the Heerengracht Hotel. There was a very nice disco with wild music and not run on an apartheid basis; it was a multiracial establishment. I was surprised but happy. Things, in Cape Town particularly, were improving. So much nicer when you can talk, dance and enjoy yourself with people of your own choice and nobody is telling you not to sit in this part of a train or that part of a bus, because that's for blacks and this one is for whites only. Mind you, I'm talking about 1977. By now everything had changed. I didn't stay very late, because I had to catch the Blue Train in the morning to Johannesburg. I enjoyed a few dances and a few beers with a black partner.

Luke Van Führen and his wife Dorothea dropped me at the railway station to board the Blue Train to Johannesburg. It's a wonderful train, very fast and clean and comfortable. On arriving in Johannesburg, I found a friendly hotel right in the middle of Highbrow, where all the action takes place. In that area you run into people from all over the globe; predominantly Indians—from India, not the USA. Most of the Indians I spoke to in Johannesburg were Muslim. Of course I had met Indians in Cape Town also, but not to this extent. Durban is also full of Indians.

In Highbrow there were a lot of dancing places. I walked into a huge, crowded dance hall and met two sisters from Windhoek, the capital of Namibia, who stuck to me. One of them was beautiful, blond, about 5'7" and with an attractive smile. Then the music changed and she shouted above the din, 'Oh, that's a nice number, let's dance to that one. Come, Bob!' She had a soft, easy style; it felt good to move with her. After a couple of more dances, we sat down, asked for some drinks and chatted for a while. Her name was Vera. They had come to Joburg on a few days' vacation with their father, because so much was happening in this city.

She disappeared for a while, then returned and showed me a quaint ivory carving of an elephant which she wanted to gift me. At first I thought I could send it to Maria because of the twins' birth, but then I changed my mind and decided to get Maria something which I could choose and buy myself. Then Vera and I were dancing again and she put her head softly against my chest and asked me if she could sleep with me tonight. 'My father only comes back in the morning. He won't notice, and my sister is no problem.'

I was actually surprised; she made an impression of such decency. She definitely was no hooker. Maybe she thought it was a good opportunity to lose her virginity and that I'd be very gentle with her. But I don't really like young girls trying to push their way into my bed. I made some excuse and went back to my hotel. Before going to bed I booked an STD call to the Philippines to talk to Maria in the morning. Then I hit the sack and tried to fall asleep.

Vietnam: Battling My Own Demons

But my mind kept drifting back to Bali where I had built a hotel for an Australian syndicate, all friends. It was built in Indonesian style with wooden beams and thatching. When it was done I had prepared myself to return to Sydney. About that time I got a visit from two officers of an American liaison company, Vinell Constructions. They gave me their business cards and asked me if I would like a well-paid job working directly for the South Vietnamese army to look after their military supply routes. 'You would be in charge of the whole set-up—minesweeping, building and rebuilding bridges along the east coast of Vietnam, Talat and Danang.' I told them that I had a construction company in Sydney and a family with three children; that I didn't have time to go to work in Vietnam. One of the liaison officers put a visiting card into my shirt pocket and said, 'Just in case you change your mind, thank you.' The next day I flew back to Sydney. I waited for my wife, Helga, at the airport; she was coming to take me home, but she never came. While she was driving on the expressway to the airport she was hit by a truck coming from the opposite direction. She never had a chance. She was alone in the car. 11 p.m.

By now I have managed to get over the shock, of course; after all it has been almost forty years since it happened; but at that time my life turned into a chaotic nightmare. I became depressed and I was desperately trying to find an answer to the question 'What to do?' Then my friend Bob Fischer and his wife Karin had suggested that they'd take my kids with them to California until I had recovered from the initial shock and made a positive decision about how to continue with my life. I decided to sell my business and go abroad.

The question was: Where to? The answer had come to me when I had gone through my belongings and found the business card of Vinell Constructions Liaison Co. Pvt. Ltd (Asia). OK, I decided, I'm going to accept the engineering job in South Vietnam. That will help me straighten out my thinking. I told Bob and Karin what I was going to do and rang up Saigon. Eventually I got the phone connection and spoke to the person in charge. They called me back the same night and asked me to come as soon as possible. I requested them to give me a couple of weeks' time because I had just lost my wife and had to accommodate my children with friends in the USA. I spoke to one of the company directors who told me that they would wait for me but I must try to come really fast.

It was strange that most of my memories of the Vietnam War resurface while I'm asleep and dreaming, whether I was in South Africa or in Bangalore during a spinal operation; maybe because it was a double pain—the pain in my back and legs and the pain in my heart about the loss of my family, my children.

When I finally reached Saigon I met the South Vietnamese Army personnel. Two days later I was taken for a drive towards the area of my functioning. Apart from Vietnamese soldiers there were several Europeans—Germans, Frenchmen, Brits and Dutchmen—who were builders or civil engineers. I used to acknowledge their presence but was in a foul mood most of the time since I was still suffering from the effects of the loss of my family.

It even induced me for some time to give in to a death wish, when I heard about the availability of Russian roulette gambling organized by a Vietnamese clique. That's a dangerous game of chance in which a single bullet is loaded into the chamber of a revolver, one player takes the gun, spins the cylinder, holds the gun to his head and fires it, then (if still alive) passes it to the next person, who does the same, and so on. The spectators or gamblers can place a bet either in favour of the player's life or death. I used to play in favour of my life and always won. There they played it a little different, for them it was purely gambling; but in effect it was the same. I won a lot of money but I didn't really care. After work, when I was in my quarters, I would often look at my children's photos with tears running down my cheeks.

For me, the turning point came one day as I was watching my workers in their mine-proof Unimogs. A Unimog is a German utility vehicle which can be made mine-proof; nothing much will happen to the driver or the vehicle if it hits a mine. As the workers drove around, I was shouting at them: 'Not like this, like that!' and 'Suppose you hit a mine? Then what?' Then it happened: the Unimog I was sitting in hit a mine and I was catapulted outside. First everybody was silent, but suddenly everybody was laughing, and finally I also started to laugh. From that moment on, I began to feel better and slowly changed back to my normal self. That evening as I sat with my workers and soldiers we discussed why some men join a war and get into situations where they fight with death-defying endeavour. It eventually gets them medals and awards, but it doesn't mean anything to them at that point of time, because whatever they have lost already cannot be retrieved. After that I never played Russian roulette again and my attitude towards my men improved a lot.

I was woken up by the ringing of the phone—my STD call had been put through and Maria was on the other end of the line. I had been dreaming about the Vietnam War the whole night long.

'Yes, my darling, how are you feeling, feeding two babies at the same time? Do you have them drinking one on each breast?' I asked her fondly. 'I'm so happy that you're well. Have you found a name for the babies yet? Why don't you call them "Baby"? Or do you want to give them separate names?' I joked. I told her I was in Johannesburg and that I'd be taking up the offer in Muscat. Then we chatted some more, about this and that. I asked her if the Jag was all right and told her to give Eddy a call if it ever gave trouble. 'Now take good care. Say hello to Dino from me, and I love you! I shouldn't really tell you this because you're a married woman now, but I miss you so much. With all my love, bye-bye, baby.'

I had to make another call to Auntie and Zia. Auntie was unhappy with my absence and I had to convince her that they could manage quite well without me. I wasn't entirely successful; Auntie was still worried about how they would run the company without me. I told her to try for some time, and if it wasn't working out, they could pay themselves off and quit.

Kenya-Ethiopia: Moving On

The next day I decided to buy myself some eye-catching clothes and some good music cassettes for my new player. The Carlton Centre downtown was the best place. I also had to buy myself a good stock of biltong; I wasn't sure if it was available readily in all the African countries and I relished that stuff—it gives you instant energy. I'd book my flight to Nairobi for the next afternoon.

I'd been to Nairobi once before. I had gone through Kruger National Park. On the other side of its border was a big farm. Just by chance I had met the farmer, and while we were chatting he talked about a lion that had been attacking some of his livestock some months before. So he had shot it. He had felt sorry to waste the meat of that beautiful lion, so he'd made biltong out of the ham area. As he was telling me the story he recalled that he had never

110

even tasted that lion biltong. He looked at me with a twinkle in his eye and asked, 'Would you like to taste it with a glass of South African wine?'

'Of course, I would love to,' I said. And that's where I spent the rest of the day with that adventurous farmer. We knocked off three or four bottles of wine. The biltong was of a real strong taste. I enjoyed it. Maybe I could find that farm again; I'm sure I could, but there wouldn't be any biltong left by now!

I went to the bank and changed all the rand I had into US dollars and Deutschmarks. Then I purchased my tickets to Nairobi, Addis Ababa and from there to Bahrain; all open dates.

That night, I was just leaving the hotel for a drink when the phone rang. It was Bob Harman on the phone, frantic. He had finally tracked me down, after calling a few hotels in Highbrow that he had recommended to me. 'Bob, be careful, Kepler has got in touch with his friends from the Joburg police; they are trying to find you! Better change your hotel.'

'Thanks, Harman. Don't talk to them and don't worry about me,' I said.

Next morning I was in Kruger International Airport, Johannesburg. I had accumulated quite a bit of luggage, so I had excess weight, for which I'd have to pay 1 per cent of the first class fare per kilo of excess luggage. I checked my luggage and found that I had a lot of books in there. When I saw the books, I wondered why I'd put them in my luggage at all. I tried to sell them to the ground hostess but she didn't want to buy them, so I gave them to her as a present. I hoped that she wouldn't want me to gift-wrap them for her as well! Anyway after I removed most of the books, the excess became affordable.

By evening I was in Nairobi in the Holiday Inn. I had a relaxing evening with a few drinks and a nice big steak. Then I leafed through my address book and found the name I wanted: Wally Thomsen. I called up the number and he answered the phone. He was surprised, but he sure remembered me. I asked him if he had shot another lion since we had polished off all that lion biltong many years ago. He said, 'No, I haven't, but you're welcome to pop over in the morning and I'll take you for a drive. We can have a drink at the tree house.'

We had a beautiful drive and saw lots of wild animals: zebras, giraffes and lions. There were a lot of jeeps and Land Cruisers on the roads—tourists driving through the countryside. It had become a big business. There were special places and special times to see particular animals in the water like hippos, crocs and elephants. It was quite interesting, but it had become very commercialized. I liked the times when you could go trekking through the bush quietly for days. Now you had to be careful about poachers, and you had areas which were cordoned off with 'No Entry' signs. The Tarzan days were over. But there were still plenty of snakes around.

The flight to Addis Ababa took off at night, arriving in the morning. The Addis Ababa airport was very disorderly and confusing. Everybody's luggage was searched. They took all my music cassettes, gave me a piece of paper and said that when I was leaving the city I would have to show the paper and the cassettes would be returned. My pistol was not found like I had predicted, so that remained in my possession while I was in Ethiopia. I didn't carry it while I was moving around in Addis Ababa, of course.

I went first to the post office to get some stamps to send letters. To be able to get inside, I was bodily searched for weapons. Everybody was subjected to the same routine before entering any public building or government office. I noticed a lot of students walking around. Most of them seemed sympathetic to foreigners in their country; they smiled at me and spoke in English. Some invited me to have something to eat.

So around lunchtime I was eating with a group of four friendly students—flatbread with some vegetable dish in one big bowl from which everybody helped themselves. The students were bursting with questions for me. But we were interrupted by some shouting from a group on the opposite side of the street. Suddenly a shot rang out; the police had shot dead a man who looked like a student. I turned to my companions and this time it was I who was asking the questions: 'Why? What? How?' They put their fingers to their lips, got up and slipped away quickly. Next to the body on the road was a blackboard on which the police wrote something which I couldn't read. But as long as the police was there, I couldn't talk to the locals. When I came back to that spot later in the afternoon, the body had been removed. It was a very hot day. Wherever I went, I became immediately aware of what a poor country Ethiopia was. The buildings were dilapidated, most of the people were in rags, and there were beggars and prostitutes loitering around. I didn't feel like staying in Addis Ababa any longer.

The Middle East: Transit Points

Next day, I arrived in Bahrain. Coming from Ethiopia, Bahrain represented a big jump in prices. I searched for an Oman consulate, but they didn't have one in Bahrain. That meant that I'd have to phone Berooz's friend before leaving.

Bahrain in 1977 looked very old. The streets were too narrow; the shops in the main streets were decrepit. It was difficult to walk on the tiny footpaths. At almost every corner you could buy doner kebabs from the shawarma stalls. I loved them—and apparently so did everybody else. I noticed that there were cars stopping outside the snack bars, blocking traffic. It would have been easier to walk like I did, but if you had a new car, you had to flaunt it. There was a stream of brand-new cars—everybody was showing off their new possessions thanks to the economic boom after oil prices had catapulted with the formation of the Organization of the Petroleum Exporting Countries (OPEC) cartel. If you visit Bahrain now, it's a difference of night and day; the same goes for other Arabian countries like the United Arab Emirates (UAE). Dubai for instance has developed to an unbelievable level.

Anyway, it was interesting to walk through the city. But I couldn't find any English newspapers anywhere, including in my hotel. In the evenings, I would sit in the hotel's lounge to guzzle a few beers. The waiters were very busy serving all the people and everybody drank beer, including the locals; drinking seemed to have become accepted along with their increased standard of living. I noticed that when the waiters collected the money for the bills, one hand deposited money in the right pocket, and the other hand always went to the left pocket with the tip. There were not too many people one could talk to, because in those days there were not many tourists, and the Arabs seemed to prefer making conversation with their own ilk. Perhaps most of them were not comfortable conversing in English.

Four days were enough for Bahrain. Then I was on my way to Muscat with a transit stop in Abu Dhabi, the capital of the UAE. With my Australian passport I could land in almost any part of the world without a visa.

When I went to the arrivals counter at Muscat airport, I caught sight of an English newspaper with the front page dedicated to the death of Elvis Presley. I think it was August 1977. Staying in a place where English was treated as a minor language, I had had no inkling that the famous singer had passed away.

After ten minutes a man greeted me, introducing himself as Alwani, the friend of Berooz Nejad. He was Lebanese and was the manager of a construction company. I was happy to finally have someone to talk to. He told me that there should be no problem getting work with his construction company because they were so busy and urgently needed civil engineers. However, I had to have a work visa for the Sultanate of Oman. While this visa was being processed, I would have to be out of the country. I had to give Alwani a copy of my passport and my contact address, and the visa would be ready in two to three weeks. Alwani took me to the airport restaurant for lunch and said he'd be back at night to take me to a restaurant for dinner. By then I should decide where I'd go till the visa was ready and keep my contact address and the passport copy ready.

I saw a big map on the wall of the arrival lounge and went over to get my bearings. After some scrutinizing of the map I realized that Muscat was not far away from Mumbai. I still had that *Time* magazine in my briefcase. I immediately decided that I'd go to Mumbai and try to meet Parveen Babi. This was a great opportunity.

I got talking to a person who worked in the lounge, a tall man of about forty with blond hair and blue eyes. I told him that I would be travelling to Mumbai. 'If there is a flight tonight or tomorrow morning, I shall take it.' He told me that the first flight to Bombay would leave at 8.20 a.m. the next morning. I said, 'I'll take that.'

Blondie asked, 'Where are you going to stay?'

I replied, 'I'll know when I get there. There is no problem; I'm only going to stay for two weeks until I get my work visa for Muscat.'

'Sir, may I request you to do me a favour?'

'Go ahead, what favour?'

'My name is Eddie Kotwal. My two daughters, my sister and my maid live in Bombay in the suburb of Andheri. I'd like to send them a parcel with some gifts. If you'd be kind enough to take it for them, I will let you stay in my house until you have your work visa.'

115

'I'd be very happy to carry your parcel, but tell me, why do you live in Bombay?'

'I'm an Indian, I'm born in India.'

'Well, I've never seen a blond Indian with blue eyes!'

'Sir, I am a Parsi.'

'What are Parsis?'

'Oh sir, Parsis come from Persia, they are originally Zoroastrians; they came from Persia around the year 600 AD.'

'Oh, yes, now I remember, the Zoroastrians are the disciples of Zoroaster . . .'

'. . . Or Zarathustra, the God of the oldest single-God religion in the world. Yes sir, you are right.'

'OK, Eddie, if you tell me where to go to book my ticket to fly tomorrow morning, I'll buy it right now.'

By the time Alwani returned to take me for dinner, I could give him my contact address in Bombay and my passport copy. After dinner we said goodbye. 'I will be sleeping in the arrival lounge for one night,' I said, 'and hopefully we'll be meeting again in about two weeks.' Eddie Kotwal gave me a parcel and a letter for his daughters in Bombay, and I left Muscat in the morning.

Bombay: First Impressions

When I arrived in Bombay, it was still morning. I took a taxi to the address of Eddie Kotwal. Eddie's sister, Frennie, read her brother's letter and welcomed me to their home. The maidservant was from Madras and spoke English. She took me to the bank so I could encash my traveller's cheques. She showed me the bus stops and the railway stations and advised me to buy a monthly pass so I could get downtown easily and fast.

When I checked my luggage, I realized that I was missing my

large shapeless bag which also contained my firearm. I inquired with the airline, which sent me to the airport to have a look in the missing-luggage department. There was nothing, so I guessed that it must have been left behind in Muscat and decided to wait until I got my Oman visa.

Meanwhile, I had a good look at Bombay city, doing a lot of walking which helped me find my way around pretty soon. On the second day in Bombay I saw a group of people filming in the street and I stopped to watch. After a while, they started winding up their work, shaking hands and kissing one another. I heard them saying that the shooting part of the film was over.

I started to talk to them and found out that the director's name was Prem Kapoor. I told them that I had also worked in movies; I'd just worked for a big Hollywood film in the Philippines a few months ago. Prem Kapoor invited me to come to their hang-out in a tea house on Veer Nariman Road near Churchgate station in the evening. I went there and met Prem and some others of that group. I had heard that anybody with the name Kapoor was big in the Bollywood film industry, but Prem Kapoor explained that he made only documentary films. 'This joint's a meeting point for art film-makers and documentary producers.' I asked him if anybody could help me meet Parveen Babi. I described how I had found the *Time* magazine in Rhodesia with a big write-up about the Indian film industry and Parveen Babi. Prem said he'd tell his workers and friends, and sooner or later somebody would introduce her to me. From then on I used to drop by at that tea house regularly and listen to them talk about their film stories.

A few days later, one of the cameramen who came to the tea house occasionally spoke to me. His name was Zuber Khan. He and a sound man, Chakravorthy, who also used to come there, worked for big feature movies for BR Chopra Productions. He told me that there would be a 'mahurat' for a movie called *Burning Train* the next day. 'Parveen Babi is one of the heroines.'

I asked, 'What is a mahurat?'

'That's an inauguration. I'll pick you up tomorrow at 9 a.m. at Andheri and take you to Bombay Central station. I'll introduce you to Parveen Babi.'

'Great, 9 a.m. at my place.'

When we arrived at Bombay Central railway station the next day there was a train on the first platform and a lot of people carrying boxes and cameras and megaphones. Zuber ordered me to stand where I was, in front of a pillar. 'Parveen Babi will come here.'

After about fifteen minutes a lady stopped in front of me and said, 'Hallo, I'm Parveen Babi.'

I looked at her for a moment and then answered, 'You're not Parveen Babi!' Pulling the *Time* magazine out of a pocket, I pointed at it and said, 'This is Parveen Babi!'

The lady laughed and retorted, 'In the magazine I'm in make-up and full get-up. Normally I don't wear make-up when I am not working. Now, before the mahurat shot, I'll have to go for my make-up first.'

I apologized and said, 'Actually I was only pulling your leg. I've been admiring your beauty. Ever since I read this magazine I've wanted to meet you personally. I'm really happy to meet you like this. I've been carrying this *Time* since I was in Rhodesia in March this year, and thanks to that cameraman over there, I was lucky enough to meet you today.'

There were a lot of people standing around listening to our conversation.

'Thanks for your compliments,' Parveen said, 'but now I have to go inside the train to get ready for the shooting of the mahurat. I hope we'll meet again. Bye.'

'Bye, Parveen. I have to go back to Muscat now but I hope we'll meet when I return some day. Good luck.'

After she left, Zuber Khan pointed out different film personalities to me. 'This is Dharmendra, walking next to him is Hema Malini and over there, the lady with the ponytail, is Shabana Azmi. That young man is Ravi Chopra who is directing the movie. *Burning Train* is his directorial debut. He is B.R. Chopra's son. The young man walking behind is Vinod Khanna, a very popular movie star.'

The mahurat shot was being taken inside the train. I waited for some time outside the train, talking to someone from the production office of B.R. Chopra who told me to drop in and say hello whenever I was near their office. He gave me a business card.

The next morning I decided to go to Juhu Beach. I went by bus, got off at the last stop, Juhu Beach, and walked down to the sea. On the shore I saw a dilapidated old building. People were coming out of it, so I thought I'd go inside and see what it was. It turned out to be a Holiday Inn hotel, functional but still under construction. The top floor was yet to be erected. The outside looked all old and grey, but I had seen so many buildings in Bombay that had that grey-blackish colour. I had been told that it was due to the monsoon, which was not over yet. These types of structures were painted only rarely. New buildings in the city were generally coated with polished stone, like granite or glass.

As I stood in the lobby of the 'new' Holiday Inn, Juhu, I observed a man, of about fifty years, who was walking in my direction. He seemed familiar to me. Then he suddenly stopped in front of me and said, 'Bob?'

'George? George Marzbetuny?' Yes, it was him. I had met this Armenian-American in Universal Studios, Los Angeles, doing some stunt work for a movie for which he had written the script. The film was called *Too Late The Hero*.

'Well, what a surprise!' he said. 'I recognized you as soon as I stepped out of the elevator. What are you doing here?'

'I needed a work visa for Oman, to work for a construction company there. I had to be out of the country while the visa was being processed and I needed a contact address. Now I've got one.'

'Are you staying here in the hotel?'

'No, George, I'm staying with an Indian actress called Parveen Babi,' I lied.

'Oh, I can see you're kidding, Bob. I know Parveen. I'm here for an Indian film director–producer–actor who bought my script for a movie he is making. Parveen was in his last movie called *Chandi Sona*. Now I'm not sure yet whether the heroine for the next movie will be Parveen or Zeenat Aman. Tomorrow is going to be the mahurat of that movie. It's called *Abdullah*, it's a Hindi movie. You must come; I'll introduce you to the producer Sanjay Khan.'

'Another mahurat? OK, let's go together,' I agreed. 'George, do you live in this Holiday Inn?'

'Yes, I've been here for two months. I'm gonna shoot an English version of the film.'

The next day, we arrived at 10 a.m. at RK Studios, Chembur. The studio belonged to Raj Kapoor, the famous producer, director and actor. He would be playing the title role of Sanjay Khan's *Abdullah*. It was 26 October 1977. Sanjay Khan was in make-up, because he had to face the camera in the mahurat shot. He played the hero. His wife Zarine was also in the make-up room, but she was not an actress. She was just present to grace the occasion. George Marzbetuny introduced me to Sanjay Khan and his wife. When I asked if Zarine was an Indian name, she said, 'Yes, but I'm a Parsi by birth and Parsis, who are originally from Persia, have their own names.'

'Yes, I know about the Parsis already, because the owner of the place I live in is a Parsi; his name is Eddie Kotwal,' I said.

Sanjay Khan was a tall man, at least six feet, and handsome, with black hair and a strong build. Yes, judging by his looks, I could easily believe that he would cut a very charismatic hero on the screen. He and his wife made the perfect picture-book couple; she was about 5'8", very appealing and sympathetic, and of a classy demeanour. At that time she was the mother of three girls. We chatted for a while and then descended to one of the studio floors, where everything was ready.

The mahurat started with some of the music of the film and a poem read by Sanjay's mother. In the Indian film industry, I was to learn, the music of each film is just as important as the screenplay. It contributes to the success of the film in an essential way. When there is an inauguration, the presence of a priest, or pandit, is usually required to request God's blessings or to express thanks by chanting spiritual text in the ancient Sanskrit language. This goes for any inauguration, be it for a new house, where the pandit prays for a happy and healthy life of the occupants, or a shop for a business. After the religious part of the *Abdullah* inauguration was over, some camera shots were taken of the essential components of the story. After that refreshments were served and hands were shaken and good wishes extended for the success of the movie and its songs.

After the mahurat was over, George and I drove through parts of the city, marvelling at the traffic and the hordes of people; not vehicular traffic so much, in those days there were only two types of cars manufactured in India—Ambassadors, which came to be synonymous with government vehicles, and a kind of Fiat. But there were a lot of buses, handcarts, carts pulled by bullocks or horses. And the people on the road made everything look so colourful, mainly because of their multi-hued clothes—saris, salwar kameezes, kurta pyjamas. It seemed to me that everybody was carrying, pulling or pushing something. If somebody who hadn't travelled much came here from a sparsely inhabited country like Australia, he would suffer severe culture shock during his first few weeks of stay!

Eventually we arrived at the Holiday Inn and had some lunch in the outdoor restaurant looking over the Indian Ocean. We had the all-time favourite of almost everybody as long as they are non-vegetarian: chicken biryani or mutton biryani, served with an onion or vegetable yogurt called raita. There is also a variety of vegetarian biryani with seasoned rice and, instead of meat, some tasty vegetables. Indian beer is also quite nice, especially when one is thirsty. And one is often thirsty because India is a hot country, especially along the coast and towards the south and in some of the northern states like Rajasthan.

After our lunch I went to my temporary home in Andheri. Reena the maidservant was there with her two young daughters. She seemed happy to see me. I slept on the sofa in the living room. The other rooms accommodated everyone else. The custom was that everyone else would sleep on the floor on mattresses or blankets. Whenever I ate in the house with the other inhabitants, I used to give the maid some money so she could go and buy some more provisions for the next few days because I used to eat a lot. Usually she put a bottle of beer on the table for me, because I used to tell her, 'Why drink water, if there is beer?'

Once I came to the house quite late, about midnight, because I had met some people who had taken me to a party. When I stood outside the door, I noticed that the light was on in the living room. I would have expected the maid to be asleep by then. I knocked very softly from outside and within ten seconds Reena opened the door. She came with me to my sofa-bed and asked me if I was tired or if I would like to eat or have some beer. I told her that I had eaten and would go to sleep. As I undressed she turned the key in the lock of the room where the other occupants slept, then she came back to my sofa and said goodnight, but she didn't leave.

She came very close and then she was also lying down, right next to me. She started stroking my whole body and feeling my manhood. We didn't talk. I put the blanket on the floor so that our lovemaking didn't cause any squeaking; we continued for about half an hour, then she kissed me and I fell asleep. Whenever I was there during the night or when I was there during the day and everybody else was out working or in school, she came to me full of passion asking me to make love to her. She had a strong desire.

Goa: Arrack and Brandy

So far I had not received my work visa. I decided to take a trip to Goa by train, thinking that the beach season must have started. I went to Victoria Terminus and bought my ticket to Goa. In 1977, it took twenty-three hours to reach Goa from Bombay! The train was full and I had no seat. There was a compartment with two benches filled with a group of Goan teenagers. They adjusted the seating in order to squeeze one more seat out of a bench and offered it to me. As thanks, I took the guitar from the guy sitting next to me and started playing and singing a few songs:

Pack up all my care and woe
Here I go, singin' low,
Bye, bye, blackbird.
Where somebody waits for me,
Sugar's sweet, so is she,
Bye, bye blackbird.

No one here can love and understand me,
Oh, what hard-luck stories they all hand me,
Make my bed and light the light,
I'll be home late tonight,
Blackbird, bye, bye.

Then,

Don't be so sad, I know it's over
But life goes on and this world will keep on turning,
Let's just be glad we had some time to spend together,
There's no use to watch the bridges that we're burning,
Lay your head upon my pillow, hold your warm and tender body
close to mine,
Hear the whisper of the raindrops blowing soft against the window,
And make believe you loved me one more time,
For the good times.

And,

Smile though your heart is aching,
Smile even though it's breaking,
When there are clouds in the sky you'll get by,
If you smile through your fear and sorrow,
Smile and maybe tomorrow, you'll see the
Sun come shining through for you;

Light up your face in gladness,
Hide every trace of sadness,
Although a tear may be ever so near,
That's the time you must keep on trying,

Smile, what's the use of crying,
You'll find that life is still worthwhile
If you just smile.

The ones who knew the songs joined in, and the others hummed or clapped; but suddenly everyone was happy—even without a Filipino musical band! Then I returned the guitar to its owner. He played pretty much the same tunes that I'm used to playing. My travelling companions took out some eatables, so I also shared some of Reena's sandwiches. Anyway, we did a lot more of singing and chatting and the time passed very quickly. We had a change of trains somewhere on the way and had to wait for about an hour, and then continued until we arrived at Margao at about 6 a.m.

I checked a few small hotels for daily rates and found them very reasonable. One of the group of teenage students followed me and showed me where to go if I would like to spend some time at Colva Beach. I liked the area and spent the whole day at Colva Beach. The sand there is white and the sea is beautiful that time of the year. I swam far out, then walked along the beach. For lunch I ate at one of the shacks that you find all along the beach and enjoyed the tasty fish which they prepared.

Towards evening that student came and met me at Colva. He invited me for a local drink. He said, 'It's called arrack—it's a fantastic drink and you'll feel very good after it.'

I drank some of it. The boy said, 'Now let's have something to eat, because the drink is very strong.'

I said, 'OK, let's have some fish. I liked the Goan fish curry I tried this morning.'

He took me to another seafood place. The moment the food came and the boy started eating, he asked me if he should order another drink. I said, 'No thanks, I'll have the fish curry.'

At that moment he gulped and then he threw up right into his plate. I jumped up, put some money on the table and walked right out of the restaurant!

I sauntered to a small hotel nearby and asked if I could make an STD call to Bombay. I wanted to call Eddie Kotwal's sister to find out if my work visa has arrived from Muscat. She had given me the number of her office.

There was a girl in her twenties who looked as though she was in charge of the hotel, because there was nobody else. I asked her for the tariff, and it was very reasonable, considering the prices I was used to paying. I questioned the girl if that included breakfast and she replied in the affirmative. I took a second look at the girl as she replied and realized that the light of the day was already on the wane; that's why I probably hadn't noticed her beauty at first glance. She was smiling, her eyes were large and black, her skin, spotless, the colour of brandy. Her hair was black like ebony with a dark-brown sheen. She had high cheekbones, and she displayed a kind of vulnerability that made me want to take her into my arms and protect her from all the ills of this world.

I asked for her name. She softly responded, 'Cecilia.'

I ventured, 'Do you mind if I call you Brandy?'

She pondered. 'Not really, but why?'

'Your skin is the colour of brandy. See, your face, your arms——and if one comes close enough, your aura——have the effect of brandy. You are beautiful.'

As I spoke, I moved my hands close to her face and her arms, and when I mentioned her aura, I almost encircled her with my arms. She smiled a very sweet smile. I couldn't help myself; I continued flirting outrageously. 'This could only be the result of the magic mix of Indo–Portuguese, am I right?'

'You are right, and my grandparents are still alive.'

I said, 'I'd like to stay for tonight, but please help me make a call to Bombay.' In 1977 it was difficult to get a clear connection when calling from city to city; you had to shout at the top of your voice and I've seen people throw the phone against the wall or out of the window in frustration! It took about another six years for inter-city calling to become less difficult. Brandy tried the number for about an hour but she couldn't get through. By then Frennie would have left her office in any case, so I decided to try again tomorrow.

I went to my room to have a look at it. Then I showered, changed my clothes and went down to the lounge-cum-bar-cum-dining hall. I decided to have my drink in the place where that most attractive girl was serving. However, the most attractive girl had apparently left for the day to return for work in the morning. How disappointing. But then, I had kept her trying to make my phone call for a whole hour. I didn't feel like doing anything extraordinary because my mood was spoiled. My mind saved me with the nostalgic thoughts of my Maria in the Philippines and with these thoughts I went to sleep.

Next morning, I took a leisurely breakfast with fruit, boiled eggs, omelettes, bread with hot sausages, sardines and porridge with prunes. I had my coffee while Brandy tried the phone again and eventually got me Frennie, Eddie Kotwal's sister. I spoke to her but could hardly hear anything, the line was so bad. Then I finally understood that the visa for Oman had arrived. 'Oh, I have to return to Bombay,' I said aloud.

'Sorry, did you say something?' Brandy asked.

'I was talking to myself, Brandy, because I got a message to come back to Bombay.'

'Oh, I thought we could do something tomorrow because it's my day off,' she said.

'Well, last night I was looking for you everywhere, but there was neither Brandy nor Cecilia. So this is goodbye my darling, maybe we shall meet again sometime in the future, eh? '

Back to Muscat: Change of Plans

I made inquiries about how to get back to Bombay and without much ado and waiting, settled for taking a Goa-to-Bombay bus. The bus trip was somehow quicker than by train, but it was not much fun with the rattling and banging through a lot of potholes. The driver had to be kept awake by the passengers because he had driven all the way from Bombay to Goa and had reached Goa just an hour before. He then had to take the bus back right away because there was a shortage of drivers! On reaching Bombay I went straight back to Eddie's place in Andheri and took a shower and packed my bags and then got some sleep after having booked my seat for the flight to Muscat.

As soon as I arrived at Muscat airport, I reported my missing bag to the airport authority. They told me to go to the hall with all the missing luggage and search. I found my bag lying in a corner, dirty and dusty. It was not locked and I checked immediately if everything was there. My pistol was in between all the clothes; I was really surprised that it was still inside the shapeless bag.

Meanwhile, Alwani had spotted me. He called me and we drove to his house where I would stay for the time being until they found something separate for me. The place was absolutely satisfactory. I was served breakfast and then we went on a tour of the company's construction sites. It took the rest of the day. We also went to the company office; they wanted to see my graduation certificate and some other documents. The next day they took me to one particular building site—it was at the foundation stage. It was an eight-storey office building. I almost asked them if I should do the work together with the sculptor but I stopped myself in mid-sentence. I didn't think they would understand my little joke; I would have to start telling them about *Apocalypse Now* and the foundations in the Pagsanjan River. Anyway, after that eight-storey office building I would be rotated to several other structures.

While I was having a look at the architectural drawings, I heard my name being called. It was somebody who had a telegram for me. It read: 'Papa George massive heart attack on way from Bangalore to Bombay. Nanavati hospital Bombay in ICU. Please come back.' I showed the telegram to Alwani. He asked me if I wanted to go back to Bombay. I told him that George Marzbetuny was well known to me, and that I wanted to go back. 'It'll probably take two or three days. You can get me a return ticket, if you don't mind.'

'That's not a problem, as long as you return to us. We'd be happy to have you in our company.'

India

'When I have a few songs to sing with a decent band, I always get in a good mood.'

In his early
days in
Bollywood.

Raj Kiran and Bob Christo in *Star* (1982).
'. . . I was trained in martial arts by an original Japanese master, but I have never hurt another actor during a film fight. I always controlled my blows . . .'

A poster of the film *Nastik* (1983). 'I always ensured that I devoted enough time to exercises and water sports to keep myself fit and flexible.'

In *Kaalia* (1981).
Bob is '. . . a "dada" type who terrorizes the other convicts . . . "Line mere peeche shuru hoti hai!". . .'

With Sanjeev Kumar.

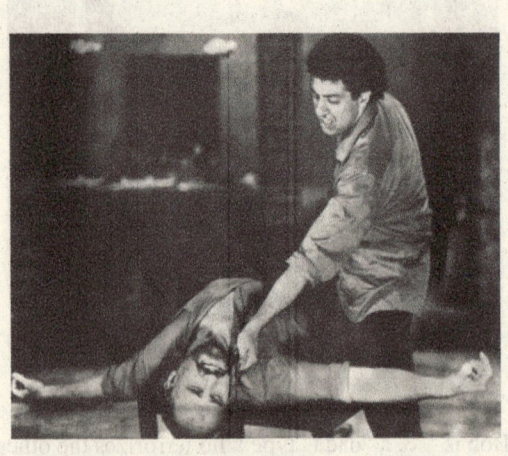

With Sunny Deol.

In one of his better-remembered roles in *Mard* (1986).

(*From left to right*) Sanjay Khan, Bob and Shabaz Khan were a team in *The Great Maratha*.

As General Matthews, an
'anti-Indian British army general', in *The Sword of Tipu Sultan*.

Playing Ahmed Shah Abdalli in *The Great Maratha*.
'I never had to learn so many dialogues in any other film
before, and in a language not my mother tongue.'

(From left to right) Bob's wife Nargis, Bob, son Darius, and son Sunil with daughter-in-law Mona. 'My family is well settled, though scattered around the world.'

'There were happy times and sad times like in every life, but it was a life fully lived.'

With his extended family.

A Friend in Need

That same evening I was on another plane to Bombay. I was wondering what I was to expect in Bombay this time around. Would George be alive when I saw him the next day? I hoped so!

At 9 a.m. I was at the hospital asking the staff to let me in. The door to the ICU was open, but they still wouldn't let me in, they had to get some special permission. Having travelled all this way, I was frustrated at being thwarted at the destination. So I shouted, 'George, good morning. George, I just came back from Muscat, shall I come in?' Some nurse said, 'Please don't shout.'

Meanwhile, George had heard me. He got out of his bed and came shakily up to where I was standing. We shook hands and then he embraced me—or maybe he just wanted to steady himself! The staff opened an empty room and ushered us in there.

'Bob, please don't make me laugh again. That hurts in my chest. I started laughing when I noticed that you were making a ruckus when they didn't let you come in to visit me. They're so stupid here, they don't know who is friend or foe; anybody can tell that you're not an enemy!'

'OK, George, now don't get excited, you've just had a heart attack. How did it happen? Was it in the flight? Are you feeling better now?'

'Much better since you burst into the ICU! See Bob, I was sitting with Sanjay and Zeenat Aman in the aircraft. Zeenat had a window seat, the middle seat was kept free, Sanjay was in the aisle seat and I had the aisle seat across from him. As I looked over to have another look at Zeenat, I thought to myself, "I'll be damned, she really is a knockout!" Even a man of my age can see that!' George's voice rose excitedly. 'That was the moment when my chest started hurting and I passed out! Luckily there was a doctor aboard who gave me a heart massage. When I came to, I thought that the massage had been given by Zeenat and I said thank you to her. She just looked at me quizzically.'

We both doubled up with hysterical laughter. Still chortling, I said, 'George, please, that's enough; you are hyper, please calm down. I know I started it all but now let's pull ourselves together! Now talk slowly and calmly, tell me what was on your mind when you called me back from Muscat.'

'OK, OK. Bob, I'm in bad shape. I won't be able to stay in India to shoot the English version of *Abdullah*. My family is on the way. They'll be here any time and they want to take me back to LA.' George's brows furrowed with anxiety. 'I want you to stay with Sanjay to make sure that he sticks to my script. We translated my English script into Hindi together, and the story is the same. During shooting we were planning to take one shot in Hindi, then one shot in English, etcetera. I want you to write reports for me of what's happening during the shooting and send me the reports. Of course, now *Abdullah* will only be filmed in Hindi.' George sighed and continued, 'You can do anything else—if Sanjay wants to give you a role or asks you to do stunts, that's up to you—but I'm very particular about the film. I want to see it on the screen with English subtitles. Please help me in that way. Whenever a filming schedule is over, send me the reports. I have talked to Sanjay already; he will take you to Rajasthan with his unit in November. You can work out some special fee; he is a gentleman, he will stick to it.' At that moment the doctor entered and requested me to let the patient rest and maybe come back in the evening.

I thought about what George Marzbetuny had said. Truth be told I was not that interested in working in Muscat. India intrigued me more and I wouldn't mind having a career in Hindi films. So I decided to wait for Sanjay Khan's offer.

Meanwhile, George's wife Lilit and his two sons Vahe and Zahre had arrived. They were to stay in India until the doctor gave George permission to go back to California. Sometimes I took George's sons to the Holiday Inn health club and gave them beginner's instructions for physical workouts. And thus I met Sanjay in the Holiday Inn lobby one morning. We sat down and talked about his shooting schedule in various locations in Rajasthan, which was to begin from 23 November 1977. He offered me a lump sum of money which I agreed to happily. At the time money was not an issue for me.

Early Brushes with the Law

When I went for a trip to the city (or 'town' as downtown south Bombay was often called) one day I heard my name being called; it was a female voice somewhere behind me. I turned around and spotted her. I couldn't remember her name right away, but I remembered that she was with *Apocalypse Now* and was always trying to talk to Francis Coppola. A pretty girl. She was with another girl whom I didn't know and a young man by the name of Martin. They had just happened to come to Bombay for a holiday, they said. The girls were Filipinos but absolute bimbos. The girl I remembered from the Philippines thought that Francis had gone to Nepal and would come to Bombay after that to catch a flight to the US. So they were going to wait in Bombay for him.

The Martin guy said he stayed at the Salvation Army, which is well known in the West as a place for rovers who are down and out. The Bombay Salvation Army is in a lane by the side of the Taj Mahal hotel. When I came out of the Taj the day after I had met Martin the first time, I almost bumped into him as I walked down the steps of the hotel to the footpath. We had a chat and he told me that he was with a gang of drug smugglers and had been apprehended by the drug squad. They had held him for two or three days but didn't find any drugs on him or in his room in the Salvation Army. So they had to let him go. However, he knew that he was being followed by undercover police. Martin warned me that I would be marked now, because they would have seen me with him.

I made a mental note not to look for Martin's questionable company in the future, but it was already too late. I saw the bimbo who was after F. F. Coppola once more, and I told her to keep away from that junkie Martin, or she might be in trouble. She brushed me off with a casual shrug, 'Oh, Martin is my friend's relation. When we came to Bombay, we had to bail him out of jail.'

That wasn't the end of it. A couple of days after meeting Martin, I was in Eddie Kotwal's place after my morning shower and was getting dressed when the doorbell rang, and two men came in accompanied by some panchayat people functioning as Justice of the Peace witnesses. They entered and started going through my belongings and talking to the maid. I couldn't understand Hindi at that time, of course. They found my pistol, which had gone undetected through so many airports; it had travelled in my check-in luggage and with an Australian passport I could walk through most immigration checks anywhere in the world. In India there were no visa rules for foreigners yet; those came into force only in 1981. So I had walked into the country freely with the pistol. But within India, you needed a permit to keep a pistol, though the rule was hardly enforced strictly. I said that I had bought it in South Africa for target shooting in a martial arts school. They gave it back to me, together with a card of a narcotics agency and their names. They ordered me to come and see them at a given place the day after.

Of course, I knew what that meant. They wanted a fat bribe from me. When I met them at the appointed place, they said, 'Let's walk down the street,' and asked me if I had brought anything. I told them, 'I only have this,' and gave each of them one sealed envelope with a hundred-rupee note inside. They opened the envelopes and said, 'But is this all?' I gesticulated that I had only very little money at the moment, but as soon as I got my money from Australia, I'd see them again. Then I turned around and left. I never met them again, but I was a little shaken up.

Soon the *Abdullah* unit was ready to leave for Bikaner in Rajasthan. I got permission from Sanjay Khan to keep the luggage which I didn't require for the six weeks of film shooting in his house in Juhu until we returned. After that I would look for another place. I didn't want to go back to Eddie's flat; I'd overstayed already.

The first few days we stayed in a hotel in Bikaner. We would have breakfast in the hotel and then drive to the shooting location which was about an hour and a half away. A village set had to be built there. The village was supposed to be in the middle of a scorching desert, open to attacks by wild dacoits; *Abdullah* is the story about a gang of dacoits attacking villages and caravans in the desert. During one such attack a pregnant woman falls from her horse. A hermit named Abdullah (Raj Kapoor), who lives nearby in the desert, helps her with the delivery of her baby and adopts the child after the mother (Farida Jalal), succumbs to some injuries. Abdullah is a Muslim, so he contacts a pandit (Om Prakash) to help him with the task of bringing the child up according to the Hindu faith of his mother. The pandit advises him to name the child

Krishna. Khalil (Danny Denzongpa) is the leader of the dacoit's gang who is responsible for the death of the mother of Krishna. Khalil is visited by an evil tantric (eventually played by me, though at the time I did not know that) who tells him that he must kill the child Krishna or else he will die a miserable death. The film's hero, Mohammed Al Kamal (Sanjay Khan), helps Abdullah and Krishna survive the dacoit-chief's bloodthirsty designs, which leads to a favourable end to the story.

After we had been shooting for a few days I got sick of the hotel we were staying at. For one thing, I had to sleep in a room with four beds all occupied by snorers. The hotel was filthy; the leather of my shoes was being gnawed up by rats at night, and in the kitchen they were wiping their dirty dishes with old bed sheets. The waiters looked sloppy and dirty too. Breakfast was usually very trying; we usually had the other meals somewhere else. One morning when I was waiting for my breakfast, I noticed that many guests had come after me, but their orders were already being served. And I was so hungry! I told the waiter that my breakfast should have been brought first. He didn't understand English. Frustrated, I shouted at him and finally gave him a tight slap. Another waiter quickly served my breakfast, but that waiter who I had slapped went on to complain about me to the hotel management and to the police. When Sanjay Khan heard about it, he came and asked me what happened. I explained about the terrible service and he laughed.

Later an accusation against me was made to the collector of Bikaner also. We were told that if we didn't pay some money we'd have to go to court and we'd not be allowed to continue with our shooting until after the court case. At that time George Fernandes, the politician, was a big shot in the government. He was a friend of Sanjay, who knew that Fernandes was somewhere close to Bikaner. He tried to ring him up. That was such a drama trying to get him on the phone, because it was very difficult to make oneself understood; the connection was so bad. Finally Sanjay got the message across. George Fernandes told Sanjay not to worry; he would be in Bikaner in about two hours and he would quash the order immediately. So we just had to wait for Fernandes to make his appearance in Bikaner. As soon as the collector saw him, he went to touch his feet and apologized for bringing him all the way to Bikaner because of a stupid waiter's complaint against a foreign national. We all went back to our shooting and Sanjay asked me to stay with him in a very nice tourist bungalow where we had our own cook and some servants who kept everything neat and clean. I had my own room to sleep in and a wardrobe to put my things in. That was much better than that horrible hotel.

The work I was doing so far was as I had discussed earlier with George: jotting down all the shots taken and their cast and the art director's work like erection of new sets, etcetera. I filed them away to send them to George Marzbetuny after our return to Bombay.

In between Sanjay took me sometimes to go deer hunting. They were lovely animals and there were lots of them. We went by jeep and aimed for them from the car window or we stopped the jeep and tried to kill them from outside the jeep. Sanjay had a .375 Magnum, a wonderful weapon. I got my first deer with that rifle. Of course all the hunting we did was solely for the consumption of our unit members. Usually I cut, cleaned and prepared the venison and fried the steaks myself on an open fire. That was right at the beginning of our filming work and at that time I had heard nothing about a ban on hunting deer.

Only later did I begin to understand from the spiritual point of view that it is a sin to kill animals. I grew up in the face of death for several years, even experiencing a World War. It took time to become aware of the meaning of karma and meditation. My level of compassion toward life was developed in a natural way with my gradual call to spiritualism. In the years to come I became very impressed with Tibetan Buddhism and read books like *The Tibetan Book of Living and Dying* by Sogyal Rinpoche. I have stopped killing animals and have almost become vegetarian, but not fully yet. Probably because since childhood right up to old age my body has required large amounts of protein to sustain my high level of activity.

The Inimitable Raj Kapoor

Our direction assistants' jobs consisted, to a great deal, of reminding our artists when to be ready for their scene. They had to be called on the phone or by telegrams and the moment they arrived at the location they were given the script so they could familiarize themselves with the dialogues. According to their availability, actors came and went. Finally it was time for the most senior actor in *Abdullah*, Raj Kapoor or Rajji, to start his work. I found that in India when you are using the first name of a person you work with, you add 'ji' to the end of their name to show that you respect the person. I was often called Bobji or Christoji. Often younger members of the unit call an older man 'uncle'; but they don't say Uncle Bob, they say Bob Uncle—the other way around. Some men don't like to be called Uncle by younger members of the fairer sex; it makes them feel old or not eligible any more. Sanjay would get annoyed if an attractive girl called him Uncle. He'd say, 'You can call me Sanjay, or Sanjayji or Mr Khan, but never call me Uncle! If you call me Uncle, you have no chance to be cast in any of my films or TV series!'

Everybody was excited—Raj Kapoor had arrived and Danny was also due. Zeenat Aman was due to come on Christmas; she played Zainab, hero Mohammed Al Kamal's wife-to-be. The unit was going to Jaipur for a three-day shoot. The shooting was in a different area, about thirty kilometres away from the village set, where we had open desert and Abdullah's tent.

On Raj Kapoor's first day of shooting we started after lunch. It was a crane shot so we could catch Abdullah as he comes towards his tent from afar sitting on his camel. After the shot Sanjay said to Rajji, 'I've got a terrible pain in my upper back. Do you have any painkiller in your basket?' Rajji always had a basket with him. Wherever he went his servants would carry that basket along. It was a food basket for when he got hungry, bursting with samosas, biscuits, chocolates, fruits and medicine of all kinds.

I overheard this and ventured to Sanjay, 'Can I have a look at it?' After I had located the exact spot where the pain was radiating from, I started massaging the area. One or two minutes later I asked Sanjay, 'Do you feel any change?'

Sanjay replied, 'Yes, the pain is gone, totally gone. How did you do it?'

'You saw what I did, I massage quite well. I used to massage my mates' calves when they got cramps as we were training for the Tour de France.' Sanjay was very impressed with my massage. However, I knew what that meant—if he got a pain in the middle of the night, he'd call me, expecting a positive result each time!

Rajji came back with his basket and handed Sanjay a strip of pills. Sanjay told him, 'Bob has fixed it already; he's got magic in his hands.' Actually that was when Raj Kapoor and I met first; I don't remember him from the mahurat.

Then Rajji complained, 'Bobcock, I have a pain in my hip, you think you can check it out?'

I looked at Sanjay. He laughed and said, 'I think Rajji is joking, but I'm sure Bob will help you if you develop pains or cramps, he comes from a sports background.'

I inquired of Rajji if he liked venison. 'Oh yes, very much.'

'Right, tomorrow I'll shoot a deer for you. Which part do you like best?'

'Get the liver for me, because I have no teeth to bite into steaks.'

'OK, Rajji, done.'

The next day I went hunting with an assistant. We drove slowly in the jeep until I saw a herd of four or five running up a hill along a line of trees. I got out of the jeep and stood leaning on one side of it for support, rifle at the ready. The hill in front of me was covered with high grass; the top of it was about 500 metres away. After about three minutes I saw a deer move into my field of vision, but I could see only the head and part of the neck, the rest was covered by grass. I pulled the trigger anyway, and the deer was gone. I was sure I had got him. I sent my assistant up to check. After ten minutes he gave me the signal; he had found it. I also ran up. The shot had gone into the brain; it must have killed him instantly. It was a beautiful animal; I didn't feel good about having killed it.

We took it down, put it in the jeep and covered it with some empty sacks. At lunchtime the steaks were all ready and Rajji's liver was served together with some mashed potatoes and his favourite pickles. After that he remained my friend for the rest of his life. The only thing I never managed to find out was why he kept calling me Bobcock.

It was actually a lot of fun to shoot with Raj Kapoor. It was nice to talk to him, particularly after he had had a few drinks—Scotch, of course; in India most drinkers like whisky. It was difficult to obtain original Scotch whiskies; only after the year 2000 could you get the real thing in the liquor stores. Before that, you had to call the smuggler; he'd deliver at your house. If you didn't have any smuggler's phone number, you had to get one from a friend; but you had to be sure that he supplied you the real thing, otherwise you had to go to a store where they sold you the so-called 'Indian-made foreign liquor'.

Raj Kapoor loved his Scotch. He always had a few bottles stocked with him when he was going for shooting out of Bombay. In the evenings he used to ask Mamaji, who was his relative but worked for him as a butler, to bring him his first peg. After a few pegs Rajji lost count of how much he had been drinking and Mamaji would say, 'You've had enough. You started a full bottle in the evening. Now look, only half a bottle is left.' So Raj would say, 'Just give me half a peg.' Mamaji manoeuvred with three or four Scotch bottles, usually Johnnie Walker, of various volumes, half full, three quarters empty or almost finished, in order to reduce Rajji's consumption for the benefit of his health. The moment Mamaji opened a Johnny Walker bottle, he poured half of it into an empty bottle and automatically Rajji would drink less, thinking that the bottle was already half empty. I've witnessed the most hilarious fights between the two because Rajji wanted to drink more and Mamaji would shout, 'Raj Kapoor, if you want to kill yourself then go ahead, but I say you've had enough!'

The last time I killed an animal was during a hunt at Christmas in 1977, so that we could give our unit a memorable Christmas dinner. There was one twist: Raj Kapoor also wanted to shoot a deer. 'Please let me try just once,' he said. So we hatched a plan.

That morning as we were moving to the location from our tourist bungalow, we rode on our respective horses, because we had to cross hilly terrain on the way and Rajji wouldn't have been able to manage riding on his camel on hilly uneven terrain; he would have fallen off. So we put him on a slow horse. As we had decided, as soon as we had a sighting of deer, Rajji's horse was held steady and his rifle was handed to him. Sanjay was on his horse next to Rajji's and he helped him hold the rifle. Sanjay told him, 'You just keep your eyes on the deer. I'll tell you when to pull the trigger.'

But Rajji's forefinger was actually on the trigger guard, while Sanjay had his finger on the trigger. As planned, I was sitting off to one side behind Rajji, Sanjay and two other riders, out of view. I was aiming at the same deer as the one Rajji was looking at. Then Sanjay counted softly one . . . two . . . three . . . and I shot at the count of three, simultaneously with Sanjay. It was fantastic; Rajji saw his rifle firing, and the deer falling. He shouted, 'I got him, I got him, didn't I?' We all congratulated him: '*Shikaar mubarak ho!*'

The Circling Vultures

It was a nice Christmas day. I asked somebody to get some Christmas decorations and decorated the rooms in the tourist bungalow. In the evening we sat down in Raj Kapoor's room and sang a number of Christmas carols and other songs. I had my guitar with me. Meanwhile, Zeenat Aman had also come and everyone was very much aware of her. She was a glamorous and stunning young lady and everybody fussed around her. Sanjay's family had also joined us for a few days and would stay until after New Year.

After the holidays were over we continued our normal shooting without interruptions. One day Sanjay, Danny and I decided to go on a deer hunt without a car and firearms; we went on horseback armed with only a spear. The spear had been presented to us by Nagaland natives during a festival of the north-eastern states in New Delhi a few days earlier.

We left in the afternoon after our shooting had been wrapped up. Since we only had one spear, we took it in turns. Each of us used the spear for about an hour. It was very interesting and we encountered quite a lot of deer, but we could only concentrate on one at a time. It was difficult to hit a moving target from a galloping horse. After all, we were not Huns! We went on for a few hours and didn't spear even one deer. It requires a lot of practice, which we did not have.

When we had had enough fun and the horses had tired, we realized that we had lost our way and didn't know which direction to take to get back to our shooting location or to our tourist bungalow. How difficult life used to be without mobile phones! We were in the middle of the desert. It became dark, and we could see very little; we didn't even have a torch with us. Luckily just before midnight we met a search party with a jeep which guided us back to the location and the tourist bungalow in about an hour.

After we had showered and were sitting together with a drink, I reminisced about another occasion where I had got lost in South Australia after my car had broken down. I had taken off from Port Augusta in the south and was headed north along the Birdsville track through the desert. I wanted to try and make it all the way to Alice Springs and Ayers Rock in the centre of Australia. The Birdsville track was a hot dangerous path and it kept changing along the way depending on the winds. The track was marked with wooden pegs, but when it was windy the markers got covered by sand and you had trouble following the track. I don't know what it looks like now, but that was the end of the sixties and it was a dirt track. Lots of people lost their lives when they lost their way because they couldn't see the markers or when they ran out of water. There were some farms here and there and a few check-posts. Drivers were supposed to stop at each check-post and enter their name and car description in the book and also fill in where they were going, where they were going to stop next and how much drinking water they were carrying. Thus, if anything happened or if the persons of the registered car didn't show up at the next check-post, somebody would be sent out to search for the missing vehicle; they usually sent an aircraft like a Piper which carried repair kits and drinking water.

I was driving a VW Kombi van with an AC. I came to the conclusion too late that it was the wrong car for the desert. At that time I had thought it was an advantage that it had no radiator. It had air cooling, but that causes a lot of other problems. After I had a breakdown, I speedily went through my drinking water and then I started walking. I walked without drinking water for three days; I just managed to get some dew from a plastic sheet which I kept out at night. Then I began to see vultures following me overhead. I couldn't walk any more; I just dragged myself along. Those vultures knew that I was dying; all they needed to do was hover around, ready to pick up the pieces.

In the morning I sank into a hollow in the sand, so that I could comfortably lie in a reclining position on my back without moving. I kept my eyelids almost closed but I could still see the vultures circling. Two of their scouts flew directly above me and then landed on the sand at a distance of about fifty metres. By and by, other vultures descended to join the scouts. I made no movement. I wondered whether they thought I was dead or whether they could make out that I was breathing. One more scout flew over me and perched ten feet away from me, watching. Then it took off into the air, swooped down and suddenly landed right on my chest. This was the most dangerous moment for me because next thing I knew, the vulture would hack its beak into my eyes. Thinking quickly with the desperation of a man at death's door, I grabbed the scout vulture at the back of its neck with my left hand and brought up my right hand with my extra-sharp Buck knife, slit the vulture's throat and brought it over my face, all in one movement. I started drinking the vulture's blood, as much as I could suck out of its artery. Then I tossed the stinking bird away and watched the rest of the flock escape with an uproarious noise.

I got up, blood all over me. I hadn't realized that vultures had so much blood inside them. I picked my knife out of the sand and stumbled along until I caught sight of—you wouldn't believe it, barely twenty minutes after my fight with the vulture—two buildings and a pub behind a sand dune just half a kilometre away! I made it to the pub and collapsed. Somebody looked after me and I was flown to a hospital, put on a drip because I was suffering from severe dehydration and given a tetanus injection because I had scratches from the vulture's claws. But I had survived by the skin of my teeth.

A Villain is Born

The next morning Sanjay requested me to massage his back, legs, arms and hips. Apparently racing the horse to spear a deer had left its mark on Sanjay's body. After a twenty-minute massage he said he felt much better. Then somebody knocked on his bedroom door. It was Zeenat, dressed in a t-shirt and pants, and with a question about the day's shoot. He told Zee that I had just given him a great body massage because he was aching from the deer hunt on horseback. 'It's just amazing how good I feel now. Would you like Bob to give you a sample of his skill?'

'Well . . . if he doesn't mind?'

'I don't mind, Zeenat. Any particular area?'

'Just my back and hips will do. Actually I do feel a little stiff.' So I got to work on Zeenat as well. While Sanjay was talking about the day's shot with Zee, which was to be a picturization of a song between the hero and heroine, he mentioned that the previous night he had decided on the casting of the evil tantric who keeps advising Khalil, the robber. Sanjay looked at me and asked me if I would like to play that character. I asked how much work it entailed.

He said, 'At least three important scenes and climax fights. You'll be playing a through and through evil character—if you do it well, you'll be noticed by the audience, for sure.' I had to shave my head for the role and grow a full beard. I'd get a good costume and get-up, and a mention in the film's credits. Zeenat was also happy to hear this news, especially since she had enjoyed my massage.

I agreed to accept the offer and decided that I would start to learn Hindi as soon as we were back in Bombay. One of the direction assistants, Qadir Roomi, would teach me how to read and write Hindi. I would be given the dialogues well in advance, but my scenes would only be shot at the end of 1978. Sanjay also said, 'From now on, when Zeenat feels that she needs a massage, it's one of Bob's jobs to oblige and I don't think that he'll ever refuse her, right Bob?'

'Absolutely.' Then we went for our breakfast which had already been served on the outside patio.

After that day's song sequence, we still had one and a half weeks more of shooting in the desert near Jaisalmer before returning to Bombay via New Delhi. But the tourist bungalow was booked out by Italian tourists. We were accommodated in tents by the Border Security Force (BSF) and every night we drank Old Monk rum with their officers. The tents were erected outside an old fort near the Pakistan border, about 125 kilometres from Jaisalmer.

One morning, when it was time to get ready and start moving towards our shooting location, Zeenat screamed from inside her tent. I went to have a look and she pointed at her sleeping bag. I inquired, 'Yes?' and she lifted the top of it up. Underneath were two scorpions moving slowly back and forth, wriggling their stingers. Those scorpions must have felt cold and looked for warmth—at night the weather was quite cool—which they had found beneath Zeenat's sleeping bag which she had kept warm all through the night. Good thing that she hadn't put her hand underneath the sleeping bag in her sleep.

One evening I went with Sanjay, Zeenat and some others to have dinner at the Jaisalmer tourist bungalow. At the same time a group of Italian tourists arrived at the place. They sat down and ordered dinner and started asking me questions about Jaisalmer—what was interesting to see and whether it was safe to walk around at night time. 'After dinner we want to go for a walk through the town. Can you come with us for one or two hours, because we are afraid of tigers? Are there many tigers and also snakes?' they asked.

I teased them a little, saying tigers had been here for dinner, but they had just left, they were lucky. I joked to one of the pretty Italian girls, 'Otherwise they might have chosen you for the dessert.' Then I explained to them that you'd only find tigers in the jungle. 'Jaisalmer is in the desert—the Thar Desert. It's quite a peaceful area but before you go to sleep just lift up your blankets and check the beds for scorpions—and don't cross the Pakistan border.'

We shot one more song on Sanjay on the sand dunes in the Jaisalmer area and it turned out very nice. At the end of 1978 we'd come to Rajasthan again to finish the bulk of the shooting. In Bombay there'd be a lot of work for Sanjay to do: all the editing that was waiting for him as well as the dubbing of the major artists. In India they always re-dub all the dialogues on a separate soundtrack for clarity because it's difficult to keep out outside noises during the time of the shooting. Originally it was very difficult, almost impossible, to acquire sophisticated equipment from abroad. Today, of course, the whole scenario has changed tremendously, and the film industry has jumped ahead in tandem with the country's economic development.

Most of the unit were leaving over two days. Sanjay and I were travelling to Delhi to stay for two or three days at a friend's place before continuing to Bombay. In Delhi we first went to the barber in one of the five-star hotels to change our looks to a more civilized one; I had allowed my hair to grow wild in Rajasthan. Then we visited Sanjay's friend Vinod Chopra and his family, with whom we had lunch. Vinod worked for Air India and knew a lot of politicians and important people in Delhi. While in Delhi I bought a pair of leather gloves for Sanjay for his birthday which had been on 3 January; I hadn't found anything suitable during our work in the wilderness. We also had a look at the Red Fort. The next evening we accepted a party invitation and left from there at about 1 a.m. I've noticed one thing in India, mainly in the cities: whenever you're invited to a party or to most other meetings, you are not expected to arrive dead on time. You shouldn't come earlier than an hour late! Don't leave earlier than expected; only after dinner, otherwise it will be seen as a lack of respect, and the party will get the reputation that it was unsuccessful because it finished too early. If you ask somebody why everybody is late, the answer always is: 'Indian time'.

1978: A Love Story

The next day we took the morning flight to Bombay. The car was waiting for us outside the arrival terminal. Sanjay offered to put me up at his place in Juhu for the time being. He had enough rooms, he said. Sanjay asked me if I did any exercises in the morning. I replied, 'If I am living so close to the beach, I'll jog for half an hour plus. Why don't you join me?' In the morning he was ready and we jogged and walked along Juhu beach. The water looked a little dirty but I was told the Indian Ocean was very muddy in this region. I will definitely look for a flat around this area, I decided. I'd have to check if there were any windsurfers for sale. After our walk, jog and breakfast, we went towards the city to the Bombay Lab where Sanjay normally went for his film editing. All the portions that had been filmed during our two months in Rajasthan had to be edited and checked for their quality.

This was a time for lots of parties. There used to be so many people and so many introductions. Nobody would refuse an invitation to the glamorous Hindi film industry. Sanjay took me everywhere and I learned a lot about him and from him. When we went into town together and he took me to friends or other producers, he would introduce me as his secretary. He was a wonderful person, a self-made man and a well-read man. You could talk to him about anything and everything under the sun or the moon and he wouldn't let you down, especially if the topic was history-oriented—ancient, medieval or modern, including mythology. He is a history buff. He is also always ready for a good joke at the right time, but if you rubbed him the wrong way, you'd meet a man who has difficulty keeping his temper under control.

I found another place—one large room and a bathroom—near Sanjay's. So we still went to the beach together for jogging most mornings, before breakfast. For two or three days, we noticed a lady sauntering along the beach at leisure; she was slim, petite, and looked intelligent and appealing. One day she crossed our path and she smiled. We wished her good morning and had a small conversation. She seemed to live close by and was very friendly.

The next day I jogged on my own; Sanjay had an early meeting at his house. The lady was on the beach again, so we conversed and walked together. She pointed to the first building from the beach and indicated that she lived on the ground floor; no doubt a very pleasant spot. The lady's name was Nargis and she was a Parsi as well. She said that she was married but was getting divorced because her husband had lost a fortune due to Indira Gandhi's Emergency, which had come to an end the year before.

Her father in-law had committed suicide, the mother in-law had also died and the bank had foreclosed a huge loan. Her husband had taken to drinking and beating up Nargis regularly when he was drunk. Before we parted company, we decided to meet again the next day.

When I told Sanjay about it the next day, he said, 'You go and meet her after we go for a little jog.' So I met Nargis near her house and we walked to the end of the beach and sat in the sand. Then Nargis said softly, 'It was wonderful to meet you, Bob.'

I asked, 'Why?'

She replied, 'Well, you see, suddenly I am in a good mood. Normally my mood is so bad in the morning.' At that moment we looked at one another for a while, and then I kissed her tenderly.

On the way back Nargis asked me to come and have a look inside the house. So we went into the building through a gate that opened out on to the beach. As I entered the house I saw a grey-haired man who disappeared through another door; that must have been her husband. I thought his hair had turned grey very fast after his bad luck! It was a large apartment with a beautiful view of the beach and the open sea. Nargis served me a cup of tea and asked when I could see her again. I didn't know because I was supposed to go out early the next day with Sanjay, so I said, 'As soon as I'm free, I'll come to the beach in the morning.'

When I came home to my place the next day, my landlady had a letter in her hand. She told me that a woman had come yesterday evening requesting her to give it to me. It was from Nargis and it was handwritten in a nice tidy script.

Dear Bob,

My husband is leaving tomorrow, then I will be alone with my twelve-year-old son Sunil. It would be nice if you like the house and would like to share it with me. It is like a proper home for you with music and potted plants and a lot of fresh air, and the sound of the waves on the shore will put you to sleep at night. Think about it, have another look at it and tell me as soon as you can.

Warm regards,
Nargis

I went across to Nargis's building which was named Casa Cama, after her maiden name and the surname of her father, Dara Cama, who had built all the six floors plus the ground floor. Her father had actually built it for his children—a son and two daughters. When it was at the stage of occupancy, only Nargis was willing to move in. The others found it too far away from 'town' and too quiet at night. The other flats were sold to acquaintances, who were all Parsis. Nargis was very happy with the place, and for me it was exactly what I was looking for.

I met Nargis before she left for her factory. She was using her father's factory for manufacturing knitwear ladies' garments for export to Europe and the USA. She did quite well, but it was tough for her to start because she had never done anything like that, yet she had no choice because her husband and his family were ruined. She had to do it for survival. She succeeded even though it was very stressful for her and often caused her to become 'highly strung'. I don't know if my arrival on the scene turned out to be a calming factor or if it added to her stress. Thinking about it now, I would declare that it balanced itself out.

I had another look at the whole house. There was a private driveway leading to Casa Cama. A watchman was usually there to open and close the main gate. On the sides of the compound were a lot of plants—looked after by a skilled gardener judging by the healthy appearance of all the greenery and flowers—and enough space for parking. On the beach side was a lockable door. The whole ground floor was one flat with two bedrooms, two bathrooms, a big hall/dining room, a large kitchen and servant quarters, and a big terrace lined with many plants and little fig trees and with a great view of the beach. On the rooftop was another terrace which could be used for entertainment or exercising.

I really liked the place. I mentioned that the flat seemed more like a cosy cottage than anything else. And looking at the proud owner of this 'beachside cottage', I felt like moving in straightaway. Nargis was attractively small and dainty with a pretty face, a slightly hooked nose and sensuous lips. She wore her hair relatively long when I met her. Some years later it would become shorter, matching her temper. I asked her how much she was expecting as rent and whether she had had any good offers already. She said, 'That can wait. You can move in whenever you want; about the rent we can talk later.' I asked her if I could move in the next morning. She agreed readily and told me to come early enough so she could show me everything in the house before she went to work. I also requested her to give me her code of rules and behaviour and the type of chastisement in case of any disregard. She just laughed and we hugged each other, and as I left I thought to myself that she had a good sense of humour; that was very important. And the place was a marvel.

I went to Sanjay's place and reported my story of Nargis and Casa Cama. They said, 'That's wonderful. You seem to meet all the Parsis in Bombay in such a short time!' I agreed that I was happy moving into that 'beach resort' and that Nargis was a nice and intelligent woman. On the evening of getting my new address, we had a housewarming dinner in town, just Nargis and I. Sunil was old enough to stay back alone.

154

Learning the Ropes

The next few days I accompanied Sanjay while he was doing his work at the editing laboratory and meeting marketing people regarding the sale of his film. Over the next few weeks I met a lot of the local actors like Amjad Khan, Feroz Khan, Jeetendra, Dharmendra, Manoj Kumar, Ranjeet and a lot of female stars as well.

I also got in touch with Qadir Roomi to make him come to Casa Cama every morning at 8 a.m., six days a week, to teach me Hindi. That was fun; even Nargis enjoyed watching me studying the national language. She sometimes helped me out, answering some of my questions that Qadir didn't have an explanation for. Actually I found Hindi fairly easy, especially pronouncing words once they were written down for me. It became important for my later films when I was given dialogues written in Hindi; the pronunciation had to be correct. Hindi is in a way a dangerous language, because if you pronounce certain letters or idioms the wrong way, it could mean something different, sometimes vulgar, which could cause unnecessary embarrassment.

As soon as I started taking tuitions in Hindi I tried to translate everything I could see written in Hindi script: articles in Hindi newspapers, signs over shop windows, the Hindi subtitles on the English news. It was a little too early, though. Either the subtitles were too quick or I was too slow! Anyway, I'd only just started and I was sure that if I gave it another year I would pick up the language, provided I continued with the same fervour with which I had started. In any case, I had an entire year to memorize my dialogues.

One morning Qadir brought me a sheet of dialogues for my role in *Abdullah*. That reminds me of a story of an actor who was out of work and nearly starving because, although undoubtedly a fine actor, he suffered from a problem: he couldn't remember a single line. In desperation he visited his agent and begged him for a part. 'For you, my son, I have the ideal part,' said the agent. 'You will be dressed up in Elizabethan gear and all you have to do is walk on stage, raise this rose delicately by two fingers to your face and say, "Ah, the sweet fragrance of my mistress." Surely you can remember that?' For the next three weeks the actor spent every waking hour rehearsing the line. Finally, it was opening night and, dressed in costume, the actor paced up and down nervously until his entrance. Then his great moment came and he walked to the front of the stage and said in his clearest voice, 'Ah, the sweet fragrance of my mistress.' His feelings of relief at getting his line right, however, were short-lived, because pandemonium broke out in the audience. The curtain came down amid the din and the stage manager came on behind the curtains and shouted at the actor, 'Do you want to get me arrested?' 'But I didn't forget my lines,' replied the bewildered actor. 'No!' said the manager, 'you forgot the rose!' Resolving not to suffer a similar fate, I worked hard at rehearsing my lines!

Sanjay had been taking me to so many meetings within the film industry that I had been well introduced, and a lot of people had started recognizing me and sometimes added my name to Sanjay's invitations as well, although normally he would have asked me to join him anyway. But occasionally I wanted to do my own thing, like go to one of Bombay's discos, which was not only a pleasure for me but also a great way to get a good physical workout, because on the dance floor with the right music I really worked up a solid sweat.

Not long after we got back from Rajasthan we took a trip in Sanjay's Mercedes to Mahabaleshwar where his brother Feroz Khan was shooting for his own film, *Qurbani*. That was also interesting and during our stay there Feroz promised me a small role. His film had the same heroine as Sanjay's *Abdullah*, Zeenat, and it was supposed to be released in 1980. While we were there, Feroz was shooting a song sequence on a lake near Mahabaleshwar with himself and his heroine. Mahabaleshwar is a hill station, meaning that it is nice and cool during the summer months. So during May there are a lot of local tourists relaxing during the holidays. There are excellent trekking paths that take you up and down the mountains to picturesque and cool waterfalls. We spent three days there with Feroz and Zeenat and the shooting unit, and we enjoyed the cuisine of some of the popular restaurants. It's also a good area for hunting wild boar. We saw quite a few running out of the bushes at night but we didn't go on shikaar; in any case I had already decided not to kill animals any more.

Sanjay and I returned to Bombay and continued with editing and other work for his film. We were also shooting for another *Abdullah* song in RK Studios. The remaining film shooting work would be done in Rajasthan from November onwards. When Zeenat returned from her shooting in Mahabaleshwar, she took Sanjay and me to a preview show of her film *Don* with Amitabh Bachchan, who had also been in *Sholay*, a superhit which I had seen earlier. I had also seen *Amar, Akbar, Anthony*, which featured Parveen Babi. That was the first time I had seen Parveen Babi in action. I immediately liked Amitabh as a hero; he struck me as very sympathetic. I felt that these three films were the beginning of the Amitabh Bachchan era and I realized instinctively that Amitabh was or would be the top star of Indian cinema.

War Memories

Around this time I received a letter from Karin and three letters from my children: Cliff, Monique and Nicole. I hadn't seen them in four years—a long period of time for growing children. They were thrilled to receive mail from me from India. My daughter Monique asked me in her letter, 'Are you an Indian now, with feathers on your head and your skin painted?' They were all living in Santa Rosa, California, and they must have seen a lot of movies about Red Indians. Anyway, since I had a few months before we continued shooting in Rajasthan, I decided to ask Sanjay if it was OK for me to travel to the USA to visit my children. I had to check that they were fine and going to good schools, and that Bob and Karin were not tired of them yet. Sanjay said it was fine for me to go, but urged me to be back after six weeks, for he wanted me to generate some popularity while he was trying to work on my film career. I thanked him and got my tickets done immediately. Nargis was slightly upset since I'd only recently moved into her apartment, but she understood, since I hadn't seen and heard much of my kids and missed them sorely.

I chose to stop over in Germany to visit my mother and then continue from Frankfurt to San Francisco via New York. From San Francisco I booked onwards to Hawaii, Tokyo, Hong Kong and Bangkok and then the return to Bombay.

Within four days, I was in the air. Next morning I arrived in Frankfurt and was met at arrivals by an old friend, Mike. He had come with his wife and they drove me to my mother's place about eighty kilometres away, a one-hour drive. My mother was so happy to see me after so many years; but even if one hasn't seen loved ones for only one or two years, it may seem a much longer time. My mother had prepared a nice breakfast for me with eggs and bacon and some fruit and German bread rolls, plus tasty pastries and cheesecake. We sat together for a long while chatting, until I was defeated by weariness and had to get a few hours' sleep. In the evening we chatted again over a few glasses of wine.

I was also determined to visit my Aunt Else, with whom I had stayed as a child in the forties during the World War. She had been staying for the past two or three years in an old-age home, after getting permission from the East German government to live for the rest of her life in the West; they had acquiesced because she was retired and had become useless for the East German communist system. She lived in the historical city of Heidelberg, a very pleasant old university town by the river Neckar and close to a very popular mountain area called Odenwald. I knew she would be thrilled to reminisce about all the adventures she went through with me at the end of the War.

I was born in Sydney, Australia, in 1938, a year before World War II began. In 1943, my father took me to eastern Germany so I could stay with his mother and sister who had not seen me since I was born. My father didn't realize how bad the war was in Germany due to Hitler's endless propaganda that Germany would soon win the war and everything would be well. Meanwhile, the Japanese had started to infiltrate northern Australia with their mini-submarines and the general fear was that Australia was going to be taken over by the Japanese. This was a great miscalculation because the USA was ready to save Australia. So I should have stayed in my birthplace, but instead I spent the next two years in Germany till the end of the war.

At the time, my aunt lived in a village called Zeithain in the countryside outside Dresden. She was the principal of a primary school, and her school was still open, while in West Germany schools had been made to close down because of the heavy bombings in the years between 1943 and 1945. My father had taken me by train from West Germany to Dresden. On the way I had been surprised to see whole townships destroyed and in ruins, like after a heavy earthquake, all from Allied bomb attacks. In Dresden my aunt and my grandmother (on my father's side) entered our train and welcomed and kissed me; I was only five years old and quite timid, because it was the first time in my life that I had met them. My father stayed with me in my aunt's house for a few days and then rushed back to Australia to look after the rest of the family.

My aunt and grandmother were such lovely and kind people that I became very attached to them. I stayed with them for two years and learned to read and write, and basic arithmetic. However, the school where my aunt was principal did not stay open for very long; it was also closed down after six months, because the bombing attacks by air intensified soon after my arrival and it became as bad as in West Germany, if not worse. For example, I remember one whole night of terrible attacks on Dresden by thousands of Allied aircraft. The entire city was obliterated. My aunt and grandmother had taken me to the zoo in Dresden on that day to give me a treat. I had had so much fun. In the night, looking out of the air-raid shelter, I could see elephants running past, trumpeting in misery because they were getting burnt from the fire of the bombs; they ran into the river Elbe nearby to douse the fire on their bodies, but a lot of the animals in the zoo must have died a horrible death.

The next day when we walked to the railway station we could see workers brick up whole streets full of dead bodies. The railway station had been destroyed also and it was difficult to get a train to take us to Riesa and further to Zeithain. We had to keep waiting for different trains because a lot of the tracks were bombed out of place. For a trip that usually took us two hours one way, we needed more than a whole day on the return trip. My grandmother had been totally distraught and I had felt so sorry for her.

When we were back in our village, there were a lot more attacks than earlier, because there was no defence by the Germans who were in other areas. Even in our small village we had to go down into the air-raid shelter and stay there for as long as one hour at a time.

About two months after we came back from Dresden, my grandmother fell ill. She started to suffer from some nerve problem around her hip area. It gave her a lot of pain and she had to lie down in bed most of the time and my aunt had to apply bandages on her hip and give her medicine. Since my aunt didn't work in her school any more, she had started to work in the army hospital in our village. A lot of wounded soldiers were transported there from the war front. Sometimes some of the soldiers she was looking after came to our house to thank her after they were discharged from hospital. They would usually bring some chocolate for me as a present. Once an ex-soldier from the hospital came offering my Aunt Else marriage. He wanted to take her to the West, but she declined because she had to look after her sick mother.

Finally, the Russian army made a breakthrough across the German border and people started fleeing from the border areas and crossing the river Elbe. After hesitating for one or two days we also joined the long line of refugees. We used a cart on which we sat grandmother and our luggage. Aunt Else pulled it along together with her cycle and I walked behind and was pushing. Suddenly, I heard a noise like some kind of shots. I looked around and saw a German soldier aim with his rifle at people who were trying to get away before the Russians arrived. I told my aunt, 'Look, that soldier is shooting at us.' Then there was a commotion and some other soldiers disarmed him, explaining that he was drunk. After some time we crossed the river on a large makeshift pontoon bridge and continued walking to the next town, assembling at the marketplace where a woman told us that we could stay with them in their house because, she said, we had a sick old woman and a small child. I asked, 'Where is the small child?' and my aunt replied, 'They mean you!' I retorted, 'I am not a small child, I am a General!' I often used to play war games.

We stayed with that family for two or three days and then there was a radio transmission from a man with a loud voice and everybody shouted, 'Der Führer, der Führer.' It was Adolf Hitler addressing the German people and exhorting them not to worry, they would win the war in the next few days. Everybody seemed to be happy after that.

We packed our luggage cart and started to walk back to see if our house was still standing or if it had been destroyed. We were a long way from Zeithain and our house. We walked the whole day and then also during the night. There were masses of people walking and many seemed to have lost members of their families, because fathers and mothers and children were calling out names continuously, but in the dark it was difficult to identify anyone properly. There were big fires from burning houses and tanks, and soldiers running with bazookas. Then there were a lot of explosions and sounds of cannons shooting in the distance; it was really frightening and I could imagine how terrible it was for children to lose the members of their families in that hell-like chaos. I was scared that I would also get lost. So I clung to our cart, while making sure that my aunt would not fall down and my grandmother was comfortable. Soon after, we were informed by some kind locals that we were on the wrong road; they showed us the proper route and directed us to the right approach to Zeithain.

After the sun rose, my aunt mentioned that we were very close to Zeithain. Soon I began to recognize the area and ran ahead until I could see our house in the distance. I couldn't see anything wrong with it; only when we were inside did we notice that it was quite dirty; there were chicken bones lying all over the place and somebody had shat on the floor and in one of the beds. They probably didn't know what the toilets were there for; our neighbour commented that Russians didn't have toilets. Anyway, all the Russians had left our house; we only had to clean it up again.

We were still not sure if the war was over or not. Hitler didn't know himself. At the time he must have been insane. When our house was clean again and the news came that the war was really over and Germany had been divided into four zones which were occupied by the US, British, French and Russian military forces, my aunt told my grandmother that she had to take me back to my parents who were waiting for me in West Germany, which was then occupied by the American forces. That would require quite a bit of paperwork. But in the meantime the Russians returned to confiscate our house again, to be occupied by two officers for an indefinite period. We had to stay with friends who had a farm and a flour mill and a lot of pigs in the neighbouring village. I was happy, because there was always something interesting to do—like riding on the pigs on a filthy, muddy ground. The people who had to wash my clothes were not so happy.

At that time I started to learn Russian. My aunt gave me a vocabulary book. There were so many Russians now that I could practise on them; the only thing was that they never understood what I was saying! I also had a girlfriend; she was the daughter of our friends, one or two years older than I, but she always wanted to play doctor with me and examine my private parts, which I didn't like at all.

After some time most of the Russians were withdrawn from our area and my grandmother could move back to sleep in her own bed, after having it thoroughly cleansed. My aunt came to the conclusion that it would be too much trouble to get an official permit to cross three zones and get into a fourth one; in the East Zone they were very bureaucratic. So she decided to take me across to my parents without papers, but with lies and her nephew's sweet smile; and that's what we did.

'It's so nice to see you, Aunt Else, and talk about the old days in Zeithain,' I said now, as we sat chatting in the old-age home.

'Yes,' she said. Thinking back, she continued, 'Some years after the war your grandmother died.'

'And you never got married at all . . .'

'No, what was the point? After the war I used to look after grandmother. That person I met at the army hospital asked me again to tie the knot with him and live with him in northern Germany, Hamburg, but by then I didn't want to get married at all; my eyes had started to become weak. Now I can hardly see. If I want to see your face, I have to bring my face very close to yours, about two or three inches away. Officially I am blind, that's why I have to walk with a white stick. Most of the time I stay here in the old-age home; people are nice and I get visitors. Now, let me get you another cup of coffee and some more of the cake.'

Slicing another piece of cake, she continued, 'When your father brought you, he took just about one day, but when we went back, we took seven days and we never knew where we would find a bed to sleep or where we would get something good to eat. There were no regular trains; most railway lines were damaged. We had to walk a lot, and often we had to travel small distances by goods trains. These goods trains were usually full of other travellers who had to find their own families in different parts of Germany. Whenever we were in the countryside we would go to some farm, because there I was able to get milk for you and sometimes some sausage to keep you strong. Often, when we had to cross a zone border without being stopped, we walked through the night and you were so tired afterwards that you fell asleep the moment you sat down somewhere!'

I recalled that one night my aunt asked in a small hospital if they had two beds free and if we could sleep there until morning. The lady gave us two beds but I chose to sleep in my aunt's bed because I was a little scared. In the morning my aunt noticed that

I had wet the bed and she felt embarrassed that the hospital lady might think that it was she who had peed in her bed! So she wanted to leave quickly, but the hospital lady insisted that I drink a glass of milk first. In general I found that people were very nice with us. I suppose they all were happy that the war was over, and they must have felt that it was very difficult to travel, especially with a child, when nothing was functioning properly anywhere in the divided country right after such a dreadful war.

Near the American Zone border we were stopped by the military police. They wanted to see my aunt's ID. She showed them her pass which was from Zeithain in German language, but they wanted to see a special pass written in English. We had to sit in a little office until a German-speaking person came and translated for them that my aunt was taking me to my parents, who were waiting for me near Frankfurt. Eventually, they let us proceed and gave us some kind of No Objection Certificate which we were to show anybody who stopped us.

I was finally reunited with my father who had come to pick me up. Soon after, he took me back to Australia; I enjoyed the long journey home by ship. I continued my education in Australia for a few years. In Germany my aunt, being a teacher, had ensured that my education continued, even with the schools closed.

Around 1950 my father, who was a cook by profession, lost his life during a mountain-climbing accident in the Alps. After that my mother took me back to Germany with my two brothers, Mike and Helmut. I went through my high school education there for the next four years.

During this time I managed to get a well-paid job as an extra in the Düsseldorf National Theatre. I worked every evening, rehearsing and performing. In 1954 I was selected from the theatre by the German movie director Bernhard Wicki to work in a German film. This was my first film and I learned a lot during the shooting in and around Düsseldorf. I don't remember the title; the subject was about the youth of the day. I have not seen the movie—just some of the rushes.

I later returned to Australia to study civil engineering in East Sydney College. During my four years of working with the Düsseldorf National Theatre, I had become very friendly with a German girl by the name of Helga. She had also been selected for the movie with Bernhard Wicki and had become the director's favourite. She followed me to Sydney about two years after I'd left Germany and we got married in 1958. A year later I graduated and our first child, Clifford, or Cliff as we usually called him, was born in 1961.

My aunt was so elated to talk about all these long-past days with me that tears ran down her cheeks. I invited her for lunch to one of the nice Heidelberg restaurants and when we returned, she took me to see the beautiful garden that was part of the old-age home and the brand-new piano in the hall where the members of the home had regular musical evenings. I sat down and played some of my jazz tunes for her, which she seemed to enjoy thoroughly. After that I would always drop in to see her whenever I went to Germany. She died at the age of eighty-nine almost twenty years ago at the same old-age home in Heidelberg.

After that memorable day-long visit, I remained for another three days in my mother's place before I took the Lufthansa flight to New York and then, the next day, another flight to San Francisco. My three children were waiting for me at the airport with Karin, their foster mother. They were very excited. Cliff was already sixteen, Monique, ten and Nici, seven. I spent ten days with them in their place in Santa Rosa and took them for walks to different beaches, to the famous redwood forest with the huge 1000-year-old trees, to the roller-skating and ice-skating arenas and to nice restaurants in Chinatown. Every day we ensured our day was full. We also went to Napa Valley for wine tasting. I sent a case of wine to Bombay for Sanjay and his wife, for which the winery printed labels and fixed them on the twelve bottles: 'Specially grown at Napa Valley for the wine cellar of Mr and Mrs Sanjay Khan, Bombay'.

After the ten days were over the whole gang accompanied me to the airport. Then Monique insisted that she would come with me. 'Nonsense, you can't go with your father just like that without preparations! A trip like this needs to be planned,' said Karin. Monique started crying and threw a tantrum. After I talked to her and promised her that she could come to Bombay and stay for a few months when the time was right, she calmed down and I could leave.

A few hours later I landed in Honolulu and took a taxi to Waikiki Beach, where I booked into a hotel. I spent five lovely days in Hawaii bodysurfing and windsurfing. Two out of the five days were spent at Hookipa beach on Maui Island where you can see waves fifty feet high. It was just amazing. Every morning and evening PR staff from hotels would welcome me and offer me passes for a free breakfast, lunch or dinner at their hotels, so as to fill up their dining areas and coffee shops at the beginning of the season. In those five days I spent hardly any money for food! In the evenings most of the hotels had great Hawaiian barbecues. I improved my windsurfing skills and returned to India with an unbelievable suntan.

I stayed over in Tokyo for two days to do some shopping and then I stopped over in Hong Kong for three days. I called Jimmy Shaw and we spent every day together exchanging accounts of the previous few years of our lives. He was doing very well working as the Kai Tak Airport food and beverage manager and had made a fortune. He said he'd invested his money with Merrill Lynch and probably wouldn't have to look for another job for the rest of his life. He promised to visit me in Bombay, perhaps the next year or in 1980.

From Hong Kong I flew directly back to Bombay. I didn't feel like making another stop in Bangkok. Nargis was ecstatic that I had returned before the six weeks were over and invited me the next day for lunch at the Polynesian buffet lounge in the basement of the Oberoi, which was in those days my favourite.

Scene 1, Take 1 . . .

The next day I met Sanjay and Zarine. Sanjay was satisfied that I was already back in Bombay. One of the first things he told me to do was to have my head shaved and try my costume for the *Abdullah* role. When Zeenat Aman saw me with my new hairstyle, she shuddered and exclaimed, 'Oh Bob, you're looking so evil!'

I said, 'I know, perfect for my role in *Abdullah*!' Others thought that my bald pate suited me very well and that it would be an advantage for my new career. With my new look, and particularly after we were involved in a road-rage fight with some boisterous motorbike goons, the press used to portray me as Sanjay's bodyguard.

Sanjay showed me the rushes of the film, whatever had been edited. I was looking forward to the end product of *Abdullah*, which was slated for the next year, but there was still much camerawork to be done and he had to strike a good deal with film distributors for the sale of the film in all the territories. He had also made some changes in the script. George Marzbetuny has written the original script in English with Abdullah being a Muslim character but the child Krishna being a Christian. Even if the changes were for the benefit of the movie, everything had to be rechecked to see that the new script would be in everyone's interest, most of all in Sanjay's with regard to the box office. I too was keen on its box-office success as it would help my new career. Once the film was ready for release we would invite George for the premiere and give him a copy with English subtitles.

By the end of October 1978 everything was ready to continue shooting in various areas of Rajasthan like Bikaner, Jaipur, Jodhpur and Jaisalmer and in the sand dunes of the Thar Desert. Till now, Nargis and I had been quite happy together but sometimes my flirtatious nature caused her occasional fits of jealousy that resulted in a few days of a subdued and reserved atmosphere. Now, of course, I couldn't help but stay away from my new home for two to three months, but I knew Nargis would make sure that I got plenty of her exceptional letters that hopefully would prevent me from falling victim to bouts of serious homesickness! Before leaving for Rajasthan, I requested Nargis to manufacture fifty *Abdullah* T-shirts with some scene prints on it. Nargis did them beautifully and Sanjay appreciated the gesture.

As soon as the shooting started, some of my shots with dialogues were taken. I was thrilled; I remembered all my dialogues. One dialogue I still remember partly after all these years: 'Accha hua tum aa gaye Khalil, ek bahut burri khabar hai tumhare liye, tumhari barbadi aur maut, ek bache ki wajah se; hason mat, meri baat suno . . .' (Good that you're here Khalil, I have some very bad news for you, your ruin and death, all because of a child; don't laugh, listen to me). My tutor congratulated me and told me that my Hindi sounded good and when we returned to Bombay in January 1979, he'd start to teach me Urdu. Qadir was a Muslim and all Muslims learn Urdu from childhood. The script is written and read from right to left. Hindi is from left to right, like most other languages.

Later on we did a trial run with our horses. For the dacoit scenes we were using about twenty horses and galloping across barren land. There were no trees or bushes, only stones and some leftover wooden sticks. I'm a good horse rider, but I wasn't paying attention. In my path there was a trunk from a chopped young tree, only about three or four feet high, which I didn't take any notice of. I trusted the horse. But my horse wanted to get rid of me—I hadn't realized that Indian horses were so smart! He galloped an inch away from the broken-off tree trunk. It hit me on my shin and lifted me out of the saddle and on to the ground. I scrambled back to my feet and had a look at my leg. The shin was badly scraped down to the bone and bruised. And the horse didn't even stop to say sorry! From behind the camera Sanjay saw me go down. He stopped the shoot and told me to take it easy. In the evening in our tourist bungalow, he called the unit doctor to treat and bandage my wound because it was pretty bad and swollen. I still have a scar from that incident. Somehow I have a feeling that the horse didn't like me. Maybe it resented my weight and wanted to teach me a lesson, not to eat too much in the future! But I appreciated the way Sanjay and the unit members looked after me after that mishap.

In the evening Brigadier Fardoon Billimoria came for a visit. I remembered him from the previous year. He had been stationed in the Rajasthan area with his battalions and had become friendly with us when we were shooting in the vicinity. We often met him in Bombay as well, because his brother lived in Malabar Hill. Fardoon was a typically British-type army officer, exuberant and buoyant; he and his wife were Parsis.

We had one more military connection who was very helpful during our *Abdullah* filming: Ashwini Kumar. He was a general of the Border Security Force. He allowed us to use a very important part of their headquarters near the Pakistan border as a climax location. We also used some of their manpower, including their extra weapons. The predominant part of the BSF soldiers and officers were Sikhs.

When they stand side by side for their morning roll call and you walk along in front of them looking at their name plates, you'll find that everybody is a Singh—A. Singh, B. Singh, C. Singh etcetera, all wearing a military turban with their uniform.

From the time we had started shooting again at the end of 1978, I'd been using the camels a lot to ride around in the desert. My favourite camel was Abdullah's camel Selma. Whenever I sat down in the sand to relax, Selma would stand next to me and lick my bald head. It must have enjoyed the salty taste of my sweat! Those camels used to make awfully funny gurgling noises which I enjoyed imitating.

One of the scenes in the movie had Abdullah searching for Krishna. When Abdullah finds the dead body of a boy, he believes it to be Krishna's. He approaches his tent and sees Selma standing next to his well. Suddenly Selma collapses and dies, adding to Abdullah's woes. It took some time for Sanjay and his cinematographer to manage that shot with the camel. We had called a veterinary surgeon to give the camel an injection to make him fall asleep. That injection had to be given ten minutes before the camel was to fall. It was to coincide with the sun disappearing behind the horizon for the camera. The first time the camel did not fall at the right moment, so we had to try again the next day at about the same time and on that day the camel fell too early. Only on the third day did the camel fall on time, as the sun sank behind the horizon right in front of the desperate Abdullah who thinks that not only is Krishna gone, but his camel has also breathed its last. But meanwhile Krishna, who is lost, has found the right track leading to Abdullah's tent. He sees Abdullah sitting on a stool in front of the well and shouts, 'Papa, Papa, Papa,' and starts running to him. Abdullah, who has already resigned himself to his fate and is ready to die, opens his eyes and can't believe that it's truly Krishna who is running towards him.

Abdullah rises from his stool to meet his beloved boy in a happy, grateful embrace.

After that scene, we had to shoot the beginning of the film's climax. We were not able to finish the total programme; the balance would be taken at a later date. Again we celebrated Christmas in Rajasthan with Raj Kapoor, Zeenat Aman and the rest of our unit. Only this time we did not shoot any deer. We reduced our non-vegetarian menu to chicken and mutton. But we did a lot of singing. I used my guitar and sang a song for Rajji which he did not know yet, but he liked it so much that he requested me to sing it for him again and again till about 3 a.m. The song was *The windmills of your mind* from the sixties film about a clever bank robbery, *The Thomas Crown Affair* with Steve McQueen. It has brilliant lyrics and until today that's still one of my favourite songs.

After wrapping up the schedule, we stopped over in Delhi for a few days before returning to Bombay. It was nice to come back to Casa Cama and walk on the beach and go swimming. When Nargis saw me, she noticed that I had put on quite a bit of weight. I hadn't realized it myself, but she was right. I usually weigh around eighty-seven kilograms but I was about ninety-three kilograms when I returned!

High Society

I spent a lot of time with Sanjay and his editors in the Bombay Lab. That was also interesting. In the evenings Sanjay and Zarine did a great deal of entertaining. They also went out to friends' places. That's how I met the Godrej family, Adi and Parmeshwar Godrej. Adi's was the largest privately owned factory in India, manufacturing refrigerators, locks, washing powders, soft drinks and many other goods. Adi is Parsi and his wife Parmesh, Punjabi. She loved company and parties and together they were on top of the social ladder. Anybody with an interesting background who had been featuring in the media and had come from abroad would be invited to ensure a great turnout at the Godrej's. Some Hollywood stars like Richard Gere, Goldie Hawn and Sally Field were regulars on their guest list, along with the top stars of Bollywood and the top cricketers.

In the beginning of my stay in India, I was invited many times and I used to enjoy myself. Quite often I met Amitabh there and had several interesting conversations with him on some of these occasions. I was always happy to talk about water sports, particularly in the earlier years when Amitabh's brother Ajitabh used to come with his wife Ramola and their children would be jumping about in the pool. Amit was not much of a water-sports man but he always wanted to know whether his brother's children and of course his own kids, Abhishek and Shweta, were waterskiing already; I used to teach them occasionally when we met at Adi's place or at the beach. Amit was a pleasant person with a great sense of humour and good to talk to. He always wanted to find out the real reason behind my visit to India. He made it sound as though my appearance here had some mysterious background; I think he asked me once if I had anything to do with the CIA. Of course it was all in jest. On my part, I was hoping he'd give me some tips that could help me transform myself into a worthwhile actor, because I regarded Amit as a phenomenal thespian.

Eventually, I started declining these social invitations, so I didn't meet Amitabh as much, though I saw him often enough during film shootings or on flights to or from film locations. My association with Adi Godrej concentrated on water-sports activities. Adi and I discussed sailing, waterskiing, windsurfing, jet-skiing and parasailing in which he was very interested and together we would go out every weekend with our latest gadgets. Adi built a speedboat in his factory and every few years he would update his equipment and we really used to have a wonderful time together, sailing from Juhu beach and all the way down to Chowpatty at 'Queen's Necklace', often with the Godrej children: Tania, who's been married for years now, and Babu and Nisa.

I taught many of the high-society children swimming, including Sanjay's children. I taught Adi waterskiing and he loved it so much that he wouldn't miss a good day on the weekend to ski, parasail or windsurf or take out his sailing boat. Juhu Beach was the favourite meeting place for everybody who liked water sports, right outside our building Casa Cama. We even used to have official windsurfing regattas along Juhu beach. Now Adi has all his equipment and his boats at Walkeshwar beach in the city and I am in Bangalore. So we don't see each other much now (but we sometimes do on our birthdays, because we share the same birthdate).

I had bought my windsurfer from a German sportsman who worked for a company in Bombay. When he moved back to Germany he sold the windsurfer along with two good sails to me. I enjoyed that sport very much and I made good use of the beach being right in front of my nose. I started a windsurfing club in the Palm Grove hotel in Juhu where I also got a life membership at the gym, which was very handy, being close to my home. The Holiday Inn, Juhu, which was even closer to Casa Cama than the Palm Grove, also gave me a life membership. The owner, Ramesh Khanna, was a good friend of Sanjay and me.

Nargis was happy when I was out in the sea windsurfing. She knew that I was a good swimmer and was not worried about me when I was in the water. Sometimes people would rush up from the beach and get carried away by the strong current into the sea, and I would swim out and pull them back on to the sand. But occasionally dead bodies were also washed up on to the beach. There were not many people in Bombay who knew how to swim. And that in a city surrounded by water! In Sydney children are forced to learn if they were not able to swim by the age of seven.

One day when I came up to the house after windsurfing, Nargis showed me a car in our compound. It was an Ambassador, one of the original old-style cars which were particularly used by government officials and inland where the roads could really be rough. She asked me whether we should buy it. I tried it out and found it quite adequate. One had not much choice in those days in India, unless one could afford to import a vehicle from abroad. So we bought the Ambassador which served us well for quite a few years. It made me think of the E-type Jaguars that I had bought in Hong Kong and had repaired in Manila. I was glad that I had presented mine to Maria. Here in India it wouldn't have been good on the rough roads.

Sanjay said he wanted to buy a good car from Dubai and bring it to India by the carnet scheme. 'But then you'll have to re-export it after six months,' I pointed out. 'But maybe you'll be able to get an extension.'

Anyway, one day Sanjay told me, 'Let's go to Dubai for a few days. I would like to buy a new car and a few other things. I have friends there; they will arrange a visa for you if necessary.'

Half a dozen Arabs received us at arrivals. That was my first time in Dubai. Coming from India, it looked so clean; the streets were spick and span. We stayed with Abdul Rahim Karam and his family in Sharjah, just a few kilometres away from Dubai. Abdul Rahim had gone for a few years to college in London. Now he had a furniture factory and a beautiful country estate. In many parts of the UAE they have desalination plants where the seawater is desalinated and used; no wonder they can grow lawns in the desert! While some desalinated water is used for drinking, most of the drinking water is imported bottled.

In the UAE many domestic employees are from India. Earlier,

India was employing Arabs as servants until the oil revolution reversed the tables. Now there were many nouveau riche Arabs who kept Indian or Pakistani servants.

In the evenings arrangements were made to feed visitors, should they turn up. Our hosts were usually ready for twenty persons. Sometimes, if nobody visited, the food was just disposed of.

Abdul Rahim had invited the chief of the transport department and introduced us. We were told to go to the transport department whenever we had the car which was to be exported to India. The transport chief would then do the rest.

The next day Sanjay and I selected a new car, which he bought. Then we went to the transport department for registration. Sanjay had to fill in carnet papers and furnish a bank guarantee in order to avoid having to pay tax upon entering India. When the car went back to Dubai for re-export, the bank guarantee would be released. Over the years we bought quite a few cars by the carnet scheme. Some of them were entered in my passport for customs to know by when I had to re-export that car. One was a Mercedes, and the other a Chevrolet Camaro which we brought to India for another film, *Kaala Dhanda Goray Log* (1986), which Sanjay made after *Abdullah*; it was used for stunts and car chases.

Before returning to Bombay, we did some shopping, particularly for things that were not available in India those days, like video players and some other electronic gadgets and a big food hamper full of delicacies like cheese, meats and caviar. We also visited Abdul Elah and his family at their house. Abdul was a businessman who had a nice bungalow, and an apartment which he used as his den where he met his cronies for playing games and watching porn movies. We met him often over the years, in Dubai and in India. One day he and his friends took me for an interesting way to go fishing. Here's how it worked: everybody puts a certain amount of money in a kitty. Then the boat takes off and each person has a roll of thin nylon line with hook, sinker and bait at the end. Whenever a fish takes the bait, you start pulling and manoeuvring the line and pull up the fish. You are only allowed to pull the nylon line with your bare hands, so if you catch a big fish it would only be with great agony that you get your catch up and into your bucket in the boat. The line may cut into your skin and if you get a really big one you might draw a lot of blood. You have to have hard hands; it's not for Portuguese poets with tender hands. But by the end of the trip, whoever has caught the heaviest load of fish pockets all the money. It can be a lot a fun. In those days I was doing a lot of workouts in the gym, with many pull-ups and push-ups. My hands were like leather. But I had injured my supraspinatus tendon in the shoulder. So I was only watching; otherwise I am quite sure I would have won. On that evening we had fish biryani prepared by Abdul Elah himself, made from all the varieties of fish everyone had caught and it was so tasty that I'll never forget it as long as I live.

The day after we went to Elah's house, I went to the souk, which is an Islamic shopping centre, where I selected a smart pair of earrings for Nargis; then we were on our way back to Bombay.

Nargis looked happy when I said that I felt like staying at home for some time, relax and maybe do some cooking for her, so she could give the cook a holiday. I've always liked cooking and usually use the ingredients of the country I am staying in at the time. That's when I start experimenting with new dishes. There're so many interesting substances that can be added to meals to enhance their taste and quality like all the Indian spices, ginger and garlic paste, etcetera. I do the same when I live in Hong Kong or the Philippines or in Latin American countries.

When I gave Nargis the earrings after dinner, she tried them on and liked them. The colour matched a lot of her clothes. Then she came and wanted to measure my ring finger with some kind of gauge. She remarked that she wanted to have a ring made for me, but since I was hardly ever at home, she could not take the proper measurement of the finger's circumference to give the jeweller. The jeweller had given her a finger gauge so that I didn't have to go to him myself. After a few days the ring was ready. It had seven diamonds on top in a setting of white gold. She said my fingers were too thick to make the ring in twenty-two- or twenty-four-carat gold, so she got it made in twenty-carat gold. But when I tried it on, it was too big. I told Nargis that I would go with her so the jeweller could take the measurement of my pinkie; it would then be a little smaller which would look better. It took about a week and the ring was beautiful, though in a masculine way. Actually it looked like a knuckleduster, but I liked it.

Close Shaves

Towards the end of 1978 I also got an offer for a film by a Calcutta production. It was being shot in Bengali and in Hindi. I was to play the villain in the same get-up as in *Abdullah*, meaning bald and with beard. Danny Denzongpa was the hero with Kim as his heroine. The title was *Pehredaar*, which is 'watchman' in English. In the film, Danny is the watchman of a very valuable religious statue in a temple. I have paid a gang of bandits to steal it for me. The watchman manages to track us down after I am already in possession of the statue and it comes down to a wild chase. Most of it was also to be filmed in the Rajasthan desert. I negotiated a fair fee and accepted.

After about two months we started the shoot in Rajasthan; at the same time I was shooting more scenes for *Abdullah* there.

During the chase scene in the desert Danny tries to catch up with me. We are both on horseback and I have the statue on me with a cloth wrapped around it and tied with a rope which is attached to my arm. As Danny overtakes my horse, he grabs the rope, trying to pull the statue away from me, but I fall off the horse with the statue. I fell exactly on the right place, and the cameraman had me in his frame. It looked like sand, but it was as hard as concrete. I hadn't checked the sand before the shot, because it looked so soft and we hadn't wanted to leave footprints. But it had baked in the sun and was rock-hard. I was in real agony for a few days. I didn't say anything, but I hoped that I hadn't broken my hip bone or my spine.

I had another close shave in the same movie when we were galloping fast. I was supposed to fall again right in front of the camera. I saw the camera about twenty feet away and I let go of the horse's reins and rolled over on to my back; that position brought me under the horse and the horse's left front hoof was coming down on to my head. I couldn't avoid it. However, the horse stopped suddenly; he froze his leg in mid-air. The only thing I felt was a light touch on my forehead. Then the horse bent down its head, looked at me for a while and walked away. Afterwards I gave him a carrot. The stunt master—Shetty with his clean-shaven pate—was standing nearby and saw the whole thing. He looked at me and said, 'God is great!' Unfortunately, I had come riding towards the camera so fast that the cameraman had got scared, picked up the camera and run. So we had lost a good shot!

While shooting in Rajasthan I used to get glimpses of the most extraordinary views. The sunrises could be remarkable. When the sun made its appearance above the horizon, you couldn't take your eyes off it. Though they say not to look into the sun directly, you can look into the sun for the first eight to ten minutes after sunrise. And in acting classes they say that if you keep your eyes trained on the sun for a few minutes just after it has crossed the horizon, you will not have any problem with the glare of the lights or reflectors that are focused on you for the rest of the day. The sunsets can be even more amazing when the sun is huge and red and has just touched the horizon. Stretching into the horizon is desert as far as you can see; and in the distance there is a camel pulling a loaded cart with huge wheels. The camel, the camel cart and its wheels look black against the setting sun with a faint orange reflection. There is no noise except the cawing of a vulture.

One day during the *Pehredaar* shooting I noticed a lot of vultures in the distance. I strolled towards that place about two kilometres away. There was a little stone house and in front of it was the skin and part of a camel carcass lying on the ground. The vultures were busy with that. Then I took a look at the other side of the house. There was a heap of the camel's body parts and bones and half a dozen people were chopping the body parts into small pieces and throwing them inside that little house. The house had an oven with a fire and a huge pot of camel flesh and bones that were being boiled. One of the workers asked me if I would like some camel meat. I asked him if they had killed the camel. He replied that it had died of a disease. That was it! There were vultures, crows, dogs and humans feasting on the remains of a camel that died of a disease! When I got back to the shooting location, they inquired where I had gone. I pointed into the distance and announced, 'I had been invited for lunch to have camel biryani but without rice.'

When I came back to Bombay, Sanjay and his family were celebrating their son Zayed's first birthday. (He was born on 5 July 1978, one week before his mother Zarine's birthday). That day was the mundan ceremony. The barber had come to shave the child's head. At the same time goats were being slaughtered and the meat was being given to the hungry people who waited outside the door in the street. It had just been a year ago that Sanjay had announced a holiday while we were shooting for *Abdullah* at RK Studios and had gone to the hospital to visit Zarine and have a look at the baby. Time had moved fast.

Yet another close shave occurred off-screen. Sanjay had a friend who owned the bungalow next to him. He also became an actor. He was quite popular. His name was Ranjeet; his friends called him Goli. One evening Sanjay, Goli and I were sitting together having drinks and snacks in Goli's place. Other members of the film industry joined: Prem Chopra, Shatrugan Sinha, Subhash Ghai and some others. Somehow an argument started; after a few drinks moods often change and tempers rise. I am not interested in fights really; as long as I'm not involved, I keep out of the way. However, Sanjay was my friend and whatever Shatru said did not go down well with Sanjay. Since it appeared like the majority of those present were supporting Shatru, I stood up and stayed near Sanjay. That was immediately looked upon as a threat by the others. One person went into the kitchen and came out with a knife in his hands. I disarmed him and told them to control themselves. Several minutes later Sanjay and I left.

That very night I received a call from Sanjay at about 5 a.m. Sanjay said, 'Come over and bring Betsy,' which was our code word for 'gun'. I went right away and Sanjay explained that shots had been fired from Goli's property across to his bungalow and someone had also fired at least two shots from outside Sanjay's front gate. The watchman had been slapped by somebody, but he hadn't seen who it was, since it was still dark. We picked up the spent cartridges of the bullets and handed them over to police after they arrived. After that we had some breakfast and later we visited Dilip Kumar to ask for his advice. Then I went to my place to take a shower and brush my teeth. Nargis had left a letter for me on the table.

My Darling Bob,

When you left for Sanjay's house this morning, I was petrified. It doesn't even occur to you, Bob, but it takes a very special type of person who'll answer a friend's SOS as unhesitatingly as you did last night. God bless and keep you exactly as you are. You are the most beautiful man on earth!

Also, thank you for phoning to say all is OK. It's gestures like these that really touch me. In a way, they are as reliable evidences of love as a night filled with your tender lovemaking. I'll be home early, though home without you is no home for me any longer.

I love you,
Nargis

It took a few days to sort everything out. Subhash Ghai had to spend one day in the lock-up until he was bailed out. The seniors of the Bombay film industry and Sanjay had a final meeting and that was the end of it. But from that time on Shatrugan Sinha was called Shotgun Sinha, although it also had something to do with his fast dialogue delivery.

Glamorous Liaisons

Abdullah was shaping up well. We had quite a few special preview screenings and the viewers' reports were encouraging. But Sanjay was waiting for better offers from some of the territories where there was a large Indian population like London, South Africa, Canada, the Arabic Gulf, Fiji and some of the Caribbean Islands.

So we had enough time to fly to Goa and stay for three or four days. Sanjay wanted to meet some friends there: Nusli Wadia, owner of Bombay Dyeing and Britannia biscuits, and Russi Modi, owner of a couple of movie theatres in Bombay and Pune. The first person we met as soon as we walked across Calangute Beach was Zeenat Aman. She was shooting for a big film there. She was happy to see us and said, 'After lunch I'll be free. I'll come and meet you.'

Sanjay commented, 'Is that a promise or a threat?' Zeenat laughed and ran away. When we went back to the Fort Aguada Hotel where we were staying, we almost fell over two deckchairs, only to find them occupied by Nusli Wadia and Russi Modi. That was fortunate, now we didn't have to search for them. It was already pretty hot. The season officially only started in October—then Goa would be packed with foreign tourists. Anyway, we all ordered a few tender coconuts to rinse our kidneys and then went for a nice walk from the hotel all along the beach to Baga Creek.

Zeenat, who was also staying at the hotel, came out to have a look around. She wouldn't sit down alone, but when she saw us, she felt more comfortable. Sanjay made the introduction. Zeenat didn't know Nusli and Russi Modi, but she seemed quite interested in Nusli. He is Parsi or half-Parsi. His grandfather was Muhammad Ali Jinnah, one of the founders of Pakistan during the partition of India.

A voice floated to us from behind. 'Darling, shall we have lunch here, or do you want to come inside?' All heads turned.

'Oh, sorry,' responded Nusli. 'This is my wife Maureen. Maureen, meet Zeenat Aman and Bob Christo. You know everyone else, I believe.' Maureen keeps telling me that she's Australian, but I always felt that there are some other genes as well; she could be Anglo-Indian.

Anyway, before the furniture was shifted and lunch was served, I excused myself and went for a pre-lunch swim in the sea. The waves looked pretty good; maybe I could ride some of them right down to the sand. The sea in Goa looked cleaner than the sea in Bombay; I had noticed that already when I had come here in 1977 while I waited for my Oman visa. I could see some jellyfish lurking underwater. I made a mental note to be watchful; I don't like the way they embrace you with their tentacles. Jellyfish stings cause severe burning sensations and can cause fever as well. They usually remain near the shore for some time when the monsoon is not quite over. The most uncomfortable of jellyfish stings are those of the Portuguese men-of-war. They are small and blue and have very long, thin tentacles and the burns are painful and cause a severe itchy sensation after a few hours. They can also get into your mouth accidentally during swimming, in case you open your mouth for breathing. I knew a surfer who was riding his board at Sydney's Bondi beach during the monsoon. He fell off his board when a big wave hit him and he was dumped into the sea. When he finally came back to the surface, he had his mouth open because he was short of breath. The moment his head came to the surface a whole bunch of Portuguese men-of-war (we call them blue bottles) were washed into his open mouth. He swallowed half of them and the other half got stuck in his throat and suffocated him. He died before he reached the shore.

I left the water and joined Sanjay and the others for lunch. I just ate fish; when I'm in Goa, I stick to seafood. But it has to be cooked—and no jellyfish! By the way, the Chinese make soup from jellyfish.

After lunch everybody went for a snooze. Sanjay requested me to give him a fifteen-minute massage until he dozed off. Then I also slept for half an hour. Later, Russi Modi and I went for a jog along the beach. It was very refreshing even though I was sweating a lot, but that I didn't mind; actually sweating makes me feel good.

Towards evening we sat again outside with Nusli and Zeenat until Nusli went to his room. I noticed that Zee paid extra attention to Nusli. She told him that she'd be shooting in London after two days. Nusli responded that he was also supposed to travel to London, maybe a day later. 'Oh, that's great, let's meet,' squeaked Zeenat. Sanjay didn't like that at all.

I left Zee and Sanjay alone and went to the bar to have a drink. When I went looking for Sanjay two hours later I found him in the room we were sharing, still talking to Zeenat. I asked where I should sleep. Sanjay told Zee to give me her key so I could sleep in her room because they'd have to discuss a few more things. So I slept in Zeenat's room. She came in at about seven in the morning and she climbed straightaway into her bed, put her arms around me and said, 'Good morning.' I also wished her, but I got up and made to go and get ready. But she requested me to give her a wake-up massage. I agreed and asked her if she managed to get any sleep. Her estimate was about two hours, that's all. 'Well, I'll give you a leg and back massage plus shoulders and arms. After that you'll have to brush your teeth and your tongue and then drink a nice cup of coffee; that should do the trick. If it doesn't, call me and I'll give you another massage.'

Sanjay wanted to go back to Bombay halfway through that day. A film distributor from Indore in Madhya Pradesh was waiting for him to negotiate terms for *Abdullah*. When we arrived at Sanjay's house we came to know that George Marzbetuny had died of a heart attack with liver complications. His wife had phoned and was talking to Zarine, sounding very upset. I silently prayed for his soul.

When I reached Casa Cama I received a call from the production executive of *Pehredaar*, saying that I was required at the sound studio to dub my dialogues in Bengali the next day. I told him I'd be there at 9 a.m. The title of the film *Pehredaar* was going to be *Lal Koti* in

Bengali. Next morning I met Danny at the sound studio. He was also dubbing. Danny was born in Sikkim, one of the north-eastern provinces closer to the China border. He had oriental features, was well built and a proficient actor. We chatted for some time and before he left, he suggested that I drop in at his flat in Juhu and have a beer with him. He gave me his address: an apartment in Kalumal Estate, Juhu, close to Sanjay's house, opposite the Juhu post office.

Two days later, I rang his doorbell in the evening. He was there and seemed happy to see me. He told me about his childhood in Sikkim and his love for acting and talked about some of the films he had worked in. Then, as he asked me about what made me come to India, I mentioned Parveen Babi; that I'd read about her in the *Time* magazine in Rhodesia and that I had met her in the first few days of my stay in Bombay and was very impressed by her. He laughed and reported that she was living right there in that building; I was shocked. I asked him to give her a call. 'See if she's at home. I am sure she'll recall our meeting at Bombay Central during the mahurat of *Burning Train* if I mention the *Time* magazine of March 1977.'

Danny dialled a number and spoke to somebody. He spoke for a few minutes and told me that Parveen was there, but she had a cold and was lying in bed. 'She remembers you and told me that I can give you her phone number. You can call her up after a few days when she's feeling better.' Then Danny confessed that he had had a close relationship with her for some time. I said, 'That calls for another beer, cheers! Do you mind if I give her a call? You know, I'm a bit of a flirt, but I've travelled halfway around the world to meet her. I'd like to meet her again.' Danny gave me his blessings, telling me to go ahead.

After that I often visited Danny and we worked together in some more films as well. I spoke to Parveen on the phone only about three weeks later. At that time she was not free, but after another month or so I met her in person at Sanjay's house. She was surprised, but remembered Danny calling her up on my behalf. After that we met quite often. I'd give her a call and if she was alone, we chatted and had a few glasses of wine together. At the end of the '80s she sold her flat at Kalumal Estate and bought the penthouse in a block of flats on Juhu beach, just across the road from Casa Cama. I think it was called Riviera, a nice place with a good view. She enjoyed inviting me over for dinner. Sometimes we even cooked something together.

Since I had moved to Casa Cama, a number of nice residential buildings had been erected in my neighbourhood. The closest hotel was the Holiday Inn, where I used to go for a drink in the evenings and sometimes had dinner after I sang a few songs with the band. Next to Holiday Inn was the Sun 'n' Sand which had been originally built by a Swiss entrepreneur. It accommodated the Swissair crew on a regular basis until the airline declared bankruptcy in 2001. This area of Juhu beach was in great demand with visitors from overseas and buyers. The estate value of beach frontage land or properties was very high. On weekends you could see masses of people walking by the sea or having picnics or jumping about in the water and then sitting down at one of the many stalls to drink some coconut water or buy small snacks or peanuts.

On weekends we often had visitors sitting with us on the front terrace. Casa Cama was a well-known place. One of the reasons was that 'Bob Christo is living there'. After I became famous, people stood on the beach, especially on weekends, and tried to attract my attention because they wanted my autograph or to meet me. Of course in 1978, it was only the beginning of my career but friends like Adi Godrej, who was a neighbour, or Sunil's friends or Bugsi, a friend who flew for Air India and also was an avid windsurfer and water-sports exponent, dropped by for a talk and a cup of coffee any time of the day. Occasionally we had a party for close friends like Sanjay and Zarine, sitting on the front terrace unless it was raining.

Torturing Jeetu, but Amjad's Unimpressed

I think it was around Diwali 1979, because I remember hearing so many cracker explosions during the night and I dislike these noises intensely; they remind me too much of war. Some people I know like war, but most of these people haven't experienced it. I prefer peace, love and harmony. Diwali is the biggest Indian festival, the festival of lights, but it's the worst festival for pollution. The three main days take a terrible toll polluting cities and villages all over India. The government has tried to ban fireworks, which is also difficult because almost every festival, celebration and wedding has fireworks to commemorate or inaugurate in style.

Anyway, I was in Sanjay's office and it was about 9.30 in the morning. The receptionist called me over saying there was a phone call for me. It was Prasanna Kapoor, Jeetendra's brother. He asked me to come to his office between 11 a.m. and 12 p.m. regarding a role in their film that started the next week. Their office was also in Juhu. Many film personalities lived in Juhu and a lot of their offices were also located in the area. Prasanna was in his office and went briefly through the script with me. Actually it was a fight between me and Jeetu, but a super fight. They wanted something really special. The name of the movie: *Jyoti Bane Jwala*. The work would take four to five days, to be shot in AVM Studio, Madras. I had to go by the first flight the next Monday. They offered me a fair fee, considering that it was only my third film in India (plus *Qurbani* which I would shoot for later); however, I convinced them to raise the fee to a better-looking figure and they gave me a nominal signing amount immediately. Accommodation would be in a five-star hotel.

When I met Sanjay in his office later, I asked him jokingly if he thought he could manage without me for five days. Then I told him that I got another movie, with Jeetu shooting in Madras. He congratulated me. Then he said, 'Tonight we're going to a party in the city in Adi Dubash's castle. It's a high-society do; bring Nargis if you like. We'll pick you up at 8.30 p.m. at your place.'

I asked Nargis to come, but she thought it might get too late and she had to get up for her work. In any case, she didn't like to go to parties, especially the type of party that she thought was too closely associated with filmi crowds. If she knew the people, she would go. She used to come to Sanjay and Zarine's dinners sometimes.

The party at Adi Dubash's was grand. It was a palace; one of the heritage buildings at least a hundred years old which was not allowed to be sold or altered. There must have been a ton of diamonds and two tons of gold on all the invitees. The elegance, grace and beauty of the gentler sex were absolutely stunning. I've been all over the world but I am sure that the cradle of female beauty is India. As cultural changes take place in any society, so they did in India. In the mid-eighties the Indian society decided that the time had come to send their daughters to annual beauty contests and vie with other girls from all over the globe for the titles of Miss World and Miss Universe, and very successfully so. I have seen many changes in India during my more than thirty years here, economically and culturally as well.

I told Nargis that I'd be shooting for *Jyoti Bane Jwala* in Madras but only for five days at the most. She was happy for me; after all I was earning now and there'd be many more films in the years to come.

I arrived at the AVM Studio in time to try on my costume and see if any make-up would be required on my face. I met the fight master and discussed with him the outline of the fight and the scene leading to the fight. There was a group of well-trained gymnasts and they were all ready for the fight, which was to take place in an open gymnasium equipped with everything from Roman rings to parallel bars. As soon as Jeetu arrived, we started with the scene. The whole group of gymnasts and fighters are being beaten by Jeetu and that's when I come in. I'm named Black Boss because I dress in black; in the end I'll also be finished. Before starting the fight, I practised on the horizontal bar and before every shot I did at least thirty push-ups to pump up my arm and shoulder muscles for the camera. When I practised the rehearsals with Jeetu and we were doing punches and blocks, it was very strenuous for Jeetu; he got tired quickly. I was used to blocking punches firmly, because that's the way I used to do it in karate sparring, but that was so painful for Jeetu that he had to call his assistant in between shots to give him arm and shoulder massages and hot and cold fomentation. Even now he talks about it, telling everybody what torture he used to go through during and after the fight! After the shooting schedules he had to take a few days' holiday to get into shape again. I told him to start exercising on a regular basis and forget about the initial pain; then he'd look forward to his next fight, because his body would have become used to it by then and he'd begin to enjoy it. He was never really irritated about it or angry; no, he took it in his stride and laughed about it when we met on flights to Madras—he was shooting for a lot of his Hindi movies there, while I would often be travelling for shooting regional films. I became very busy with regional films in Tamil, Telugu, Malayalam and even in a few Kannada films for the next ten years. I worked with leading lights like Kamal Hasan, Rajinikanth, Chiranjeevi, N.T. Rama Rao, Mohanlal, Mammootty, Ambareesh,

Vishnuvardhan, K. Bhagyaraj and director Priyadarshan. I played the same role in quite a few south Indian remakes of corresponding Hindi films. *Jyoti Bane Jwala* was released in the beginning of 1980 and ran for a long time to full houses.

After returning to Bombay I received a call from Feroz Khan, telling me to come for two days for shooting three scenes for *Qurbani*. One was a fight with Amjad Khan who played a detective. I played a mechanic in a motorcar repair shop. One of the cars there has been identified by the police to have been used during a drug smuggling incident and they send Amjad Khan of the detective squad to investigate. He interrogates me, but I don't cooperate; instead I show my strength to impress the cop by hitting a brick wall with my fist and make it collapse in front of him. He just laughs and utters, 'I'm not impressed.' Then I hit him and he throws a tyre from his jeep at me. I throw it back against his head, but he again exclaims that he is not impressed at all. The fight continues until Amjad manages to get hold of the shawl which I wear wrapped around my neck, sticks it into a sugarcane press which is standing inside the repair shop and starts winding it, threatening to suffocate me and giving me the third degree until I disclose the licence number of the car in question. He handcuffs me to the sugarcane press and asks me some more questions.

After we finished the shot, nobody could locate the key for removing the handcuffs from my wrists. They were actually Feroz's handcuffs but the key had got lost somehow. I was in a very uncomfortable position, half standing, half sitting and bent to one side. I kept shouting for them to get me out of the inconvenient tight spot. Nevertheless, I had to wait for two hours until they brought a locksmith who was successful in releasing me eventually.

After that we spent a few days in Rajasthan for the filming of *Abdullah*, with lots and lots of sand dunes and camels, and gypsies who were working in road construction and washed themselves with sand because water was rarely available. For the same reason, they also put camel or cow's urine inside the mortar for constructing new houses in the desert. On the way back we stayed with the Chopra family again and made a plan to go for a trip to London, to eat T-bone steaks and visit the White Elephant and other gambling houses and see some of the latest Western movies. We decided to go right after New Year, in January or February 1980. In that year *Abdullah* would definitely be released.

Before we left, Nargis and I discussed how to continue with our life together. Nargis had given me a new home and I was very fond of it. However, I was not in a hurry to get married again. I had lost my first wife and then had almost got married to Maria in the Philippines; we were really close and it was quite tough for me when it didn't work out because of the circumstances that arose. Nargis had not applied for a divorce yet, so I thought of letting her take the first step, for the divorce had to come before the next marriage.

Living it up in London

Vinod Chopra was in a hurry to go, because he had some work in London for British Airways. So we took off in early 1980. Sanjay and Vinod travelled first class and I was happy in economy class. During the flight I visited them a few times in the Jumbo bar on top of the stairs and joined them for a drink. We were in a relaxed mood; Sanjay had taken his shoes off and was lying on the sofa. Suddenly the captain came out of the cockpit and took a look at Sanjay. He said in a very provocative tone, 'Take your dirty feet off the sofa!' Sanjay responded calmly, 'How dare you address me in this manner? How did you get on this flight?' At that moment Vinod introduced himself as a marketing manager of British Airways and asked for the captain's name and designation. He asked the captain if he normally greeted his passengers in this abusive, derogatory way. Everybody who was witnessing this scene was shocked and another passenger enlightened the captain, an Englishman, that the passenger on the sofa was Mr Sanjay Khan, a well-known personality from Bombay with VIP status. 'If this is the way British Airways is treating us, we all demand to be let off the flight, so we can make other arrangements,' he said. The captain offered to apologize. Before landing Sanjay was furnished with a signed apology and a copy to Vinod Chopra. Other follow-up letters between Sanjay Khan and BA were traded before the matter was settled satisfactorily and the captain was let off the hook with a few weeks' suspension.

We stayed at the Inn on the Park hotel just across from Hyde Park. While Sanjay and Vinod attended to their respective work schedules, I strolled around the city and called on some friends and rang up my children in California. At lunchtime we met and had a sumptuous steak lunch with all the trimmings and Courage Bitter, a famous British beer.

The next day Sanjay told me that he needed some more cash. He asked me if I needed a visa to Switzerland. I responded in the negative—with an Australian passport I needed only visas for a few countries like Japan, South Africa and Sultanate of Brunei. Sanjay said, 'Excellent, I'll get you a ticket for tomorrow's first flight to Zurich with Swissair. There's a man who owes me $50,000. You go to this bank right on Lake Constance with the name I've written down for you; also the name of the person to get in touch with. I've spoken to him already on the phone. Just count the money, put it in your attaché case, have a nice lunch and come back.'

I was up early in the morning and very happy to go to Switzerland. I like Zurich; I've been there many times. That particular bank is part of a very good restaurant, practically jutting over the banks of Lake Constance. I had phoned a good friend who lived about eighty kilometres away from Zurich. One hour later she was there at the restaurant and joined me for lunch. Her name was Emanuelle. We had a wonderful afternoon until she dropped me at the airport.

At London airport my name was called with a message to call Sanjay Khan at his hotel number. He said, 'Bob, listen carefully. After you left for Zurich this morning, Chopri tried to fill the trust that I have in you with the seed of doubt. At lunchtime he started by saying, "How do you know that Bob is gonna come back to give you the money? He's got $50,000, which is a nice sum. He can immediately continue to the USA and you'll never be able to trace him. I think you can kiss your money goodbye. I'll bet you £100 that he's not coming back." I replied, "I bet you £500 that he's coming back. Do you accept the bet, Chopra?" Well, Chopra had no choice but to accept. Now listen, Bob. Don't come now; wait till 8 p.m. or 9 p.m. before you walk into the lobby. That'll make his disappointment more acute. By 9 p.m. he'll be sure he is £500 richer, that bastard. I don't like him any more. He always looks for the negatives in everybody first.'

When I finally walked into the hotel lobby, I saw Sanjay come down the stairs from the mezzanine, and behind him, Vinod Chopra. I could make out the look of dissatisfaction on Chopra's face, after which he turned around and walked up again. We went to Sanjay's room where I handed over the money and we had a drink and exchanged our stories of the day. 'Tonight we'll go to the White Elephant and try to double the money that you brought,' Sanjay said. 'Tomorrow we'll go to the recording studio, where Feroz is recording his title song for *Qurbani*.'

We had dinner at the White Elephant and then gambled till about 1 a.m. Sanjay couldn't double his money, but he won a moderate amount. Before we went to the casino, I changed my attire to an Afghan-style salwar kameez because I wasn't carrying a suit. Sanjay had had it made for me in Bombay. At the entrance Sanjay introduced me as his guest. The guards insisted that I had to wear a suit and tie but Sanjay said, 'The gentleman is wearing national dress. He's from Afghanistan and doesn't speak English.' They looked at one another, then agreed to let us in.

I went straight to the bar and asked for a brandy, lime and soda, which was my favourite drink in those days if I couldn't get sangria. Actually it was not ordinary brandy but cognac, with lime cordial, ice and soda. I didn't play at the casino; I had stopped gambling the night the floating casino that I frequented on Manila Bay had burned down——I think it was in 1976. I had been at the casino shortly before the fire. So I just watched the gamblers win and lose and observed the interesting mixture and behaviour of different nationalities. I noticed that there were a lot of Indians gambling in the casino and Sanjay knew many of them. It was like a gathering of Indian gamblers.

The next morning we entered the recording studio at a corner of Oxford Street. Feroz and Zeenat were sitting inside with Nazia Hassan, the young singer, and Biddu, the Indian composer who had settled in London several years ago and become popular with all the famous hit songs he had composed during the late seventies. I had heard of him when I was in the Seychelles. I had heard songs like *Everybody is kung fu fighting* and *Dance little lady, dance* and was told that the composer was Biddu Appaiah from Bangalore in India. Later I often met him in Bombay. He even asked Nargis and me if we could rent out our apartment in Casa Cama to him and his wife Sarah; he wanted to stay for a couple of years by the beach.

The title song for *Qurbani* was *Aap jaisa koi meri zindagi mein aaye*. Nazia was a talented singer and Zeenat was surprised to see us in London. Feroz looked at me and said, 'The fight between you and Amjad came out very effectively!' The film would release in the middle of the year. Feroz invited us to his place for dinner. He had rented a place in Chelsea for the duration of the London shooting for *Qurbani*. The next day Sanjay and I watched a few new movies in the city and Vinod Chopra returned to Delhi. Sanjay and I bought a lot of clothes and food items like salamis, cheeses, chocolates and some specialities for Nargis and Sunil. Sanjay bought so many things, most of which were for his four children—toys and clothes—and gifts for relatives and friends.

In the night we went again to a casino but I excused myself because I had a date with Jacqueline. She was a Jamaican dancer known to me from an earlier visit to London. She had invited me to her place near Wembley. She was happy to see me after about six years. She kissed me and squeezed me and I noticed that she still had the same impeccable almond-brown skin which used to have such an alluring effect on me. There was somebody else in the kitchen. Jacki introduced her as Devi; she was Indian and very attractive. She also kissed me, holding me so tight that I was pressed up against her unbelievable pair of boobs. She was wearing a miniskirt and a light, short-sleeved blouse—without bra, I noticed when I became aware of her nipples as she embraced me. I just thought, 'Wow, what are we celebrating?'

She excused herself saying, 'Sorry, I was feeling so hot in the kitchen, so I tried on Jacki's miniskirt which she uses for some of her dances.' Then Devi checked on her dishes in the oven and I saw she was making paella, the famous Spanish dish of rice, saffron, chicken, seafood and vegetables cooked in a large shallow pan. Jacki must have disclosed to her some of my secrets because once I had taken her to a Spanish restaurant where I had ordered paella and she had loved it. Jacki asked me what I was drinking these days. I picked up the bottle of champagne from the table where I'd put it after entering, and said, 'I still love my sangria, but champagne is fine or you can mix me a brandy, lime cordial and soda with ice. What are you wenches drinking?'

They opted for champagne. Devi asked me when I wanted to eat. I said, 'Let's have a couple of drinks together and let me hear about some of your latest adventures. Then we can have that lovely smelling paella.' Jacki put on some nice jazzy music and I started singing with some of the tunes. In London it was winter, so they had the oil heater on in their flat and in the kitchen it was hot in any case from cooking; but after I started drinking and dancing with the girls, I started perspiring. Devi offered me a towel. She mopped my brow and advised me to take off my shirt, which I did.

Then we sat down on the sofa and relaxed, just listening to some romantic music. That seemed to turn the two wenches on, and they started to become affectionate. Devi put her arms around my neck and started putting her tongue in my mouth. We kissed passionately and I put one of my hands innocently on her thighs and noticed that she didn't wear any panties. No bra and no panties, what next? The answer came ten seconds later, when Jacki suddenly said from behind, 'Close your eyes please, I have a surprise.' The moment I closed my eyes, Jacki turned my head a little and kissed me with such emotional intensity that I just couldn't resist any more. As I noticed that she was naked, I realized that Devi had become busy trying to relieve me of my trousers. The two girls looked after me wonderfully. I felt so wanted, pampered and spoiled. And finally they served me this lovely meal which Devi had prepared. I must say, Devi was an excellent cook. Actually both of the girls were excellent in their own ways! They persuaded me to stay over and spend the night in Jacki's place. I called Sanjay to inform him about my delay. He said, 'Take your time; I'll be in the hotel!'

When I woke up in the morning, I observed that the three of us were sleeping in one big double bed. So I quickly got up and did my old trick with the cold cream again and they both woke up and caught me by my feet before I could disappear. It ended in a great fight, or may be I should say in a very sexy fight. Afterwards we had a satisfying breakfast and I returned to the Inn on the Park.

Sanjay was sitting at the table, looking at the newspaper, making notes and also watching TV. Then I realized that he was checking on the horse races of the day. 'Oh,' I ventured, 'you lost last night and want to regain your losses?'

He grinned and asked, 'How do you know? Please do me a favour. Go to the consolidated betting shop in the next street, with "Mecca" written on the door, and give them this £1000. Tell them you are betting on Swan to win. It's 20:1.'

When I came back, Sanjay was still checking horse races; but after half an hour he settled down to watch the races on TV saying, 'Bob, keep your fingers crossed that Swan wins the race.' Well, that race was very interesting. First of all, Swan didn't have a good start. It was a 1600-metre race and Swan slowly caught up with the field. About 200 metres before the finish line Swan increased his speed without the jockey whipping him. The jockey only used his legs and the horse won by a head. That was amazing for an outsider. Sanjay won £20,000. He said, 'You were right, I've regained my losses already.' On that morning Sanjay had two more wins. I wouldn't have believed it had I not paid the money myself at the betting counter. I started calling that Mecca betting shop 'Mecca Bank'.

Next morning before we went to the airport, I asked Sanjay, 'Don't you want to go to the Mecca Bank first, to withdraw some money?'

He just laughed and said, 'You know, we might need that extra money at the airport, because we have a hell of a lot of luggage. But in any case, we are not leaving today, we are leaving tomorrow morning. Tonight we promised those people in Southall that we'd join them for the party they're going to throw for us, remember?' Oh yes, I did remember. Earlier on in our trip we had met some fans from Southall who had told us that they'd host a party in our honour. They'd pleaded with us to attend and we had firmly promised to be there.

I was amazed at how many shops in Southall were owned by Punjabis. This was only a small part of a London area that was populated with thousands of Indians; there were many more in other parts of London as well as in Birmingham, Manchester and Liverpool. When I thought back through British history I remembered how India was at one time populated with British soldiers and their families. Now it's just the other way round. That small island of the United Kingdom is densely inhabited with Indians. Would they all return to India one day? Maybe one day India will become a superpower and England will become a part of India. Well, I got that impression sometimes when I realized how many Indians, and of course Pakistanis, were living in the United Kingdom. There are a lot of intermarriages between India and England and both populations seem to be quite happy with their new world.

When we reached the appointed place, we were ushered into a large hall where all the Indian weddings and other functions used to be conducted. There were other rooms as well, all spilling over with a huge mixed crowd of English, Indian and Pakistani people. They had organized a grand musical set-up and unbelievable catering facilities. Hindi films were being shown on multiple screens. There were posters announcing the Khan brothers, Zeenat

Aman and Bob Christo. There were loud announcements that the food would be better than in India and they also had a big array of Indian musicians and comedians.

It was an unforgettable experience. We drank and ate enormous quantities and enjoyed ourselves thoroughly. Some people were happy just watching the Hindi movies. I even sang a couple of Hindi songs and recited a few Urdu poems. Finally we left. I was glad because we had to get up early for packing everything properly.

Sanjay and I had to hire three cars to transport all the luggage and ourselves to Heathrow airport. And we still wanted to buy some duty-free items! When we saw that long line of suitcases and boxes accumulated at the counter, we discussed the situation. 'If we don't use any tricks, we'll have to pay a large amount as excess weight charge,' I said. Sanjay nodded.

It was an ordinary weekday, which was in our favour. There were not many passengers at the counters that morning. Sanjay said to the clerk, 'We have a bit of a problem.'

The clerk asked, 'What's the problem?'

Sanjay answered, 'We have so much luggage,' and he pointed towards it.

The clerk said, 'Let's see what we can do about it.' At that Sanjay took some notes out of his pocket and handed the British Airways clerk £40. The clerk looked around surreptitiously to see if anybody was looking in his direction and then put the money into a drawer. Then he said, 'Just to be on the safe side, I'll charge you £32 for excess weight—in case someone notices that you have a lot of luggage but didn't go to the excess weight counter. Go to that counter over there and pay the money.' We thanked him. Once we had boarded, knowing that we had saved a lot of money, we laughed as though we had successfully robbed the bank of Monte Carlo. We were quite surprised that you could do things like this even in England. Among all the luggage there were also two big television sets; in those days television programming was restricted to a few hours a day in India, so we used them mainly for watching videotapes.

There's No Business like Show Business

Nargis was happy to see me, as always. In the evening Nargis and Sunil enjoyed going through all the goodies I had brought home with me from London. At that time it was hard to find things like quality chocolates and continental delicacies in Bombay. There was only one shop in Cuffe Parade near President Hotel which sold Swiss, Dutch and Italian cheeses and different salamis and caviar. It was a shop owned by Parsis. Today you can get anything you want.

The day after I came back home, Bugsi dropped in and told me that Ramesh Khanna had asked him to send me over to the Holiday Inn to meet a photographer from Hong Kong who wanted to take some shots of me with my windsurfer in front of the hotel for their service directory. I went to Ramesh's office and he called the photographer. What a surprise! It was Dinshaw Balsara, the photographer I had met in Hong Kong over five years ago. He had shot the first lot of photos that had got me many modelling assignments in Hong Kong. Dinshaw recognized me immediately, even though I looked much more solid and beefy now. He explained that he had come to Bombay to visit his relations; he is a Parsi and the family was celebrating some festivities. I'd met so many Parsis since I'd come to India that I could tell one now by just being told his name. For the next few years you could find me on a windsurfer in the Bombay Holiday Inn service directory on every page. Two or three years later, I was told that Dinshaw had passed away in Hong Kong. God rest his soul.

One morning Sanjay rang me at Casa Cama and asked me to come over; he had a very sore back. I did the needful and thirty minutes later he was full of praise for me and my healing hands; he felt so much better. Then he made a suggestion regarding my singing. He liked my singing voice and had come across a song by a new singing sensation called Lou Rawls. The song Sanjay liked went like this: 'You'll never find as long as you live, someone who loves you, tender like I do . . .' He got me a disc and 'ordered' me to learn the song. 'Next week I want to hear you sing it when we dine at the Taj Rendezvous. They have a good band who know all the latest songs.'

Well, that was a challenge for me. I love singing with a good band. I was ready in time with lyrics and melody; it's a great song. I also learned some more Lou Rawls songs, like *Stormy Monday* (my favourite), *In the evening when the sun goes down* and *There's a time to be born*, though Sanjay's favourite tune of mine was *The windmills of your mind*, the one that Rajji had also liked so much. Sanjay and some female companions were seated near the stage where I was warbling away. The Rendezvous was packed and I got a roaring applause with encores for more songs. I was very happy and everybody at my table was beaming. Sometimes I wished I was a professional singer; I play guitar, the clarinet, the piano, and I'm not a bad dancer. But then, I used to think: I don't have to go back to civil engineering if I don't want to, I'm in the right profession. I can act: So what am I complaining about? There's no business like show business! I can sing whenever I want! Even now, I still enjoy performing. I felt bad that I couldn't get Nargis to join us for that dinner. If Zarine would have come, Nargis would have definitely given us company.

The release of Feroz Khan's movie *Qurbani* in June 1980 was a great event. The Maratha Mandir theatre in Bombay was totally packed. The film was a super-duper hit and so was the music. The celebrations went on for weeks in different parts of the country; after Bombay came Delhi, then Bangalore, the birth town of the Khan brothers. I was hoping that *Abdullah*'s success would be at least on a par with *Qurbani*.

After the excitement of *Qurbani*'s success, I received a call from Madras from a Telugu film producer with an offer for my first Telugu movie. It was a film with a lot of action. The Telugu hero was N.T. Rama Rao; also in the movie was Chiranjeevi who was at the beginning of his career. I had to jump through three glass panes in one fight scene, when the hero throws me through glass after glass. After the release of that film I received regular offers from Tamil, Malayalam and Telugu producers. I even did four Kannada movies. I was treated very well by the south Indian production houses and the remuneration was usually equal to that in Bollywood.

My work in the south Indian films usually took a little over a week or sometimes two weeks; occasionally I had to come back for several more schedules until the completion of my work. The system was not like in Hollywood. In Indian films everybody has to give the dates when they are available to shoot and the shooting can rarely continue in one non-stop schedule because every successful actor works in a number of films at the same time. I worked sometimes in four different movies on one day! The shooting locations are often in different cities. For instance, I would sometimes shoot in Madras for a Telugu film. Because of the superior infrastructure and filming equipment, regional films from other states in the south used to often be shot in Madras.

Meanwhile, Madras was renamed Chennai a few years ago. That name apparently was closer to its original one many years ago. Unfortunately, it spoiled the rhymes of some of the limericks that I used to hear at parties. One of my favourite ones went like this:

There was a young maid in Madras
Who had a magnificent ass.
Not pretty and pink,
Like you probably think.
She was grey, had long ears and ate grass.

That doesn't work with Chennai! Nevertheless, Madras or Chennai, I used to be very happy to stay there when shooting for films.

Anyway, I was happy that I had many offers of Hindi films based in Bombay and regional cinema mainly in south India. Apart from that, I always ensured that I devoted enough time to exercises and water sports to keep myself fit and flexible.

One day, as I was having my breakfast, I heard somebody call my name from outside on the beach. I recognized Sanjay's voice and went out to the terrace. Yes, it was Sanjay in jogging gear. I told him to come up because I had already started my breakfast. He asked me whether I was free the next day. 'Yes, tomorrow I have no shooting.' I had planned to go out in the sea windsurfing; I needed some more practice because I want to get ready to take part in some windsurfing regattas. I had been advocating for these regattas for some time now in Bombay. So far there were not yet enough exponents in Bombay to justify the start of competitions, but I was sure it wouldn't take long if I kept talking to the water-sports clubs.

Sanjay told me that he had planned to fly to Delhi the next morning. Mohammed Yunus, the PM's confidante, has arranged a meeting with Indira Gandhi regarding a documentary film that Sanjay Khan had made about Sanjay Gandhi's life. Sanjay Gandhi's death during a practice flight in Delhi on 23 June 1980 had been a shock for the nation. The papers were speculating that it was an assassination by Sanjay Gandhi's enemies; he had accumulated many when he began the vasectomy programme to bring the birth rate down in India. It hadn't helped at all when he'd started the sterilization programme with the males of the minority population. However, there was never any conclusive proof of murder. Sanjay Gandhi was a hard-working person whose head was full of ideas. His mother's ambition was to groom Sanjay as the future prime minister of India. This ambition had already grown roots in Sanjay's head, and he had had a lot of plans for the future. He had worked on a great project—the Maruti project—to manufacture hundreds of thousands of cars: Maruti cars. In a German magazine I'd read about the similarity of his vision to Hitler's Volkswagen project before the Second World War. The article in that magazine was headlined 'The Hitler of India'. I think it had been published in 1978. Sanjay Gandhi never got the opportunity to implement his grand idea. The Maruti 'people's car' project was finally given the blessing of the Congress government; Maruti cars flooded the market in the early 1980s and gave a name to a whole generation: 'The Maruti Generation'.

In the afternoon of the next day we met Indira Gandhi at the India Exhibition Grounds in New Delhi. Mrs Gandhi shook our hands and then the documentary film was shown. There was a lot of coverage of Sanjay Gandhi and his brother Rajiv from their childhood right up to Sanjay Gandhi's last photograph before his death next to his aircraft. After that followed Mrs Gandhi's address to the visitors. I felt sure that the Congress party would be coming back shortly and the Emergency would be abolished. I was never a politician and had not much interest in politics but I was influenced by Sanjay Khan's opinion, because he knew many of India's leading politicians personally and I valued his quick mind and his ability to come to correct conclusions. I learned the facts from the media; then they had to be digested and brought into the right perspective by Sanjay Khan's thinking process.

Chacha and the King of Creoles

Abdullah was released in December 1980. It did very well at the box office and was highly praised by the critics. We had a long night celebrating the premiere and I was in high spirits and performed many songs in the Supper Club of the Oberoi Towers accompanied by the Soft Rock Revolution band. Several days after the premiere, Sanjay, Zarine and their four children and I travelled to Mauritius for a twenty-day vacation in one of the beautiful resorts. The rooms had been reserved for us with the compliments of the prime minister of Mauritius, Sir Sewoosagur Ramgoolam, who had become a good friend of the Khan family after Sanjay had made his movie *Chandi Sona* (1977) in Mauritius some years earlier. Following this, a large number of Indian film companies also decided to shoot their films in that wonderful island and Mauritius became well known as an Indian film location.

The prime minister, who was affectionately called Chacha, met us at the airport along with an entourage of some of his ministers and a large stock for our bar in the beach resort. Everything was available, including my favourite sangria. I went to my room, put my luggage away, donned my swimwear and checked out the boathouse. There were windsurfers, waterskis, speedboats and jet skis. My most important training would be windsurfing, because upon getting back to Bombay, I wanted to organize competitive windsurfing regattas. I'd also do a few runs of mono-skiing twice a day.

The water in Mauritius is absolutely beautiful, totally clear and deep blue; I used to call it the 'Inkian' Ocean instead of the Indian Ocean. It was Christmas season 1980, climaxing in New Year 1981, and Mauritius was full of international visitors from South Africa and Europe, with a choice of the most beautiful girls in the world. I spotted at least half a dozen Miss Universes of the previous years, and many of the foreigners were lying in the sun, let us just say, in such a way that they'd soon be blessed with an all-over suntan!

One day Sanjay and I walked along the beach and Zayed was following us; he was only one and a half years old at that time. While Sanjay and I were talking, we forgot about Zayed. When we looked around for him after a few minutes, we couldn't spot him right away. But then we saw him toddle towards two pretty foreign ladies who were not wearing anything at all except for sunglasses. They were lying on their backs. We didn't call Zayed, we just watched him to see what he was going to do. When he reached those ladies, he stopped and started touching one lady's breast, playing with her nipples. The girl took off her sunglasses and, seeing the little adventurer, she called out to her companion saying, 'Look at this little sweetheart!' Both laughed and sat him down on a towel. That's when we entered the scene. Sanjay asked the girls, 'I hope he's not giving you any trouble, we lost him for a moment. Thanks for looking after him.' The girls introduced themselves and said they were from Paris. We got involved in a conversation until we saw Zarine approaching looking for her son and reminding us that it was time to have lunch.

The food was good at our resort; sometimes we cooked our own food or made special snacks when we had visitors. The seafood was delicious in Mauritius whether we were at the seafood restaurants or we had prepared it in our kitchen. One of our Mauritian friends was a good diver. He knew where the lobsters were to be found, and he dived into the sea and pulled them out from under the rocks. After that we prepared them in our kitchen. Some of them were almost as big as the lobsters in Sydney.

One night during dinner, I met some young Germans who were from Berlin and we got talking about our experiences in Mauritius. One of the Germans was called Klaus. The other wasn't really

German; he was from Africa, so they called him Afrique. There were also two girls named Melanie and Ingrid. The guys were in show business and music remixing. They had hired a motor yacht for their holiday and invited us to come with them in the morning. 'We also have fishing gear in the yacht. We could go out for the whole day for fishing and swimming. Only it would not be advisable to take the children with us, because they'd get sunburnt.' So we left all the kids with the nanny hired in Mauritius. Of course we also applied sunscreen whenever we went outdoors. We took some sandwiches with us when we left in the morning and an icebox full of beer. We had a lot of fun. The Germans took a lot of photos and kept reminding us to visit them in Berlin so we could inspect all the photos.

During Christmas there were a lot of special meals on the menu and fun evenings with local salsa dancing and singing competitions. After dinner we generally spent some time in the disco in a neighbouring hotel. Sometimes in the morning I went to one of the other big hotels that had parasail equipment and went up in the air for some time, pulled by one of the speedboats. There were large fishing boats for hire as well, with everything especially geared for hauling in large fish, barracuda and tuna; for example, the chairs were screwed into the deck so you didn't lose your balance when you were pulling in the catch. There was so much to do; you could never get bored for a single moment. There were also friends of Sanjay and Zarine who resided in Port Louis, the capital of Mauritius, and invited us over quite often.

One interesting character that has to be mentioned in connection with Mauritius: Gaetan Duval, who was a politician and for some time even the prime minister of Mauritius. He was a friend of Chacha. Theirs was a love-hate relationship. Gaetan had been the foreign minister for some time and he used to travel to Paris a lot in the company of other politicians. He often came to Bombay, in which case he would stay at Sanjay's house in Juhu; that's where I met him first. He was a well-liked personality, full of humour. In Mauritius people gave him the name 'King of Creoles'. A Mauritian Creole is a person of African or Malagasy descent and Mauritian Creole, a mixture of French and African, is a commonly spoken language, although the official language of Mauritius is English and French is also spoken and taught widely.

Gaetan used to entertain lavishly on his large farm on an island north of Grand Baie. It had many animals. He had about six giant turtles, two of them over a hundred years old, and a couple of huge cockatoos. There was a boat and a jetty. Guests could come by boat from the sea or by car, in which case they would be ferried across to the island. The farmhouse was very large—the dining hall had a dining table with a hundred chairs for sit-down dinners. Gaetan's party invitations used to go out all over the world to guests like Brigitte Bardot and Catherine Deneuve. He loved horse riding and had a stable on his property. Once, during a Christmas party, guests were surprised to be confronted with a horse in the middle of the dining hall. He loved giving parties with surprises and he loved his French wine. When he was in Mauritius, there was always something interesting going on. Unfortunately, he is not around any longer. He died at least ten years ago.

Our holiday was over, but all the flights were full. Sanjay, Zarine and the kids were waitlisted. I got a seat, but two days after everybody else had left. I went for another fishing trip with Klaus, Afrique and the two girls on the last day. I was lucky and caught a 450-pound tuna; we gave it to the kitchen and asked them to prepare it for dinner. Afterwards we went to the disco and had some more drinks. Then it was *Aufwiedersehen*.

The next morning some journalists had made a booking with me for an interview about the films *Qurbani* and *Abdullah*. During the rest of the day I went waterskiing and windsurfing. Then it was time to leave. Alain Wong, the diver who used to get us the lobsters from under the rocks in the sea, invited me to come on his flight in first class. He was a purser for Air Mauritius and made sure that I was given VIP treatment.

Babu Krishna, the Australian with the Amazing Voice

I had improved my windsurfing skills over the vacations in Mauritius. Back in Bombay I was absolutely perfect. Nargis was amazed with my deep tan.

She gave me a phone number to call up a production house that wanted me for a movie. When I called, they told me it was a film with Amitabh Bachchan called *Kalia*. Everything was ready and we started shooting in Film City four days later, with a fight scene in jail. Amitabh and I are both inmates. I am a 'dada' type who terrorizes the other convicts. Everybody is standing in line while food is being distributed, but I want to jump the queue. I strut up and shout, 'Line *mere peeche shuru hoti hai!*' (The line starts behind me!). I take the plate of the convict who is standing in front and whose right leg is in plaster and push him away, making him fall down. At that moment Kalia enters. At once he understands what is going on and he makes it his business to give his support to the underdog. He throws his plate à la frisbee at my head, shouting his challenge at me. With that we become involved in a vicious fight during which Kalia makes mincemeat out of my character.

I noticed instantly how professionally Amitabh worked. Before any punch, blow, knock or rap, he made sure that I understood exactly what we were supposed to do for the camera. Even though the fight master was there, Amitabh wanted to help me because I was a relatively new member of Bollywood; after all, that was my first film with him. Sometimes he corrected me when I made a mistake and he said something like, 'No, that would be play-acting.' He was always mindful of being realistic. I caught on straightaway and appreciated how his mind was totally engrossed in his work, cutting time to a minimum. The fight turned out OK. After Parveen Babi saw the movie, she told me that my movements looked a little stiff. I remembered that for my next screen fight. After I started my yoga lessons, my flexibility improved quite a lot.

The same day that I got the offer for *Kalia* Akbar Khan called me; he is another brother of Sanjay and Feroz. He was also making a film, called *Haadsa*, meaning 'occurrence'. His heroine was Ranjeeta. The dates were not yet fixed but he explained the script to me. There would be a fight between Akbar and myself, in which I'd be strangled.

In the evening when I was at home with Nargis, she told me that she had started divorce proceedings and it wouldn't take more than two months before she would be free and we could get married. I congratulated her and kissed her softly.

In the morning I woke her up and said, 'We haven't been for a beach walk for a long time, come let's go.' We both had to go to work but I could take it a little easier, because in the film industry it was not that strict—I wouldn't be required before 11 o'clock. When we came back to Casa Cama somebody was waiting; a young chap by the name of Vikram Singh who lived nearby. He mentioned that on various occasions he had heard me singing in the Taj Rendezvous and the Supper Club of the Oberoi. They wanted to have a pop and rock concert at Rang Bhavan (the popular venue of the biannual Jazz Yatra) on 18 March 1981. The concert was being organized by the Bombay Music Association in collaboration with Jazz India. 'We'd like the concert to be a triple bill featuring Vijay Benedict, an Indian pop singer who has been performing in London and Nairobi; Bob Christo, an Australian who has got an amazing voice; and the Monserate Brothers who have a nine-piece band. Would you be interested?'

'Of course,' I said. Vikram asked me to keep 18 March free, to fit some rehearsals in before the show. He said that he'd be in touch with me about other details. Nargis was surprised but liked the idea and I told her to keep 18 March free for my show.

I was already quite busy. I had got a part in another Telugu film, *Ba Buuli Puli* by Krishnam Raju. The shooting would be in Madras and would commence after another four days. Now I had to select my numbers for the Rang Bhavan show in March and allot some time for rehearsals with the band. I decided that I would sing three or four Lou Rawls songs and the rest I'd put together after I met the band.

Sanjay was working on several new scripts to decide on another movie. I usually dropped by or phoned him once a day and often had dinner at his bungalow. He was happy that I had started to get offers in other Hindi films and also in Telugu and Tamil films.

I soon started shooting for *Ba Buuli Puli*. The directorial assistants didn't know me yet, so when the director needed me for my first shot and told one of his assistants to call Bob Christo, the assistant went out and called, 'Babu Krishna!' And then again, 'Babu Krishna!'

After a while I asked doubtfully, 'Are you calling me?' He nodded. 'But my name is Bob Christo.' I protested.

He replied confidently, 'In Telugu it is Babu Krishna!' When I conveyed this to the director, he laughed so much! He even offered to use 'Babu Krishna' in the film credits if I wanted. I suggested they stick to Bob Christo for the time being; otherwise my fans might not like it!

Soon after I got another visit from a Bombay producer who offered me a role in a film called *Ustadi Ustad Se*. We would start that film now, but we'd only shoot for three or four days and finish the rest of the work the next year, in 1982. Mithun Chakraborty and Vinod Mehra were playing the main roles and I played a villain. I received another ten or twelve movie offers in the next few days, mainly in Hindi films but also in one Malayalam film, *Sangar Sham* with Prem Nazir, and in one Tamil movie. I gave them my dates and received some signing amounts.

On 18 March, I did my concert for Vikram Singh in Rang Bhavan. I sang eight songs: *Mona Lisa* and *Nature boy* by Nat King Cole; *Somewhere* from *West Side Story*, *There's a time to be born*, *You'll never find*, *Stormy Monday* and *In the evening* by Lou Rawls; and *I wish you love*. Nargis was there, sitting right in front, and the audience seemed to like my songs, judging by the applause. That was the first time I got paid for my singing; all the other times it had been just for the love of music. I was paid Rs 10,000.

After the concert I went with the Khan family to Kashmir for a week. In Bombay the temperature had shot up and it was nice and cool in Kashmir. We stayed with Sanjay's sister Dilshad's family. It was cherry season and I made a lot of cherry jam which I took back with me to Bombay and surprised Nargis with it. I liked Kashmir and the mountains and the lakes. I went waterskiing in the lakes, but I enjoyed the skiing more in Mauritius. It was nice to come back home to Juhu, where I continued my film shootings and went windsurfing whenever I had enough time.

One day in July 1981 Nargis told me that we were going to have a baby. She looked kind of guilty. At first, I didn't know why. Maybe she thought I didn't want another child. Then she confessed that she had so far never told her father about me, and the divorce from her first husband had also not been finalized. She estimated that the baby would be born in January or February. I said, 'Let's go ahead with the baby, and get married as soon as you get the divorce and introduce me to your father.'

On the Road, Again

I finished some of my movies that were under production and then left for about a month, visiting my mother and brothers in Germany and Nargis's cousin Dr Feroz Tata and his German wife Angela in Berlin, and then stopping over in London before proceeding to California to visit my children. I also wanted to visit James Casey, the sculptor from *Apocalypse Now*, and his young wife Flores in Los Angeles and had written a letter to them to that effect, so they wouldn't go away on a holiday while I was there. I can't say that Nargis was overjoyed about my leaving India for another break already, but she forgave me because I had taken the news about the baby with obvious delight and was looking forward to an extra member in our family.

At the last moment I had to change my itinerary because I had to travel to Moscow first with Sanjay's family and the Indian delegation, which included Raj Kapoor, for the screening of our film *Abdullah*. The Russians loved Indian cinema and always have been crazy about Raj Kapoor. We had to leave immediately to be there on time for the beginning of the film festival in Moscow. So my one-month break got extended to two months.

It was very nice in Moscow and all Muscovites seemed to be swimming in the Moscow River. It was the middle of summer. I liked the Russian champagne which had a sweet taste very much to my liking. We stayed in the Rossiya Hotel, which claimed to be the largest hotel in the world in those days with 2000 rooms and 4000 beds. The films screened at the festival were good. Sanjay kept buying roubles from the black market, by which you could save a lot of money if you had US dollars on you and were careful not to fall victim to cheats; it was a big racket. In between watching movies, we had enough time to have a good look at Moscow, even to visit some Russian friends from the diplomatic corps whom we had met in Bombay.

I left a little earlier than the rest of the Indian delegation because I had so many visits ahead of me and I didn't want to run the risk of staying away from India longer than necessary with so much work waiting for me. My brother Helmut was waiting for me outside the Frankfurt airport. He dropped me at my mother's place, where I stayed for a couple of days. Then I visited my brother Mike and his family at the pensione where he was cooking for about a hundred people daily. He prepared the most delicious leg of lamb for me. I just loved his cooking.

After that I continued by train all the way to Berlin. Nargis's cousin Feroz and his wife Angela got into my train a few stations before Berlin railway station to be able to meet me before my arrival. They accommodated me in their beautiful flat in Friedenau. From there I phoned Klaus, our German friend from Mauritius, at his place in Berlin Grunewald. He told me to come over immediately. When I arrived, he was lying on a deckchair on his terrace and sun-baking, like in Mauritius.

'Good day Klaus, I can see that you're still maintaining your "Inkian" Ocean suntan.' We greeted each other warmly and sat down to chat. We reminisced about the good days in Mauritius and I advised him to visit Seychelles the next time. 'It's just as beautiful.' Klaus asked if he could get me anything to eat, but I had had something already at Angela's place. Klaus went to get me a glass of beer and brought along a box full of photographs. He had some great photos of me, Sanjay, Zarine and the kids. I selected the best ones and gave the negatives to the photo shop for copies to take to Bombay. I stayed with Klaus for one day and he took me to their recording studio where I met Afrique as well. The area around Klaus's place was lovely, green and with little lakes and forests. It was the top suburb as far as real-estate values go.

I spent another two days in Berlin, during which Angela and Feroz took me to the Berlin Opera House in the evenings; during the days I used to go to some wonderful German *konditoreien*, which are huge cake shops full of freshly prepared cakes and tarts, and buy those rich sweet tarts made with cream and cottage cheese on a biscuit base. I also went to the East German side of Checkpoint Charlie on the Berlin Wall to see if there were any changes since the last time I'd visited. I wished that that horrible wall would come down.

The next day Angela took me to a few more places. There was a beautiful lush park; the summer sun was shining and I couldn't believe my eyes: there were about fifty people lying on the grass totally naked and sunbathing. It was like Mauritius. The people on the street didn't even bother to look. Angela explained, 'Originally, you were not allowed to take your clothes off but eventually the authorities got fed up with putting up restriction notices everywhere, so they let them take their clothes off. Now there are no complaints and everybody is minding their own business. That's the way: if you can't beat them, join them! And it's not only in Berlin; you'll find the same in other cities like Munich.'

Opposite the Tatas' apartment was a bar with a big sign reading 'Genuine Australian Pub'. Feroz and Angela told me that it was a new bar, only about two months old. I asked them to join me for a drink there. Inside, I ordered three beers and told the waitress that I'd like to see the owner of the place. I mentioned that I was from Sydney and I'd like to know where the owner was from and how long he'd been living in Berlin. The waitress said, 'The owner is not here and he's not from Australia. He is Turkish.' We burst out laughing. Some twenty years before, a lot of Turkish immigrants had settled in Berlin, but which Aussie wants to chat with a Turk about Australia? There's nothing 'fair dinkum' about it! And the beer didn't have that flavour reminiscent of a good Aussie beer.

I said goodbye to the Tatas hoping to be able to come back soon. This time I took a flight from Berlin directly to London's Heathrow.

I arrived in London, which was preparing for Prince Charles's wedding to Diana. At the time of writing this book, London was getting prepared for another wedding—that of Prince Charles's son William to Kate Middleton! How the years have flown! When I called Nargis in Bombay and asked her how she was feeling with the tummy growing, I joked, 'I think we're doing the right thing, even the royal heir in Great Britain is getting married!' I also told her that I loved her. All I could hear from her end was: 'Oh Bob!'

I went to meet Euan Lloyd, the film director, in London. I had met him the first time when I was offered a role in his movie, *The Wild Geese*, in Cape Town. I was not free to accept that role because I was too busy at the time, but I had spent some time talking to him about my period in Rhodesia with the SAS. A little earlier that year I had met him again in Bombay, quite by accident, in the Oberoi Towers hotel. He had remembered me when I mentioned Cape Town and *The Wild Geese*. He'd said that he had come to India for a movie he was going to shoot in Goa, *Sea Wolves* with Gregory Peck and David Niven. 'It's about a skirmish between the German and British navies which includes an underwater attack in the harbour of Marmagao, Goa.' He remembered the underwater activities in Beira harbour that I'd told him about and expressed confidence that I'd have no objection if he were to use it in his film. I had no objection, but I'd requested him to give me a role in *Sea Wolves*. Euan Lloyd said, 'Of course! I'll give you a good role. There's a character of a German spy that could be interesting for you.' He had given me his London phone number and urged me to give him a call. The shooting was to start in the summer of 1982, in about one year's time. He was flying back to London that very night.

I met him together with another film director at their club where they'd invited me for lunch. We talked about *Sea Wolves*, the script and cast and about my own background. Euan Lloyd was very certain in his mind that he wanted me in his film. I gave him my details and contact address and phone numbers. After that I didn't hear from him until the next year.

That was all I had to do in London. I stayed overnight with an Indian friend and booked my flight to New York for early morning. When I approached the departure lounge I heard my name being called out. I was a little late for boarding, so I thought they were looking for me because I was late. They gave me the phone and it was Nargis talking to me from Bombay, wishing me a pleasant flight to New York and hoping that I'd be back soon. She was always very good at finding out where I was, and how she could get me to answer her calls! Sometimes she caught me in situations that caused me embarrassment, but I still admired her for it.

In New York I just wanted to stay for one day in the Wellington Hotel in Manhattan, buy a few nice greeting cards and send a romantic letter to Nargis to cheer her up and let her know my feelings. The letter looked a little big as though it contained something more materialistically valuable than feelings of affection. To my consternation, it never reached her.

I went to see what was running in the Broadway theatre and in the top cinemas and checked on concerts of the new few months. The next day I arrived in San Francisco and was received by Karin, Monique and Nicole. Cliff had an important day in college; it was vacation time but he was doing a special course. He was in Berkeley studying naval architecture and marine engineering. His future employer, Chevron Oil, was paying for all the costs until graduation, including for his Ph.D. I'd see Cliff in the evening, when he came back from college.

My girls had grown quite a bit and their pretty faces were wreathed in expectant smiles. As we were all catching up, Karin told me about some Indian people from Punjab who had big businesses in California. She had seen a lot of them lately. I told her that India is spreading all over the world very fast and one day it would become a superpower together with China.

It was in the middle of summer, so I took my girls for a few days to the 'Doom Floom' where they had to slide down a slippery spiral dip and crash into the swimming pool at the bottom; that was one of the big enjoyments of the youngsters in the hot summer days. One day later Cliff could also join us after his special programme at the university was over. We went to some Californian beaches where the huge waves were perfect for bodysurfing.

I went to Francis Ford Coppola's San Francisco's office, but since he was not in town, I just left him a message. In the evenings I sat in the house in Santa Rosa and chatted with Bob and Karin while the children were watching TV. We talked about our respective work, lifestyles and enjoyment; well, you can say we talked about the past, dreamed about the future and enjoyed the present.

As I was leaving for LA to visit James Casey, it was Nicole who made a scene this time because she wanted to come with me to India. She clung to me and didn't let go, until I sat down with her to explain that each of them would get a chance to stay with me for a few months. I arrived in Los Angeles towards evening and Jim and Flores were waiting for me outside the airport. We went for dinner right away, had a few beers and talked about our latest adventures. I told them that I was now knee-deep in the Indian film industry and it looked like I would be hanging in there for a number of years. Jim rang up some of the members of the *Apocalypse* crew; later I visited some of them too. I had a very nice two nights and one day with Jim and Flores. They gave me their double bed while they slept in their van outside in the garden.

The next day we went for a visit to Hollywood just to see the changes that had taken place over the years, and bumped into a few old friends in the cafeteria. Then we continued to the airport. This time I bought babies' items and special-size bras for my soon-to-be wife, apart from the usual chocolates, liquors and savoury titbits. The next day I arrived in Bombay.

Settling Down

After a shower I started calling up producers, to let them know that I was ready for work. I had three free days before I had to start shooting again. Nargis had something in a little box to show me. She said that it was my wedding ring. 'You should start wearing it from now on; no matter when the wedding will be.' It was a lovely twenty-carat gold ring, moulded in the letters B and C with a diamond in between them; it was Nargis's design, very attractive. I asked her to put it on the ring finger of my left hand and solemnly blessed her with my right. The following day, Nargis promised to visit her advocate in order to accelerate the divorce; after all, the baby was already on the way.

Soon I received another Hindi film offer: *Main Inteqam Loonga* with Dharmendra, Reena Roy and Amrish Puri, directed by T. Rama Rao. It was to start in about six weeks. I also got another Tamil film. For the Malayalam movie with Prem Nazir I had to go to Rajasthan for a whole week's shooting. I had started getting a pain in my lower back during film shooting those days. Even if I just had to stand for a while on one spot it bothered me. I wondered what could have caused it. Could I have pulled something on my recent trip? I used to lug a heavy suitcase around with me, hoisting it up on luggage racks in trains and other places. Or could it have been the time when I'd had to fall off my horse during the shooting of *Pehredaar* and had hurt myself so badly? The pain was not there all the time, only after some strain or bending. I'd have to have a check-up if it didn't stop bothering me. However, shooting almost every day, I was too busy to go to a doctor. Nevertheless, if I had the time, I would still try to go windsurfing in the afternoons when the wind was usually strong, but I often had to stop because of the pain.

Nargis's divorce had come through finally. We had to give the office of birth, death and marriages a few weeks to announce our wedding in the newspapers. Thus the wedding was fixed for 14 December 1981, about one month after Nargis's birthday on 12 November. There were not many people for the wedding, only Nargis's family and a couple of friends. We opened a few bottles of champagne and then I was expected to briefly go to Raj Kapoor's house in Chembur. Because Nargis was so advanced in her pregnancy I thought that it wouldn't look good for us to go out on our wedding day. So instead of staying at home, I went out alone. But it was a really silly idea. Nargis was not pleased. But after it was all over, we were married and we celebrated thereafter on every anniversary.

Barely one and a half months later, Darius was born on 25 January 1982. We had thought there was still plenty of time, so I'd left Bombay on 24 January for Bangalore to shoot for the Hindi movie *Ashanti*. Most of the shooting was in and around—and on top of—the Bangalore Palace. It was a big film with Rajesh Khanna, Mithun Chakraborty, Amrish Puri, Zeenat Aman, Parveen Babi and Shabana Azmi. The next day, Nargis told me on the phone that the baby was placed in such a way that a Caesarean section was required. For that they would have to wait for a few more days. But Darius had other plans; he was born on the same day.

I came to know only a day later. He was a big healthy boy; we named him after his grandfather. Nargis's parents were at the hospital looking after Nargis while I continued with my shooting. The producers begged me to stay on because a big schedule had been planned and if I left for a few days it would result in a great loss of money and time. So I stayed on as long as I was required. Parveen Babi was a very good companion and helped me keep my mind balanced through those days. I was glad that she was there. A few days later, after shooting till late at night, I returned to Bombay to see my wife and baby. But I could stay only till next morning; I had to take the early flight to Delhi and from there fly to Srinagar to shoot for *Namak Halaal* with Amitabh and Shashi Kapoor. Parveen was also in the film but not in that schedule.

We were shooting in the snow and staying at the Highland Park Hotel. It was really beautiful, but my mind was on Darius. He had been so fat when I'd seen him the first time. Nargis told me that the sisters of the maternity ward had given her three bottles of milk to last from the hospital to our Juhu residence, fifteen kilometres away. The first bottle he had drunk during the trip from his mother's hospital room to the lift, the second bottle while waiting for the lift to take him from the seventh floor to the ground floor. The third bottle he'd emptied on the way to Juhu. I told Nargis to get a cow for hire and keep it on the beach for the first year in case she hadn't got enough mother's milk!

I was in Kashmir shooting for the next four days. At night it was quite cold. The room service placed hot bricks wrapped in towels under the sheets. That kept my feet warm. During shooting and walking in the snow, my lower back hurt badly. I would have to go to a doctor before I started shooting for *Main Inteqam Loonga*, because that was a boxing picture with lots of action.

I made an appointment with Dr Dholakia, a famous Bombay surgeon. After the examination he said, 'You have a slipped disc—No. 3 and No. 4 vertebrae. You need to be in a horizontal position for fourteen days without leaving the bed, not even to go to the toilet. You can book yourself into a hospital or ask somebody at your house to make sure you have your meals in bed.' Nargis became my nurse and there was a cook named Pauline. During my recuperation, I caught up with a lot of reading. Darius would come to my bed for a little while every day. I had to take medicines two or three times a day. After two weeks I got up and felt much better, just a little pain.

When I called the doctor, he advised me to start physiotherapy. I ventured, 'As far as I know 90 per cent of physiotherapy is derived from yoga?'

'That's about right,' agreed Dholakia.

'In this case I will hire a yoga master to teach me yoga. After all, I'm in the country of its origin.'

'Sure, go ahead,' said Dholakia, wishing me best of luck.

I mobilized Bhailal Tank, the yoga master of the Holiday Inn, and got him to come every morning to my house and teach me the right asanas that would help my lower back recover. I understood that spending an hour a day for curing my back would be a small sacrifice for my health. From that day on I did my asanas every day first thing in the morning and the pain in my back subsided. Within two months I was totally cured. Later on I even started teaching yoga, when I was working in the Golden Palms Hotel and Spa. I never had any more problems with my back until 2005, twenty-three years later.

During those two months I continued with my film work and fights in movies. However, once I felt that I'd recovered, I took a hiatus and spent a week in the Maldives, living on an island and windsurfing and diving. That made me 100 per cent fit again and after I returned to Bombay, I threw myself back into work, toiling for days and sometimes also at nights.

The Premier Studios Tragedy

That year Nargis's factory burned down, so she decided to call it a day and stop her garment-manufacturing and export business. She had much to do bringing up our infant son, and in any case, I earned enough for the family. I looked after Darius whenever I was free. I often walked with him on the beach and as soon as he turned six months old, I dropped him into the swimming pool at the Holiday Inn and he started to swim. I used to start kids off like this in Sydney; just drop them into a calm pool and watch. They would instinctively paddle like frogs and float. At that age they were not scared of the water; it is said they are still used to water from the time they've spent in the mother's womb. Darius became a very good swimmer, but he didn't put in enough practice to excel in the competitive field. I didn't have enough time to spend with him because my movies took up so much of my presence. I taught him waterskiing at the age of five and he was very good at it.

I also travelled with him abroad, to Europe and the USA. His sisters Monique and Nici came for a few months from California, one at a time. Mo was in Casa Cama for nine months in 1988 and made many friends in Juhu. Nici came shortly after for about four months and she came with me to Bangalore when Sanjay had the mahurat of his big TV serial, *The Sword of Tipu Sultan*—in which I played the character of General Mathews, a real nasty, anti-Indian British army general without any respect for human beings.

Then the shooting shifted to the Premier Studios in Mysore,

where a terrible explosion occurred, triggered off by an electrical short circuit which resulted in a fire that raged on inside the studio where the set was erected. Sanjay risked his own life to pull people out of the fire to save them, but fifty-four people died. Later, he voluntarily paid large amounts of compensation to the victims of the tragedy.

I had stopped the night before at the studio, coming from a shoot in Ooty for a Tamil film with Rajinikanth, but I had carried on to Bangalore where I had to shoot the coming day for a Kannada movie. The date was 9 February 1989. In the morning I read a little news item in the morning paper. It mentioned that there had been a fire during the shooting of Sanjay Khan's TV serial *The Sword of Tipu Sultan* but nothing serious had happened. Just to be sure, I rang Sanjay's Bombay phone number. One of the daughters picked up the phone and urged me to go to a particular nursing home in Bangalore. 'He will be there. And Mummy is on the way to the airport.' I called up the nursing home and asked to speak to Sanjay Khan. After a while his brother Ahmed, also called Sameer, came on the line and told me to come to the hospital. I asked him to give the phone to Sanjay, but again Ahmed just asked me to come to the hospital.

So I went. Ahmed showed me where to go. I went into the room which Ahmed had pointed out to me but had difficulty recognizing Sanjay. His head was bigger than normal and his hair was burned down to a length of about half an inch. His hands and feet were raw flesh and the rest of the body was covered with cloth. The face was not so bad; he must have covered it with his hands when he went through the flames. I spoke to a few doctors; most were afraid that his chances of survival were only about 10 per cent. Sanjay had suffered 65 per cent third-degree burns, and even 20 per cent third-degree burns on your body can be life-threatening. Age was also an important factor, they said. Sanjay was at that time forty-eight. He was not unconscious; he was talking to me.

I asked the doctors if they could transfer him to a specialized hospital for burn injuries. They got an ambulance ready and sent him to St. John's Hospital, which had a burn ward. I accompanied him. I spoke to Sanjay on the way; he asked me how long by my estimate he would have to stay in hospital. I said at least thirty days and wished him best of luck.

Then I went to the airport and made my way to Bombay. Zarine had also arrived by then and was already entering Sanjay's room in St. John's hospital. She was calm and controlled and spoke to her husband in a reassuring voice.

Sanjay's doctor from Bombay and the relatives got together and worked out a comprehensive plan for Sanjay's treatment. In the evening of that same day, Sanjay, his family and doctors boarded the J-class of an Indian Airlines Airbus. The plane had a special bed for Sanjay with a hook-up drip to prevent dehydration. Two nurses were also with him. From Bombay airport he was transferred to an ambulance and ferried to Jaslok Hospital, where seven years earlier my son Darius had been born.

For the next three months Sanjay was on the ninth floor of the hospital. He went through a total of a hundred blood transfusions, donated mainly by college students, and auto-donor skin transplantations were performed at regular intervals. As soon as the donor skin has grown firmly to the surface of the body, it could be removed again and transplanted to a different area. Work was also done on his hands and feet. The last of the donor skin transplantations was performed on his back. For that he had to rest on the front side of his body for thirty days. Before that he was allowed to leave the hospital for about two weeks.

During that fortnight of rest, Sanjay stayed, along with his family and me, in a house that he had acquired some years earlier about twenty kilometres from Bangalore. He and Zarine talked about what they would do with the fourteen acres of land on which the house stood. At that time they were only growing fruit and vegetables on it. Sanjay and Zarine decided they would use that beautiful place to set up a hotel and spa. Before this project took off, Sanjay had to go back to hospital and then travel with his nurse to Washington, DC, where his hands would be operated on again at the Georgetown hospital.

I travelled with him, together with my son Darius, who was by then seven years of age. We stayed with Sanjay at his rented house in Bethesda, Washington, DC, for two weeks. Before that we travelled through Germany and witnessed the fall of the Berlin Wall, which was a very big event, followed closely by the disintegration of the USSR.

We stayed as long as Sanjay needed us and then Darius and I travelled to California to visit Cliff. In the intervening years he had married and his wife Carry was seven months pregnant with her first baby, Natalie. We stayed with them in the township of Walnut Creek. The day after we reached, we all went to the beautiful Vallejo Zoo. Karin had sent me her car in case I had brought along a lot of friends from the over-populated Hindustani peninsula! But the day together in the zoo was really great and Cliff amused us with a few super jokes in the evening. I think this was one of his:

> *A young woman visited a doctor, asking for a check-up. The doctor*
>   *said, 'My dear lady, you are pregnant!'*
> *'Oh no, Doctor, that's not possible.'*
> *'Why, are you not married?'*
> *'No, I'm not.'*
> *'Do you have a boyfriend?'*
> *'Yes, I have, but we never do anything.'*

'What does he do when you're together?'
'He just looks at me,' the woman said.
'Oh,' exclaimed the doctor, 'then he must be cockeyed!'

In the evening, Darius and I left for New York. I had to visit a friend on Long Island who had some great jazz music; I used to joke that you just follow the sound of the music and it takes you right up to his place. On the next day we took Darius up to the Statue of Liberty. He was thrilled walking up all those stairs. He wanted to go to the top of some other high buildings, so we took him to the top of the Empire State Building. It's really no point climbing high buildings now; the moment you've climbed a structure thinking it's the highest in the world, you'll find a notice on the top that tells you the highest building is now such and such in Kuala Lumpur or in Chicago or in Dubai!

From Kennedy International Airport I rang up Sanjay to say goodbye and wished him a speedy recovery. He said that he missed my massages. When I massaged his tortured body I had to be very careful not to touch the areas which had not yet totally healed. In between Sanjay used to get itchy sensations, which I concentrated upon. We talked about the *The Sword of Tipu Sultan*; Sanjay was supposed to play the adult Tipu and because of the accident and the delay in Sanjay's appearance on screen, the script would have to be amended several times. Before hanging up, I urged him as I often did that he must play Tipu Sultan himself and not give it to another actor; I thought it would help him with his recovery and to regain confidence.

Nargis was very happy to see her son return from his first overseas trip. By this time, I had worked in some top Hindi movies like the Manmohan Desai hit *Mard* with Amitabh and Amrita Singh in 1986, and the Shekhar Kapoor hit *Mr India* with Anil Kapoor and Sridevi (also in 1986). I was still going strong with an ever-growing number of films. However, I had been disappointed when Euan Lloyd came from London for the *Sea Wolves* shooting in Goa and in spite of sending a letter to the *Sea Wolves* unit's address I received no reply. I almost decided to go to Goa to investigate, but when I told Sanjay, he cautioned me not to sell myself cheap. 'Let them call you first, then you go.' I did as he said and finally received a reply that I should give them a proper contact address the next time. I *had* given them a proper contact address! But by then it was unfortunately too late; they had given my role to somebody else. I had missed out on the film *Gandhi* (1982) as well—I had given my dates, which Richard Attenborough had accepted, but then I was suddenly requested to advance my dates. But I was in the middle of an important Telugu film in which I played the main villain and the role went to somebody else.

From the mid 1980s and through the nineties I went quite often to Sharjah and Dubai in the UAE for cricket. An Arab sheikh by the name of Abdul Rehman Bukhatir had built a cricket stadium in Sharjah in the early 1980s, and then a few years later, another one in Dubai. Cricket teams were invited from India, Pakistan, Bangladesh, Sri Lanka, Australia, New Zealand, England and the West Indies. The crowd-pulling matches were usually those which featured India or Pakistan, particularly when they played against one another, because a lot of Indians and Pakistanis were employed in the Gulf and would be there for the matches, which were tough little wars. They are all cricket-crazy. Bukhatir used to send airline tickets and free hotel accommodations and entry passes to VIPs from India and Pakistan to fill the VIP enclosure with film stars, industrialists, politicians and even crime-syndicate members. Only one-day international matches were played. Test matches were only played in their respective countries; they were considered too boring for Sharjah and Dubai. I too only got interested in cricket once ODI matches became popular, because you could see the result on the same day. These cricket matches in the Gulf were so successful that Bukhatir built another cricket stadium in Morocco in the late nineties.

Sanjay Khan, Comeback Kid

Sanjay was to be back soon from Washington, DC. The shooting for *Tipu Sultan* had been going on steadily. For the time being Sanjay's youngest brother Akbar was directing. All the shooting of Tipu Sultan was taking place at Samod Palace and in and around Jaipur. I would only be required again in Sanjay's presence.

I had to go to Mauritius for twenty days, for the shooting of *Agneepath* with Amitabh, Danny Denzongpa and Mithun Chakraborty. The film schedule was placed across Xmas and New Year 1989: my second time in Mauritius over the Christmas holidays, only this time I was working. The film was directed by Mukul Anand and produced by Yash Johar. The Mauritius government cooperated with us in letting us use their helicopters and speedboats, which were required for our shooting.

In Mauritius the shooting went well with all the fringe benefits of windsurfing, parasailing and waterskiing. Amitabh came with Abhishek and his sister Shweta. In those days I saw a lot of Amitabh and Jaya's, and Ajitabh and Ramola's, children, often at the Godrejs' or at gorgeous shooting locations like Mauritius. Yash Johar also brought Karan Johar and his brother, little boys then, and of course his wife Hiroo. Karan became a big name in the film industry after his film *Kuch Kuch Hota Hai* (1998). He is now one of Bollywood's most famous and successful directors.

After Mauritius, Bombay was pretty chilly. For windsurfing and waterskiing, I had to wear my wet suit because of the cold wind splashing the water right over me. Still, I had to catch up with finishing quite a number of films. Sanjay had returned from

Washington, DC, and was working on the amended script. He still had to take a lot of rest combined with light exercises.

In August 1990 I arrived with Sanjay at Samod village for the filming of the scenes of a grown-up Tipu Sultan. The earlier episodes featured Tipu Sultan as a child and then Tipu Sultan in his teens. From his late twenties Tipu's role was played by Sanjay Khan. Tipu was a very important king in the eighteenth century. The British didn't like him. In the end they killed him but he didn't die easy; in fact he defended his fort with his weapons at the ready and history says that he was the only Indian king who died on the battlefield fighting until his last breath. Sanjay gave an extraordinary portrayal of the legendary historical figure. It was a great success, a mega TV serial. After the ordeal he'd gone through during and after the fire at Premier Studios in Mysore, he'd made a remarkable recovery and even did his fight scenes himself, including every close-up shot, without a stand-in. He went for regular workouts in the gym and walked a lot, but he had to keep out of the sun.

In December 1990, our son Sunil married Mona, who was also residing in Juhu. We bought them a small apartment in a housing society next to the Juhu post office called Pandurang Wadi. A little later even Nargis and I bought two one-bedroom flats, situated next to one another in the same housing society, and converted them into a very nice three-bedroom apartment. Casa Cama was our favourite but it used to take a lot of beating during monsoon days. We liked to keep the doors and windows open and the rain caused a lot of damage and everything got spoilt by fungus deposits. So we decided that we would rent out our Casa Cama apartment and reside in our Pandurang flat. It was also close to Juhu beach but protected from the rain.

During his stay in Georgetown hospital, Washington, Sanjay had met a young NRI entrepreneur who had developed a new type of tear gas which he was trying to sell. India with its large and sometimes unruly population seemed to be an ideal market. Finally it was decided that the entrepreneur would come to Bombay with a sample shipment of different sizes of the Cap-stun tear gas-containers for a presentation. Sanjay called me so I could be present and give my opinion as to the practicality and advantages of this weapon for riot control. In several of the states of the USA it was already a mandatory part of the highway patrol officers' outfits. The tear gas was manufactured from the oil of hot peppers (oleum capsicum). The moment it hits the eyes, they can't be opened for about fifty minutes. If you want to reduce this time, all you have to do is wash your eyes with cold water, without soap. It gives the police officers enough time to unarm and arrest dangerous persons when necessary.

We realized that we would have to make inquiries regarding the laws of India. One fact was that mace, the tear gas in existence at the moment, could cause severe injuries to the eyes, even blind people. Cap-stun, however, is harmless, without danger to your health. Moreover, whoever wanted to use the Cap-stun weapon had to undergo a course and also had to get it sprayed into their own eyes in order to familiarize themselves with the symptoms of being exposed to Cap-stun and the treatments thereafter. Thus, I was to visit the state of South Carolina in eastern USA, stay at the home of Charles Budd, who was in charge of Cap-stun marketing, take the course and spend a week with one of the highway patrols to observe the way they used their weapons.

I could leave our new place with a good conscience because the civil work was done and the rest was safe with Nargis on the job. I was there in January 1991 when Budd's bungalow, situated next to a lake, was totally snowed in. It was a beautiful part of South Carolina, not far from Columbia, the capital. They fitted me out with highway-patrol uniforms and boots and sweaters. In the mornings it was very cold and I could never understand how my highway-patrol mates could drink iced tea from glasses full of ice pieces. I was glad they didn't mind me drinking cups of hot coffee. After my training, the Cap-stun company gave me a nice farewell party and a certificate of completion of the course for handling and proper use of the tear gas from the highway patrol.

When I returned from Carolina, Nargis and Darius had just finished moving into our new flat in the ground floor of Pandurang. The new flat had turned out very attractive; Nargis is an excellent interior decorator—I had noticed this when we had made alterations at our Casa Cama flat before Darius was born. It looked so good, our big bedroom and Darius's room plus a guest room, and a large hall with a bar and an attached dining room, a nice kitchen and servants' quarters.

Meanwhile, we had to organize several training camps for Cap-stun in Bombay and Pune, and ask the police and military representatives to give us their feedback. Their overall opinion was that for a big country like India, where large masses of people have to be controlled, Cap-stun did not have sufficient and quick enough output of gas. So, unfortunately, we couldn't do business with Cap-stun. It was an interesting experience though, to be working with the South and North California highway patrol for a little while.

Before the Mysore fire, Sanjay had invested heavily in cinematographic equipment from abroad, particularly for *Tipu* and also for future projects which were already in the pipeline. After about a year of shooting for *Tipu Sultan* a spare part for our big movie camera had to be replaced. It was not available anywhere in India. So I had to travel to Japan. With my Australian passport I didn't need a visa; my credit card was enough, so I was always given the jobs that involved travelling. I didn't really mind, I was ever ready to go abroad. Nargis was not that happy to see me go abroad so often, since I was travelling within India frequently as well. That was not the only time I had to go to Japan; two or three years later I had to go again for a number of small spare parts. After that it became easy to get everything involving spare parts of electronic or cinematographic nature in India. The world's becoming smaller day by day.

Finally, we rented out our Casa Cama flat. We used to get so many requests from foreigners, and we eventually gave in. Brokers often came with European and sometimes Australian people who were interested; they always preferred to stay close to the beach. Renting out to tenants again cost us a lot because there were repairs like water leakages, drainage problems and resurfacing of walls. Because the place was on the beach exposed to monsoons, salt water and fungus, the annual maintenance bill could be quite high, especially if you left the windows open, which is so tempting once the rain stops and everything smells so fresh! This was the reason why we ourselves had changed our residential location. For the tenants it was heaven; they didn't have to undertake the repairs, which was our annual responsibility if we wanted to keep them happy. Generally we kept good relations with them and managed to sort out any problems concerning the flat in an amicable manner. Whenever any of our tenants gave a party, they would make sure to invite us.

Once a broker told us he had somebody interested in our flat. He was from the Seychelles but wanted to stay for only six months. I'd often been thinking of the Seychelles. After the coup, Albert René had turned out to be a much better President than Jimmy Mancham. In the eighties a gang of mercenaries under the leadership of the famed Michael Hoare flew in from South Africa and entered the Seychelles airport with weapons. However, they were discovered and identified before doing too much damage. Apparently that had been an attempt to bring Jimmy Mancham back from England, where he was still in asylum. When the mercenaries were ordered to open their luggage, they pulled out their weapons and started firing inside the arrival hall. Eventually they had no other option but to run back to the aircraft which had brought them to Seychelles and was almost ready to take off again for its return to Johannesburg. They hijacked it but were arrested in South Africa on arrival. Two of the mercenary team were caught in Victoria before they could get away and were jailed. One died in prison, while the other was released after eight years. The rest of the gang, including Michael Hoare, was jailed in South Africa after pressure from the Seychelles and some other countries. However, they were also released because of good behaviour after serving a shortened jail term.

The last film made by Sanjay Khan as producer and director was *Kaala Dhanda Goray Log* (1986) with Sanjay, Akbar Khan, Amrita Singh, Sunil Dutt and myself. After that Sanjay only produced and directed historical and mythological mega serials. After the shooting of *Tipu* was over, he got busy with the script of his next TV serial, *The Great Maratha*. The great Maratha was not Shivaji as it was supposed by a large number of people, but Mahadji Scindia (or Shinde), played by Shabaaz Khan. I was thrilled to be given the role of Ahmed Shah Abdali, the Afghan king. That was a true challenge for me. With the help of director Sanjay Khan I did well. I managed to get into the character and I enjoyed it. I never had to learn so many dialogues in any other film before, and in a language not my mother tongue.

I will never forget one particular scene. It was the build-up for the battle of Panipat—where the Marathas suffered a terrible defeat against Abdali, after which the Afghan king eventually returned Delhi to the Indians and only kept Punjab in his possession. Abdali could not sustain the hot climate in India and preferred to stay in Kabul. I too suffered much, especially in the scene where I had to ride in front of Abdali's army during the heat of the day. The camera was on top of a hill to capture the snaking line of soldiers on their horses, about two kilometres long. It took time to get everybody in the correct position and one single take was not enough. By the time the director was happy with the take, everybody was soaked in sweat. My costume was of thick black cloth with furry trimmings in different layers and leather-like battledress, and my head was covered with a thick black turban. I had never experienced sweating like this even in a sauna.

The Great Maratha was also filmed at Samod Palace and its surrounding fortresses and at the Red Fort in Delhi. Before Abdali retired to Afghanistan, he gave a speech while sitting on the Peacock Throne in the Red Fort. Since I was playing Abdali, I had to sit on the Peacock Throne after they managed to open the old padlock. There was a write-up in the morning paper with the heading: 'What is happening to India?' The gist of the article was that another foreigner was seen sitting on the Peacock Throne in the Red Fort and that the editor had received reports that the foreigner had been identified as being Bob Christo, who was shooting for the TV serial *The Great Maratha*!

The same morning I received a phone call from my friend Gavin Bromilow, the former Australian consul general to India in Bombay who was now an attaché with the Australian High Commission in Delhi. He told me, 'Bob, you better get out of Delhi. You were spotted by the authorities in the Red Fort sitting on the Peacock Throne as though that was your birthright. But if you're still free, drop in and see me later for a cup of coffee!'

Which I did. He surprised me with the news that he had decided to stay in India. He was just in the process of getting married. I was very happy to hear this and wished him bliss and contentment with his wife.

Then I went to the airport to get back to Bombay for the shooting of the film *Gumrah* by Yash Johar, who had also signed me for *Agneepath*. The film was based on an English film, *Bangkok Hilton*. It was an action film about drug smuggling. I was the jailor in Hong Kong. (In the English film the jail was in Bangkok.) The film featured

Sanjay Dutt, Sridevi, Anupam Kher and myself and was directed by Mahesh Bhatt. Since the shooting was in Bombay, I could spend some time at home; it was nice to be home again for a while. Darius was now going to the fifth standard in primary school.

My shooting for *Gumrah* was supposed to take three weeks, but in between I had to give three days in Ooty for another action film with a new actor who had trained in martial arts and kickboxing in Bangkok for four years. This was his first film in Bollywood and his first fight with me and the actor Manek Irani. The newcomer's screen name was Akshay Kumar, and I found him to be a very nice person. I felt that he would become one of Bollywood's top actors. I did some more films with him during the year ahead.

From Ooty I had to rush back to Bombay for the climax shoot of *Gumrah*. It was set below the jail in the underground sewers with all the drainage and water pipes and lots of water. I catch Sanjay Dutt and Sridevi as they are about to escape through this underground route. The climax ends with my death, of course, but I didn't have to go to Hong Kong to die; the set was built in Bombay's Mehboob Studios. While in Bombay, I got all the reports about the status of my TV serial *The Great Maratha*. I was in the first eighteen episodes and the TRP rating was good. I received a lot of praise for my work; many viewers were in favour of prolonging the work of Abdali for a few more episodes, but it was not possible—the serial would then have had to be renamed *The Great Abdali*! In India Abdali was the villain, so it was up to Shabaaz Khan to keep the rating high without the character.

Vocational Hazards

It would be too much to write about the more than 230 films and fifteen TV serials that I've worked in, in India. But I want to write about a film I was working on in 1986, about the same time I was working on Manmohan Desai's *Mard* and Shekhar Kapoor's *Mr India*. I received an injury during the filming of an action sequence in jail. It still gives me a lot of trouble periodically; that's why I can't forget it. The film was *Geraftaar* with Amitabh, Kamal Hasan, Rajinikanth and Manek Irani. The action was between Amitabh and me, but a stand-in was used for Amitabh. It was Amitabh's regular duplicate of those days. The fight master was called Judo Rathnam. The substitute had to kick me in the face; or rather, from the camera angle that was used, it had to give the impression as though I was being kicked viciously in the face. After the first take Judo Rathnam cut the shot and told the substitute in broken English, 'One more, go forward more!'

Instead of overlapping my face with his bare foot, the substitute kicked me with his heel right in my eye; I couldn't manage to avoid the foot. I had to lie down for half an hour after that. My left eye felt quite sore for the rest of the day. The next day we had to shift from Madras to Kudremukh to shoot there for another three days. During this time I noticed that I was not able to see properly; after closing my good eye (which was the right one) and keeping my left one open, my view became distorted and blurred. I knew immediately that I had to go to an eye specialist for a check-up.

In 1986 the best one was Dr Ashok Shroff in Bombay. After an inspection the doctor told me that this was an emergency, and that I should have come in right after the accident. After further checking, Dr Shroff explained to me that my retina was detached and haemorrhaging. He would have to stop the bleeding first. After that laser treatment had to be done to photocoagulate the affected area in order to prevent severe visual loss. Even though the macula was also damaged, it couldn't be touched by laser treatment, because the optical nerve would be destroyed. It was quite a shock to hear all this. I had laser treatment done for all the damaged parts in the retina except for the macula. In the beginning it appeared to be much better, but after about a month it was the same as before, because the macula could not be treated by laser. I was told that there was a possibility that I would gradually lose the eyesight in my left eye.

I checked on good eye specialists in Europe and found the phone numbers of an eye clinic in Munich, Germany. The place had a good reputation, so I phoned them and made an appointment for a second opinion. I went there the same year and had both my eyes thoroughly examined and got the clinical papers. The laser treatment that had been performed was perfectly all right; however, I had to have my eyes checked regularly every three months because of the danger of developing glaucoma. My right eye was perfectly normal. During the next few years I suffered some haemorrhaging and after it was cleared I had to have further laser photocoagulation on other parts of my retina. By the year 2007, the whole retina had been operated by laser treatment. I still see my present eye specialist, but so far there are no new problems, except that I often feel uneasy and unable to focus with my left eye alone. There seems to be no solution at this stage. I just have to live with it now. The producer of the film *Geraftaar* never offered me any compensation. I don't know what the situation is like now in India, but a Hollywood producer is only allowed to produce his films if he is adequately insured so that his employees are covered against accidents.

In 1982, Amitabh himself had been hit in the abdomen during the shooting of the film *Coolie* in Bangalore. It had happened during a fight scene between Amitabh and Puneet Issar. Puneet was a well-trained sportsman and a karate exponent. He was supposed to deliver a blow into Amitabh's abdominal area but had misjudged it, putting too much power into the blow. That is the reason why we have to rehearse a couple of such knocks before performing for the camera. All blows have to be controlled when they are delivered for the camera. In Amitabh's case the damage ended in a life-threatening disease called peritonitis. While he was fighting for his life in the hospital, fans all over India prayed for his recovery. I visited him several times in hospital to wish him a speedy recovery and thought, 'Thank God that he's got so many fans praying for him.' Often people, including other actors, ask me if I was the fighter who gave Amitabh that almost fatal blow in the film *Coolie*. I don't like that particular question. I reply that I was trained in martial arts by an original Japanese master, but I have never hurt another actor during a film fight. I always controlled my blows, except when it happened in a military situation where I was meant to kill the enemy. When we had started shooting for the film *Mard*, Amitabh had fallen ill again, this time of myasthenia gravis. Thank God the illness could be controlled with medicine. He went on to do a lot more great movies, many of which are still being shown on TV at least once a week on some of the TV channels.

During my over two-decade-long career in Bollywood, I have worked with many interesting people. One such was the superstar Rajinikanth. I found him to be a very well mannered and likeable person. I worked with him in a number of films—Tamil, Hindi and also English (*Bloodstone*, 1988). He was always fascinated by my gold wedding ring in the shape of my initials with a diamond in between. Whenever we meet he asks me, 'Have you requested your wife to design a similar ring for me?' I tell him that he will have to come to our Bombay residence and speak to my wife in person and be our guest until the ring is ready. So far he has not come.

Once we were shooting together for a film in Madras. I was sitting in the Chola Hotel dining room, when the door opened and in walked

Rajini. He announced, 'I want to have some kebabs. My wife doesn't let me eat non-veg; that's why I've come here to join you!'

I said, 'Please be my guest and enjoy your non-veg meal.' He said whenever he felt like having non-vegetarian food, he came to the Chola Hotel.

I think the last movie I worked on with Rajini was *Siva* (1989), which included a fight in a tea plantation. It was a hit, like most of Rajini's movies. I noticed that he always carried some spiritual books. I think he is quite a religious person and he is looking for a way to show his gratitude towards life by way of compassion and love for his fellow human beings and worship and respect for God.

A colleague who became a very good friend was Tom Alter. After I moved to Bangalore in 2001, we'd lost touch. In 2008 I came to know that Tom Alter was going to perform in Bangalore in one of his latest plays called *Three*. He was directing the play, and the verses and dialogue, in English, Urdu and Hindi, were all going to be delivered by Tom. The team had only three actors, one of them a French jazz musician, Pascal.

I came across his Bombay phone number and called. A few days later he called me back. Of course I went to see the play. I took a friend with me, the artist Kaleem Pasha who is a sarod player, poet and playback singer. We both enjoyed the play thoroughly and after the finale Tom spoke to the audience, who were eagerly praising the performance of the artists and the idea of the play. Tom was kind enough to ask me to come up on the stage to say a few words to the audience, which I did.

Later Tom suggested that we have dinner at a nice restaurant near the racecourse. We were all in a good mood and had a great time. Tom's son Jamie, who is a cricket journalist, also joined us with a friend. During dinner Tom asked me if I remembered the first time we worked together, for a French TV serial called *The Indian Trunk*. I sure did!

This must have been either in 1980 or 1981. It was about how much faster one can reach India from England since the opening of the Suez Canal. Tom played the French consul in India. I play a British official and in one scene I have to deliver an urgent message to the French consul and his party, who are resting under a shamiana in the open. It was the first sunny day after a few days of rainfall, which had caused the terrain to become wet and soggy. I was riding on my horse in front of my 'soldiers' at a brisk pace. We were all wearing uniforms. My uniform was similar to the French consul's red and white. As I came galloping around a curve towards the consul, my horse refused to stop. I was wondering why; I had pulled the reins for it to slow down. The answer came in a few seconds when my horse—with me on top—sank into the wet muddy ground in front of the French consul. It must have been a funny sight, because nobody could manage to keep a straight face. Now, it took time to get out of the muck. My horse couldn't manage with me on top, so I had to jump off the horse. Even then the horse had to be pulled out. It took about half an hour.

Meanwhile, my uniform had changed colour; it had become black. There was no other uniform, so it was decided that in the frames where Tom and I were not together, I would wear Tom's uniform since we were of the same height. In Tom's and my combined shots I had to wear the upper part of my uniform since that was reasonably dry and not black, and something else on my lower portion. So my lower body could not be in the camera frame! There was a lot of manoeuvring involved because of the dirty uniforms.

We also had to change the original set because we couldn't retake the shots there again. The muddy ground would have taken a few days to dry up; a little further ahead there were water buffaloes happily immersed in the black mud!

A 'Golden' New Phase

I was ready to give up working in Indian films as an actor by the end of the twentieth century. I needed a change; actually I required some kind of change every twenty-five years of my life. So in the late 1990s, I worked on the production of another mythological mega serial by Sanjay Khan, *Jai Hanuman*, without accepting a role.

The last two films I worked on were *Veer Savarkar* (2001), a so-called 'freedom-fighter movie', and another one, scripted, directed and produced by two NRI sisters living in London. Even though I can't remember the title of the movie, I recall that I played the character of a priest in that film. I accepted the role because when I asked whether the character was that of a crooked priest, the reply was, 'No, the role is that of a good priest.' I thought that at least my fans could see me play one good man in my Indian film career! Alas, the film was never released.

In 2000, I left Mumbai for Bangalore, where Sanjay was building his new hotel, The Golden Palms Hotel and Spa. I started off as gymnasium manager and yoga master once the hotel was officially opened for business; in 2002 I became director of health and fitness, and of the spa.

The Golden Palms Hotel and Spa was a beautiful five-star hotel with lovely landscaping created by Jimmy Amrolia. It had 149 guest rooms and a huge swimming pool, a Chinese restaurant, a fine-dining Italian restaurant with live music, also a restaurant-cum-coffee shop called Cafe Solaire. There was a large gymnasium, a fully equipped spa with treatments of an international quality and a yoga room to accommodate thirty guests at a time for stress management and meditation, a sauna, steam room and jacuzzi, two outdoor tennis courts and a long jogging track; to top it all, a whole floor for cosmetic surgeries. Opposite the main hotel block on the other side of the street was another area for lawn games and parties.

I liked the hotel and the work. I stayed in the hotel. I was given a room, but when we were full, I had to move to Sanjay's suite until my room was vacant again. All my meals and laundry were part of the perks of my life in The Golden Palms, and for going to town I could use a hotel car with a chauffeur.

Darius was at that time doing his twelfth standard at the Canadian School in Bangalore. For the first year I saw my son every week when I picked him up from his hostel, which was always something to look forward to, until his graduation, after which he returned to Mumbai to continue his education there.

I used to visit Nargis and Darius in Mumbai every three or four months and stayed for a few days each time. Darius had always been interested in motor cars and motorbikes. He was very keen to work in this field. His teachers in the Canadian School had suggested that he should become a commercial artist because he always topped in art, so he started attending an art course at the Wigan and Leigh College. I soon realized that this was not the right career for him and wanted to make him do an apprenticeship for learning everything about motorized vehicles. Then he could eventually start his own business which would definitely offer him the opportunity to become successful. But his mother had other ideas; she didn't want Darius to start doing such dirty work. 'This is not the right occupation for our son. He doesn't come from that background,' she said. It upset me quite a bit, because I was sure that he would have excelled in it. Most of all, he liked the work and would have been happy with it.

Later, I tried to get Nargis interested in moving to Bangalore. I suggested we sell Casa Cama in Bombay and buy or build a house in Bangalore while the estate values were still reasonable, because they'd shoot up soon with the IT industry booming. She said that she had never liked Bangalore, and she was not going to change her mind now. In the years since I've moved to Bangalore, Nargis has been highly uncooperative as far as our family life is concerned.

From the second year on I was plagued with mishaps in the gym, like slipping off an upright push-up support from which I was able to balance my weight by my arms to bring my legs into a horizontal position for an abdominal strengthening exercise. This tore my supraspinatus tendon in the shoulder; it took several months to heal. Then it tore again when I was walking on the treadmill and the UPS didn't work during a power cut; I got thrown up in the air and ended with a somersault that tossed me with my damaged shoulder on the edge of the treadmill. I had to have my arm in a support for over a month to keep my shoulder motionless, and then started with special exercises (I developed them myself) which accelerated the healing process. I used to do 500 push-ups on the floor in five sets, 100 push-ups per set non-stop within half an hour. This must have weakened my supraspinatus because I was doing it every day. After it healed I couldn't do the exercises properly any more. So I had to give up my favourite fitness exercise. Maybe this is part of getting old?

I had a lot of guests from abroad who had different kinds of physical problems like osteoporosis or arthritis or thyroid problems and, most of all, obesity. One of these guests came from Germany. She came to my yoga room and groaned that she was totally stressed out. She was a tall slim lady with grey hair, in her fifties. She said that her name was Evelyn Mathews. I asked her whether she knew why she was stressed out. She replied, 'Yes, I do. I lost my husband a few weeks ago. He was an airline pilot, American, but he lived with me in Germany. He was twenty years older than me and died of pulmonary emphysema. I'm the chief rédactrice of a top international fashion magazine called *Elegance*. It comes out in three languages—German, French and English—twice every year. The collection is photographed with the models in different parts of the world every season; which is a lot of work and I had to go through this while my husband was fighting for his life for almost a year.'

After listening to this, I decided that I would help this lady and bring her back to a situation where she could enjoy peace and harmony. I immediately started to introduce her to a few light yogasanas and taught her how to relax in Savasana. Then I took her every day for meditation practice. I also started to give her company during her meals and advised her which spa treatments to take. She started to calm down and began to smile again. By the time she had to leave two weeks later, we had become friends and we stayed in touch with each other by e-mail. She continued visiting the Golden Palms twice every year and once she even did a fashion shoot in our hotel for the magazine. A very elegant, pleasant lady. Once when I was in Germany she invited me to her home.

I made the acquaintance of many hotel guests at the Golden Palms and continued to keep in touch with them and ensured that they kept visiting the hotel at least once or twice a year. It was part of my job, which may be called 'public relations', but I thoroughly enjoyed it.

Looking Back, Looking Forward

My enjoyment didn't last for too long because by 2006 I started suffering again with pains appearing in my legs, hips and lower back. I started having difficulties while walking, my ankles used to twist sometimes and occasionally I used to trip and fall. I had to go for weekly visits to my orthopaedic doctor, Anand Galgalli, who also sent me to have spinal scans. He diagnosed it as the beginning of an ailment called spinal stenosis which is triggered off by blocking of the spine from soft tissues. It causes severe pain because of the pressure on the nerves located in the vertebrae. It is usually age-related but can also be caused by trauma from earlier years—like the falls I had had during movie stunt work. The doctor put me on some painkillers and anti-inflammatory medicine and stated that he had to keep it under regular observation. If it got any worse, I'd have to have an operation on my lower spine.

At that time I was booked on a journey to Germany and Austria. I was going to see my daughter Monique's family, who lived near Evelyn Mathews near Aachen, and my mother, who was staying in a nursing home for old people in another area of Germany. I also wanted to visit a school friend from Sydney who was married and settled in Germany near Lake Constance. The main reason for my visit to Austria was to see Klaus Engelhorn in Vienna. Klaus was in the process of building an Ayurvedic resort in Austria near the northern border with Italy. He had in mind to engage me as director, after he had visited the Golden Palms the year before and we'd met. He'd invited me to show me the area and the progress of the resort. I had a great trip and Klaus and his wife treated me like royalty. We stayed for a weekend in the mountains 360 kilometres away from Vienna, which is called Wien in German. We travelled in Klaus's Range Rover, which was going so fast that people whom we overtook on the highway seemed to be standing still. We lived in a big comfortable mountain hut with amazing food. It was so fantastic to use my mobile phone from the top of snow-capped mountains to talk to friends in India.

However, it was a big problem for me to walk around in the mountains with my health predicament. It seemed to be becoming worse by the day. To reach Vienna I had travelled through Germany by train, changing trains in Salzburg. It was a long walk from the Salzburg railway station till the station where the train to Vienna was waiting, and by the time I'd reached, the railway official was already blowing the whistle for the Vienna train to leave. I had to run with a full suitcase and a briefcase, which had been very difficult for me. Luckily, the train had waited for another minute and I'd managed to climb up on to the last coach. Then I'd had to walk right through the train to the first coach in which I was booked. By the time I arrived there, we had just reached Vienna railway station.

From there I took a taxi to Hotel Residenz Palais-Coburg, where Klaus had made a reservation for me. Before I left the hotel, Klaus had generously cleared all my bills. The Palais-Coburg was not a cheap place. They charged about $1,000 per night.

On my return trip to Bangalore, I chose to fly Vienna to Bangalore via Frankfurt. The flight was quiet and comfortable. I was looking forward to touch down in Bangalore. Actually, I had planned to stop over in Mumbai, but because of the pain I didn't feel like stopping over; I couldn't wait to get back to Bangalore without delay. I arrived about midnight, 10 April 2006.

After a few days in Bangalore I had to go to my orthopaedic surgeon again for another check-up. He noticed that the symptoms had increased. My medication had to be augmented. He sent me to see a neurosurgeon. I too noticed that my thighs, buttocks and calf muscles had started to waste away. My limp had become more pronounced. One day I heard Sanjay mention to somebody that I had developed a bad limp, which was not good with respect to my designation as director of health and fitness. I immediately handed in my resignation and left my job in The Golden Palms.

I took an apartment in RT Nagar with two bedrooms, a hall, dining room, kitchen, bathroom and my own upstairs terrace connected by a staircase from my hall. I used one bedroom as my yoga room. The place was pleasant, airy and had a large area of trees, undergrowth and flowery bush and a common jogging track. It was on a dead-end street without through traffic. No traffic noise, and quiet at night.

Before booking a spinal operation I tried a number of alternative medical treatments, but nothing else could remove the blockage inside my vertebrae, except surgery. So I finally booked the operation in MS Ramaiah Memorial Hospital, Bangalore for 9 February 2007. The day before my operation, I had to go through a total physical check-up. Everything seemed to be normal except my heart; I had to see the cardiologist regarding an abnormal heartbeat. I told the doctor that I'd been taking Calaptin 40 for the last fifteen years because of this abnormal heartbeat. I seemed to have forgotten to take the two tablets which I was supposed to take every morning plus one every night. It is nothing dangerous as long as I take the tablets regularly. They control the irregularity of the beating of the ticker. It is just a magnetic abnormality. The cardiologist checked it thoroughly and then passed it as safe. It would not be life-threatening or risky for my health in any way; I just had to take the two tablets early morning before the surgery.

Dr Balaji Pai, one of the top neurosurgeons of Bangalore, performed the operation. It started early morning and lasted for about four and a half hours. I cannot remember much about the operation. I thought about how I had forgotten to take the tablets the day before and as an afterthought I decided that it didn't really matter; even if I didn't survive, it was OK with me, I couldn't go on living forever. Then I felt myself become sedate, calm. The doctors and nurses walking around seemed like shadows; then the anaesthesia made me drift away, but I felt like I'm still awake, even though I couldn't see the doctors and nurses any more. I just saw scenes and flashbacks in my mind, scenes of events that had happened many years ago in my life . . .

. . . I was on one of my building sites in the early seventies, during the time I was restoring old buildings in the Sydney suburb of Paddington. Paddington was one of the oldest suburbs of Sydney. Many of the old houses had started to crumble and fall apart. Yet, if you took a good look, you could see the old iron-lace balconies and in some places, where the lime mortar had broken away, you might get a glimpse of old sandstock bricks with variations of colours inside and outside. I knew that these bricks had originally come in the bottom of old steamships and ocean liners as ballast, to keep the ship stable on their voyage from England. The steamships had probably been filled with convicts, who were arrested for minor offences and then sent to populate this huge new-found land.

There were other suburbs in a similar state of disrepair as Paddington. However, Paddington, locally called Paddo, had the advantage of being located close to the city and a hop away from King's Cross. Being hilly, it offered very pretty views—including that of the beautiful Sydney Harbour Bridge—in the mornings and evenings. When I was young, whenever I happened to pass through Paddington, I always dreamed about owning one of these houses. And I passed through often, for in those days I was working as a Sydney taxi driver till about midnight to earn some extra money. In the mornings I used to surf at Bondi beach for about an hour, and after that I went to college. After college I joined the National Service for the military training which was compulsory for all adult men. I learned useful military and survival skills during this period; later on, I further pursued my interests in shooting and martial arts.

Right after I graduated with a BSc in civil engineering, I bought a nice old sandstock and iron-lace house in Paddington. I got it very cheap and decided to restore it on my own. I just used a plumber and an electrician and a few labourers; carpentry, joinery, bricklaying, concreting, plastering and tiling I did entirely on my own. I loved improving old buildings with the help of modern technology. I fashioned a lot of archways throughout, all in colourful sandstock bricks, sanded and lacquered, and added courtyards, gardens and fountains. It made me happy to look at the fruit of my labour. Actually I wanted to keep my first restored house as my residence; however, I received such good offers to sell that I just couldn't refuse. I made a good profit, so I could pay the deposit for two houses this time and start my construction company. I had my eye on houses in other areas too, like Edgecliff, Woollahra, Bondi Junction and Darling Point. My favourite was still the area of Paddington because that's where I'd bought my first house, and it had been lucky for me. Eventually, lots of people moved to addresses in Paddo, particularly architects, artists, entrepreneurs and actors; the real-estate values shot up and other builders also started developing there.

At one time I was so busy that I was equitable owner of twelve houses; all sandstock-brick and iron-lace constructions but in a very modern style. Now I was in a better position to invest, and banks offered me loans. I was ready to take advantage of this—there were twenty acres of land for sale on the sunshine coast in Queensland near Mooloolaba, Maroochydore. I wanted that land. I had to do a lot of running around to get the finance. In the end it almost fell through. Then somebody I knew, a man named Peter Petersen, helped me to get the required resources, but I got stuck with a big loan.

Here I was, a civil engineer with twelve prestigious projects, twenty acres of land and a wonderful family with three children. Just when I thought that everything was going well and I had made a breakthrough, life fell apart. In 1973, the OPEC hiked the prices of crude oil, triggering a year-long global recession. I still remember the mile-long queues of cars outside the gas stations because of the rationing of petrol sales.

Meanwhile, the guy who'd helped me with financing for the twenty acres of land and who I'd thought was my friend turned out to be my enemy. He had invested in the same property and managed to get his investment back with a big profit just before the recession started. He had had insider knowledge and used it for his own gain.

With the economy down, I could not sell any of the land I had bought, and I couldn't pay the interest on the big loans that I had taken from the banks. I had a beautiful house in Vaucluse on the harbour front but I had to mortgage it at the beginning of the recession. It was a bad time. I didn't realize at once how bad it really was. Thinking about it only made me sweat. When I tried to look at my situation positively, I just couldn't find any positives. I had to start using funds from my construction company in order to pay for the interest on my loans. Consequently I could not pay the earnings, wages or salaries to my workers on time, and ultimately, not at all. I was desperate.

Then my wife died. After that my friend Bob Fischer and his wife Karin moved in with me so that she could look after the kids. Bob and Karin had no children of their own, but they knew my children well. I had first met Bob when I was looking around for old houses to restore. One of my builder friends, Alan, had told me that he needed money and he had an old sandstock/brick cottage with iron-lace windows in Woollahra which he wanted to sell. One evening he'd taken me there and I'd checked it out. There was a person sitting inside; Alan introduced him as Bob Fischer, an American now living in Sydney. Alan told me that Bob was the tenant, but if I wanted to buy the place, Bob would move out. I'd bought the house but after an inspection found it to be riddled with white ants; the ones you find in Sydney are particularly destructive. I'd renovated the house and though I hadn't touched the white ants problem, the house looked so good after renovation that I had had no trouble selling it. I'd moved into my nice house in Vaucluse. Bob Fischer and Karin had moved to a house nearby—our family had got to know them well and we'd started meeting on a regular basis and played a lot of chess and war games. At the time Bob had a pizza inn and he'd offered me a small share in it, which I had bought happily as it helped with my economic difficulties as well.

Bob was always ready to help me when problems arose and the support was mutual. After Helga died, I often sat together with Bob trying to find some quick solution to all my problems, but I couldn't concentrate properly, because suddenly I just had too many problems. Karin did not fully realize the effects of the economy's downfall. She was spending most of her time with my three children: Cliff, the eldest, tall and ambitious; Monique the lazy one, although very sweet and loving; and Nicole, who was clever and liked music. Monique too was musically inclined and was learning ballet while living in Sydney. All three were born in Sydney. Our family life was happy as long as their mother was still alive. All the kids loved water sports and Sydney, with its fifty ocean beaches, was a paradise for them.

In my depressed state I visited some friends who were accountants, but they couldn't come up with anything useful either, so I went to talk to one of my bank managers. He listened, but didn't offer me a bridging loan because of the credit squeeze. He advised me not to panic. 'Don't worry; the financial crisis isn't going to last forever! If you can manage to survive a recession, you'll come out stronger than before.' This armchair philosophy was not going to help me at all. I needed a proper solution now, which would lift me up again and salvage everything I had worked for. I was so disappointed about Bob's inability to help me, but I couldn't really blame him for anything. All of us were going through a bad period, and this was not the first time. Bob used to have very progressive ideas during our earlier struggles.

So I was sitting in my office, looking at my account books, trying to find a worthwhile idea. A headline flashed across my mind: 'Robb a Bank Incorporated'. I didn't know where I'd seen it before. Maybe in a book? Or possibly in a film? Could it have been the title of a comedy film? The truth was that in my desperation I started thinking of robbing a bank. Finally I got tired of thinking of my problem any further. I got up and went for a walk. I felt thirsty and wanted to distract my mind by thinking of something nice, like a holiday in Samoa or Bora Bora. So I walked into a pub and ordered a beer.

My thoughts were interrupted by a young, well-dressed man who asked me a question. I didn't understand what he was saying, so I asked him, 'What do you want?'

He replied, 'I have a gun for sale.'

'What kind of gun?'

'A pistol.'

'I don't have a licence.'

'It's a black-market rate,' he coaxed.

I relented. 'Let me have a look at it.'

I inspected it; he named the price and said that it came with twenty rounds of ammo. I pondered for a while and wondered about the coincidence.

Was this my fate? Was this going to be part of the solution? Where was it going to get me? I asked the young man for identification, telling him not to worry ('I'm not a cop.') I gave him my card. He gave me his. My card was genuine. I don't know about his, but I went along with it. He gave me the pistol with a discount.

However, the moment I held the weapon in my hand a thought burnt itself into my brain. I felt that the instant I bought this firearm, there would be a temptation to use it. Luckily, I decided to cancel the deal immediately, returned the pistol to the salesman and apologized to him. I resolved that I would find a sensible solution to get out of my difficulties. I must not get involved in crime to try and solve my problem.

The next day I flew to Brisbane and drove to the place with the twenty acres of land that I had thought I'd lost about six months ago. When I arrived at the site, I noticed that it was fenced in and a board was displayed which read that the property was for sale. I noted down the telephone number and went to call the office at a Sydney address. They told me that the property was under litigation and that the previous owner, Petersen, had become bankrupt. So I went back to Sydney to find out all the details and how I could acquire the property. I followed up the legalities of the litigation and found out that there was a possibility that I could recover part of the money after everything was settled. Since I knew that the previous owner had turned out to be a crook and taken me for a ride, I got my solicitor and chartered accountant to look into it——because I always had the feeling that I was owed money from the time when I was the owner of the property; because in the beginning I had paid a lot of interest on my loans, which had financed the property. Somehow part of that money must have been usurped by Petersen, and I took immediate steps to get a refund.

You can imagine the relief I felt when three weeks later I was paid almost $100,000. God bless my solicitor. He didn't sleep over it; he worked non-stop until he could hand over the money to me. I didn't want the land back because at that time I couldn't afford it any longer, but with the amount that I retrieved, I was perfectly happy because I wanted to accept the offer from Vinell in Vietnam and probably join my children later on.

Bob and Karin were so happy that my financial problems were sorted out satisfactorily. They said goodbye and hoped that I'd be able to meet them after my Vietnam stint.

I called the Saigon office and left a message. They phoned me back the same night and I spoke to the person in charge. He told me to come as soon as possible. I said goodbye to Bob and Karin and Cliff. For the girls, I left a message that I'd meet them after my work was over. My camera and photographic equipment I gifted to Cliff together with my opal collection, which he used for a down payment for his first house in Sacramento, California two years later . . .

. . . I woke up after my spinal surgery was over and the doctors reported that I had been very restless during the operation and several times I had shouted and cursed while the anaesthesia was still active.

But now it was finally all over. I had gone through so much pain the previous year; I'd even had to leave my job which had led me to cut ties with Sanjay Khan, with whom I had shared such a close friendship since 1978. It was not a friendship with only Abbas (I always called him by his second name) but with his whole family, and I am sure that they must have missed me just the same as I missed them over the years. I feel that a friendship like ours cannot simply be undone by a stroke of a pen or a 'Sorry it was good as long as it lasted'. No, for me it was a large and important part of my life. I wish my friend and his family the best for the rest of their lives. Thanks and God bless you!

After my surgery, I still could not work; the physical discomfort during my post-operative period was unbearable. There were headaches, pains in my calves, thighs, buttocks, hips and back. I did some yoga exercises to help me and later I started walking, which also helped a lot.

Then my friend Farooq met some people from the European Union who were working on starting international schools in India and the United Arab Emirates. Farooq travelled to Brussels to find out more about it and we came to know that this was one of the big projects of the European Union Commission. We enrolled ourselves as Ambassador International Residential School with the European Union Commission, with me as the project director, and started looking for a large plot of land which would be required as soon as we could find suitable builders and contractors. Now we have some land identified. This is the type of company I am looking for to join for permanent employment. I am young enough and a civil engineer and this would be the right type of work for me to get into. Most of my life I've been working . . . and now I have to earn again!

My family is well settled, though scattered around the world. Nargis lives in Mumbai with our youngest son Darius, who just turned twenty-nine. Cliff is almost fifty and still working for the company he joined after he graduated, Chevron Oil. He's really smart and must be a millionaire by now, but he won't admit it. Nikki is a hospice nurse in the USA, and just visited me in Bangalore. Monique has a lovely family and is moving to California from Germany. Sunil and Mona are settled in Goa.

As I look back on my life, I feel blessed. There were happy times and sad times like in every life, but it was a life fully lived. I can only wish all my readers the great mixture of bliss and sorrow that I have experienced in my life.

Index